BUREAU FOR PARANORMAL · RESEARCH AND DEFENSE ·

B.P.R.D. HELL ON EARTH: LAKE OF FIRE

created by MIKE MIGNOLA

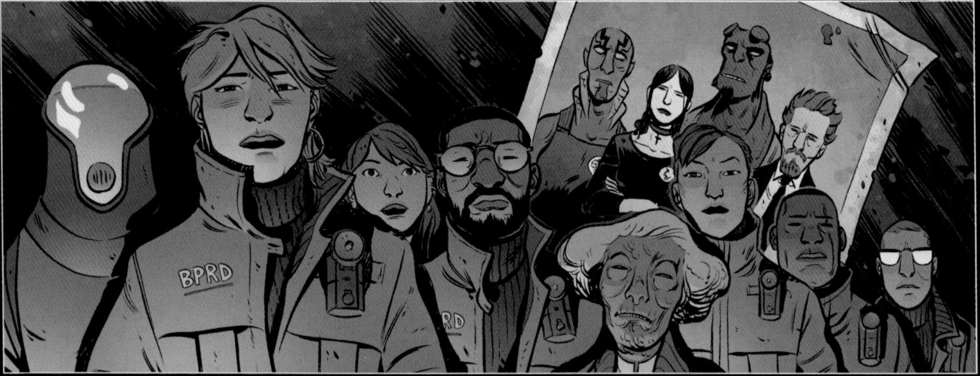
BPRD

To stop the Black Flame's attempt to raise a new race of man, Liz Sherman lit a fire in the underground city of Agartha that nearly cracked the world in two. Though the Black Flame was destroyed, new threats continue to crawl out of the earth. After Agartha, Liz went missing, and Abe Sapien was shot by the young psychic Fenix. Now Abe has disappeared, and the B.P.R.D. has joined forces with the Russian Special Sciences Service to deal with the worldwide crisis. Neither group knows that the current increase in devastation was caused by the rebirth of the Black Flame . . .

MIKE MIGNOLA'S

B.P.R.D. HELL ON EARTH
LAKE OF FIRE

story by **MIKE MIGNOLA** and **JOHN ARCUDI**

art by **TYLER CROOK**

colors by **DAVE STEWART**

letters by **CLEM ROBINS**

cover art by **MIKE MIGNOLA** with **DAVE STEWART**

chapter break art by **RAFAEL ALBUQUERQUE**

editor **SCOTT ALLIE**

associate editor **DANIEL CHABON**   collection designer **AMY ARENDTS**

publisher **MIKE RICHARDSON**

DARK HORSE BOOKS ®

Mike Richardson PRESIDENT AND PUBLISHER · Neil Hankerson EXECUTIVE VICE PRESIDENT
Tom Weddle CHIEF FINANCIAL OFFICER · Randy Stradley VICE PRESIDENT OF PUBLISHING
Michael Martens VICE PRESIDENT OF BOOK TRADE SALES · Anita Nelson VICE PRESIDENT
OF BUSINESS AFFAIRS · Scott Allie EDITOR IN CHIEF · Matt Parkinson VICE PRESIDENT OF
MARKETING · David Scroggy VICE PRESIDENT OF PRODUCT DEVELOPMENT · Dale LaFountain
VICE PRESIDENT OF INFORMATION TECHNOLOGY · Darlene Vogel SENIOR DIRECTOR OF
PRINT, DESIGN, AND PRODUCTION · Ken Lizzi GENERAL COUNSEL · Davey Estrada EDITORIAL
DIRECTOR · Chris Warner SENIOR BOOKS EDITOR · Diana Schutz EXECUTIVE EDITOR · Cary
Grazzini DIRECTOR OF PRINT AND DEVELOPMENT · Lia Ribacchi ART DIRECTOR · Cara Niece
DIRECTOR OF SCHEDULING · Tim Wiesch DIRECTOR OF INTERNATIONAL LICENSING · Mark
Bernardi DIRECTOR OF DIGITAL PUBLISHING

DarkHorse.com   Hellboy.com

This book collects the comic-book series B.P.R.D. Hell on Earth #110–#114, originally published by
Dark Horse Comics.

Published by Dark Horse Books
A division of Dark Horse Comics, Inc.
10956 SE Main Street
Milwaukie, OR 97222

International Licensing: (503) 905-2377

First edition: April 2014
ISBN 978-1-61655-402-6

10 9 8 7 6 5 4 3 2 1
Printed in China

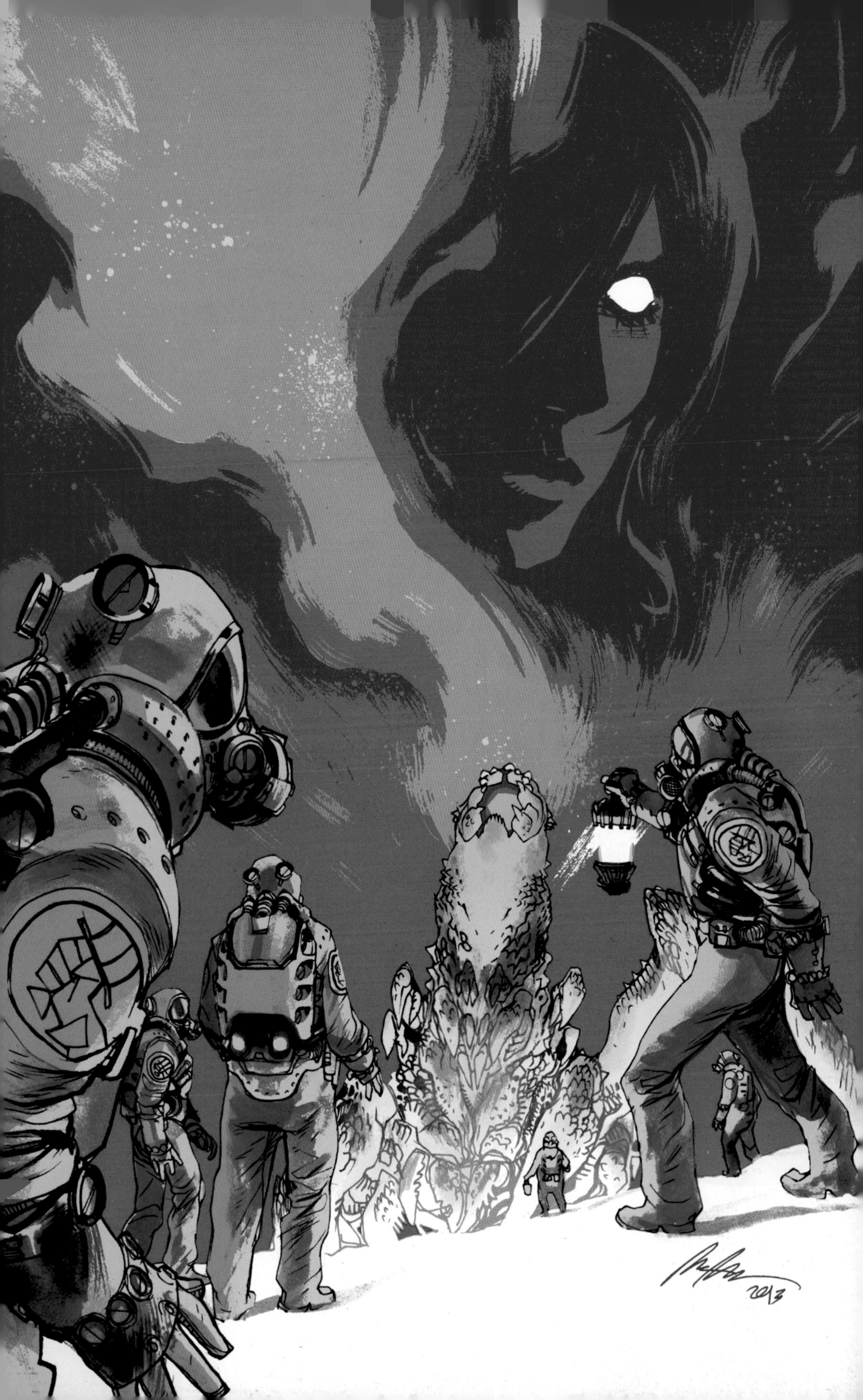

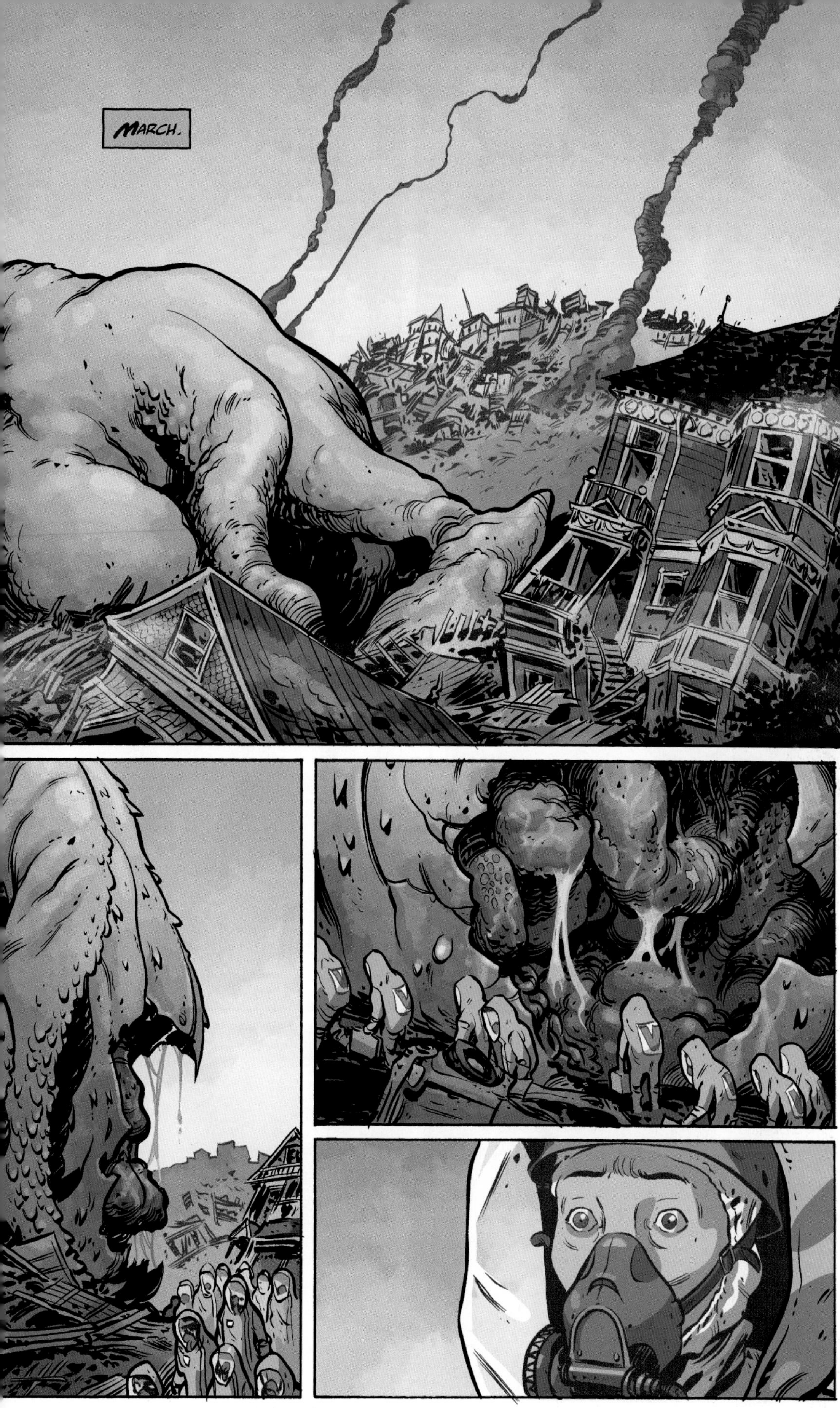
MARCH.

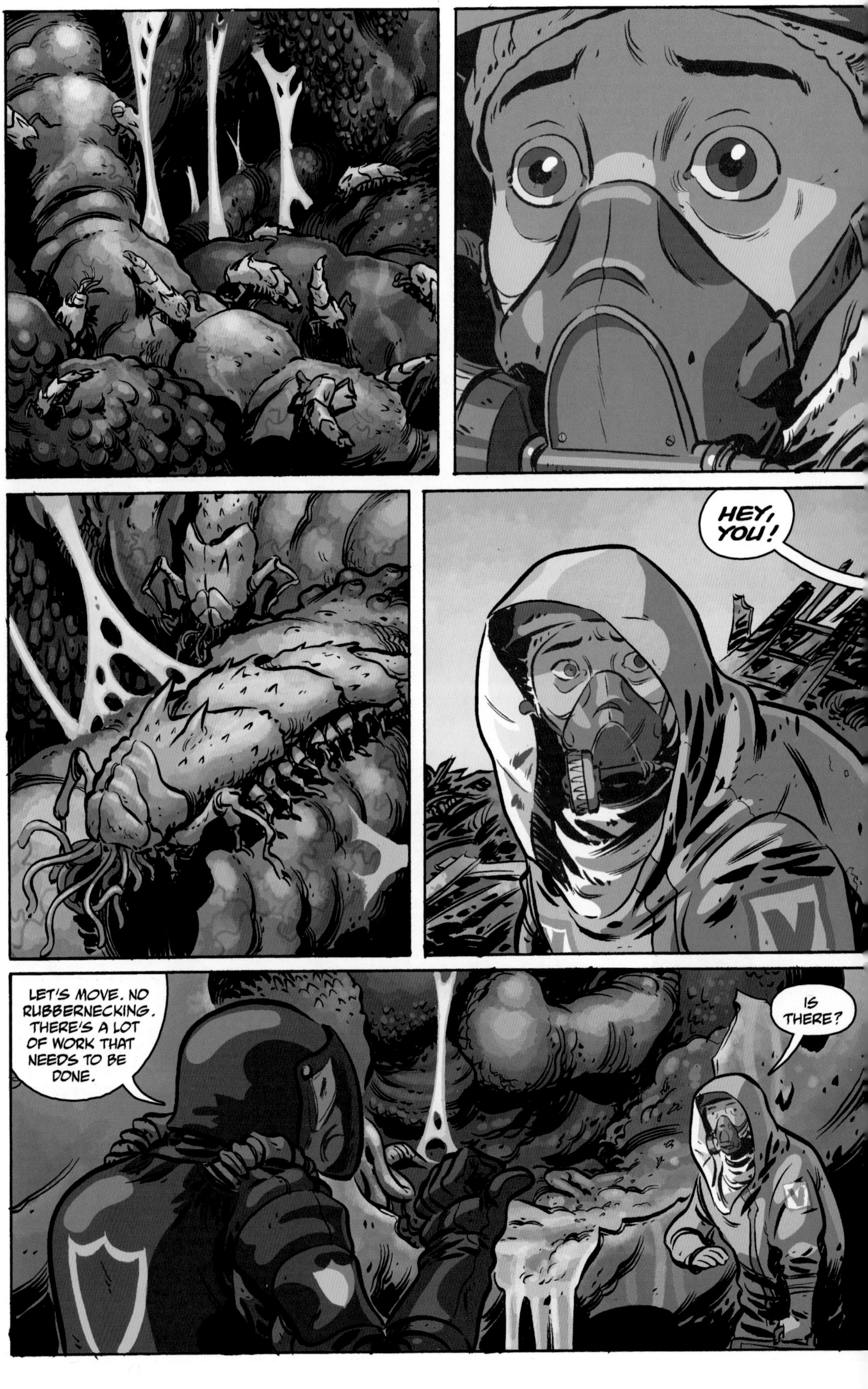
HEY, YOU!
LET'S MOVE. NO RUBBERNECKING. THERE'S A LOT OF WORK THAT NEEDS TO BE DONE.
IS THERE?

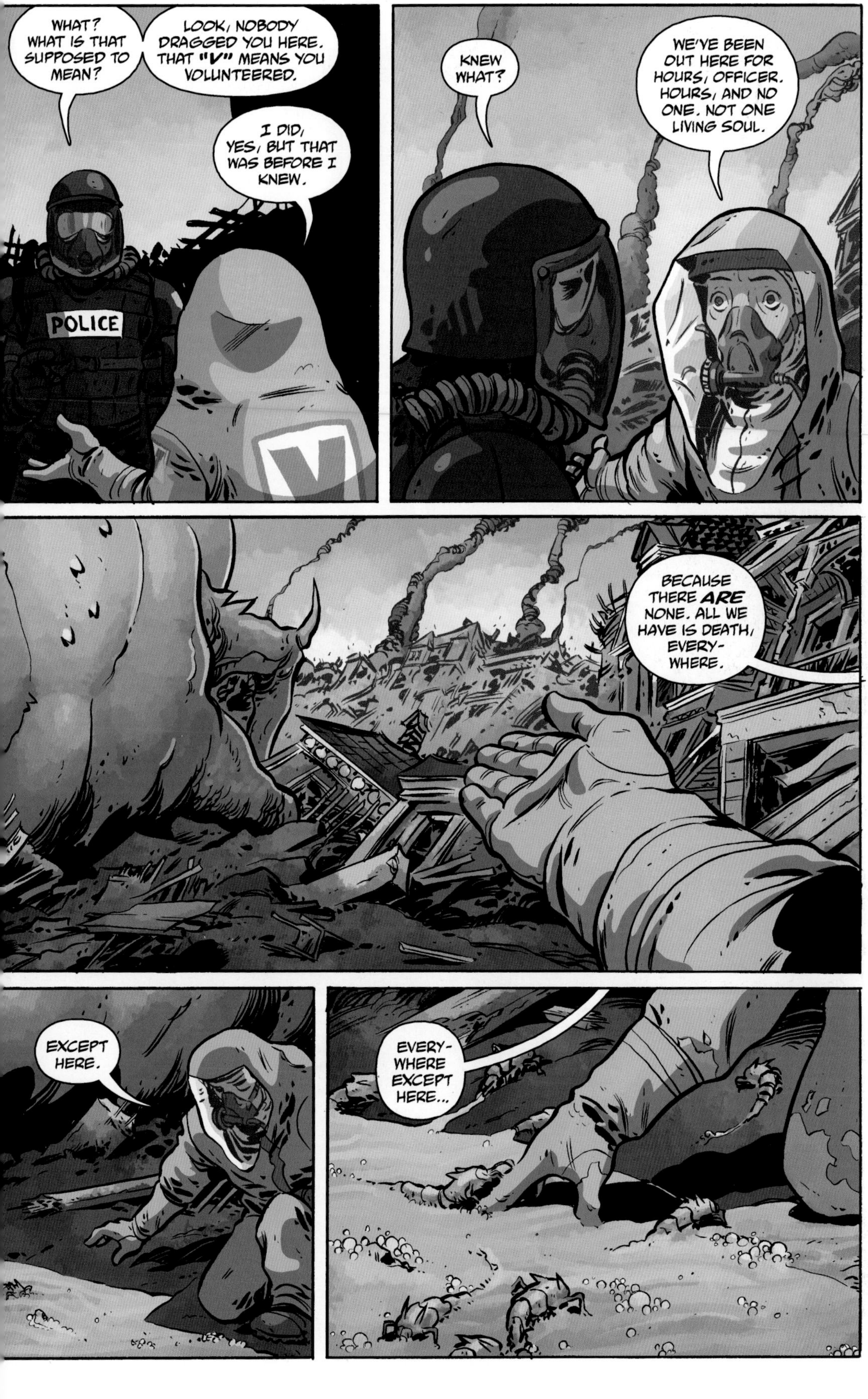
WHAT? WHAT IS THAT SUPPOSED TO MEAN?
LOOK, NOBODY DRAGGED YOU HERE. THAT "V" MEANS YOU VOLUNTEERED.
I DID, YES, BUT THAT WAS BEFORE I KNEW.
POLICE
KNEW WHAT?
WE'VE BEEN OUT HERE FOR HOURS, OFFICER. HOURS, AND NO ONE. NOT ONE LIVING SOUL.
BECAUSE THERE ARE NONE. ALL WE HAVE IS DEATH, EVERY-WHERE.
EXCEPT HERE.
EVERY-WHERE EXCEPT HERE...

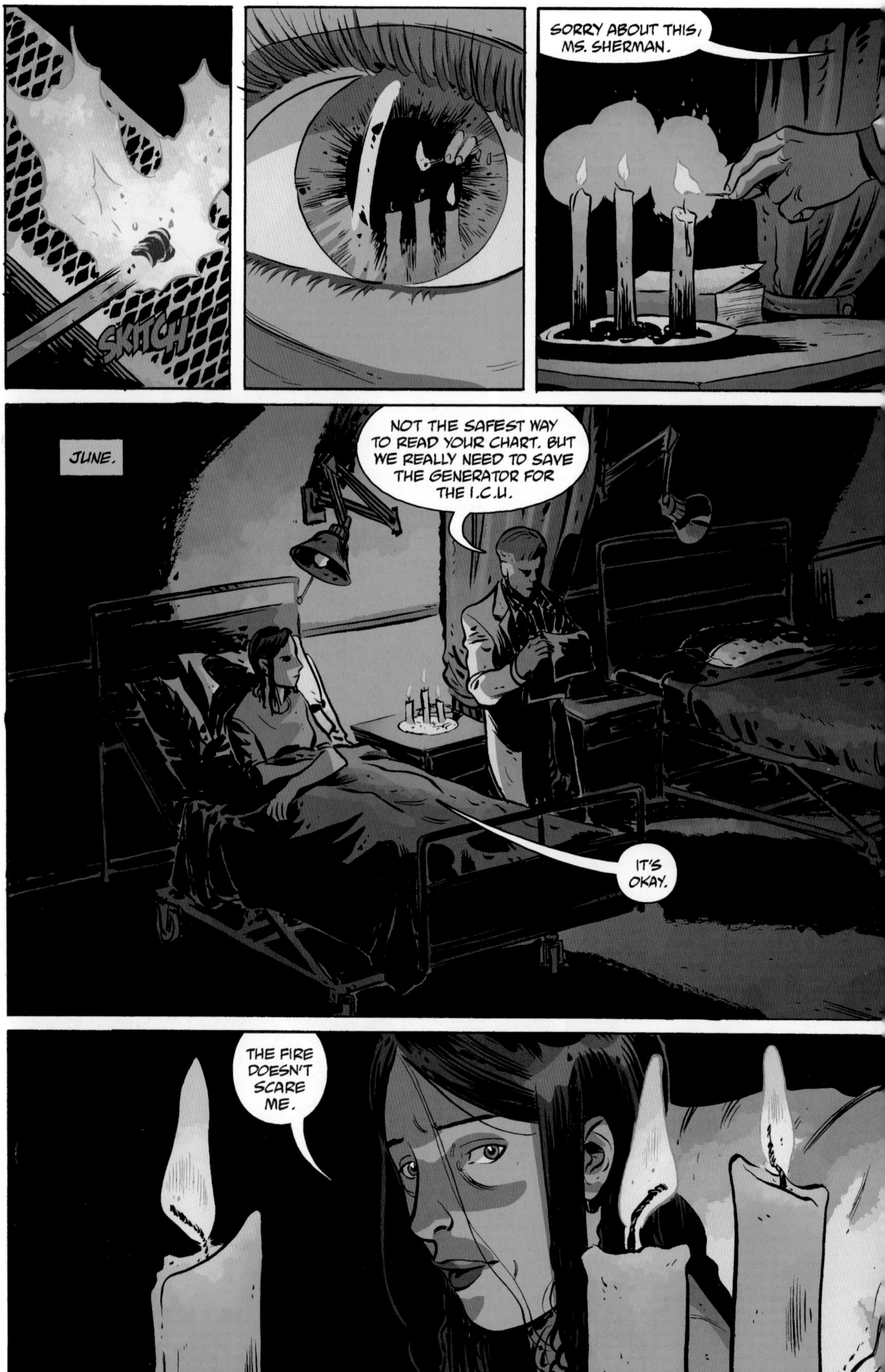
SKITCH
SORRY ABOUT THIS, MS. SHERMAN.
JUNE.
NOT THE SAFEST WAY TO READ YOUR CHART. BUT WE REALLY NEED TO SAVE THE GENERATOR FOR THE I.C.U.
IT'S OKAY.
THE FIRE DOESN'T SCARE ME.

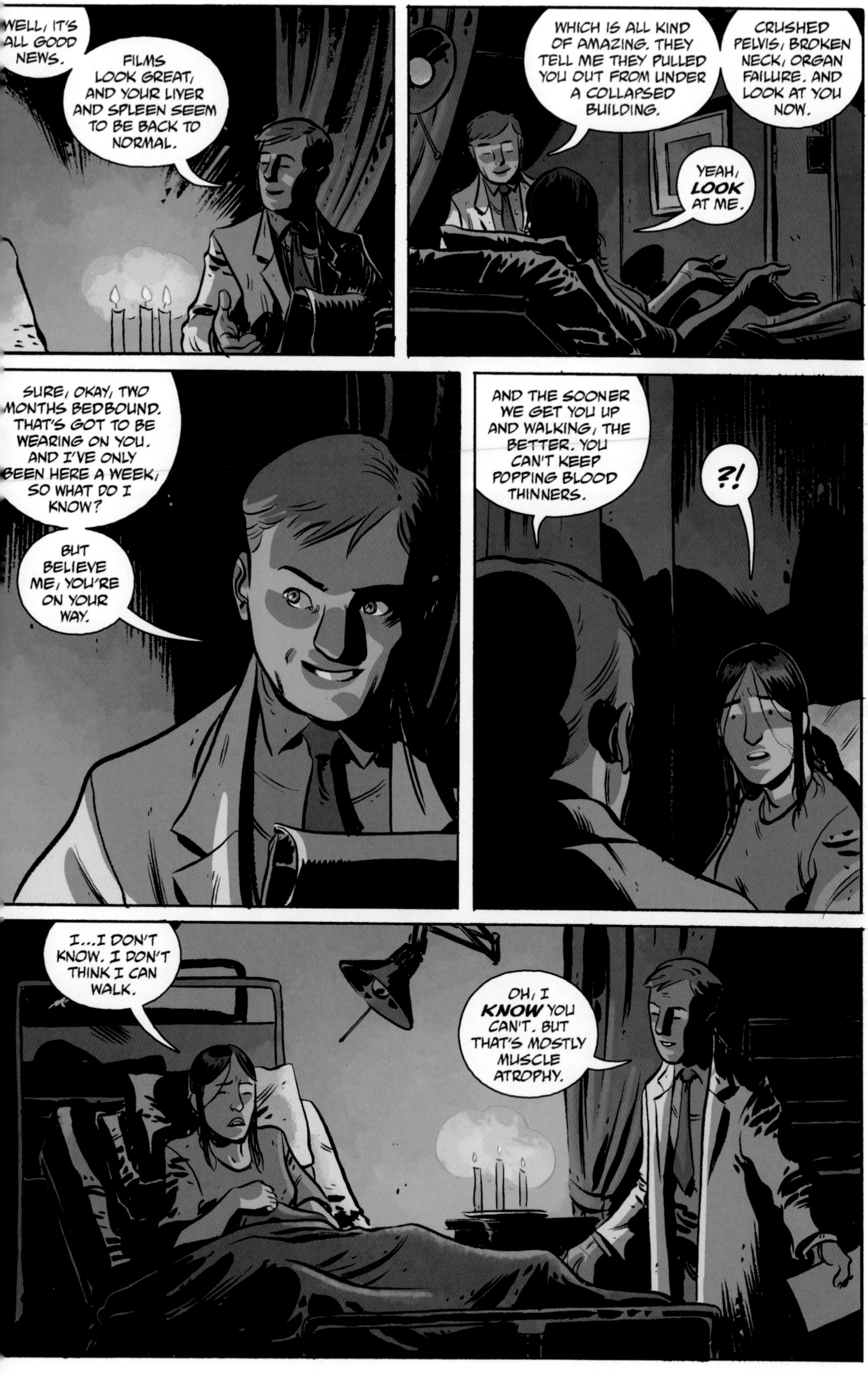
WELL, IT'S ALL GOOD NEWS.
FILMS LOOK GREAT, AND YOUR LIVER AND SPLEEN SEEM TO BE BACK TO NORMAL.
WHICH IS ALL KIND OF AMAZING. THEY TELL ME THEY PULLED YOU OUT FROM UNDER A COLLAPSED BUILDING.
CRUSHED PELVIS, BROKEN NECK, ORGAN FAILURE. AND LOOK AT YOU NOW.
YEAH, **LOOK** AT ME.
SURE, OKAY, TWO MONTHS BEDBOUND. THAT'S GOT TO BE WEARING ON YOU. AND I'VE ONLY BEEN HERE A WEEK, SO WHAT DO I KNOW?
BUT BELIEVE ME, YOU'RE ON YOUR WAY.
AND THE SOONER WE GET YOU UP AND WALKING, THE BETTER. YOU CAN'T KEEP POPPING BLOOD THINNERS.
?!
I...I DON'T KNOW. I DON'T THINK I CAN WALK.
OH, I **KNOW** YOU CAN'T. BUT THAT'S MOSTLY MUSCLE ATROPHY.

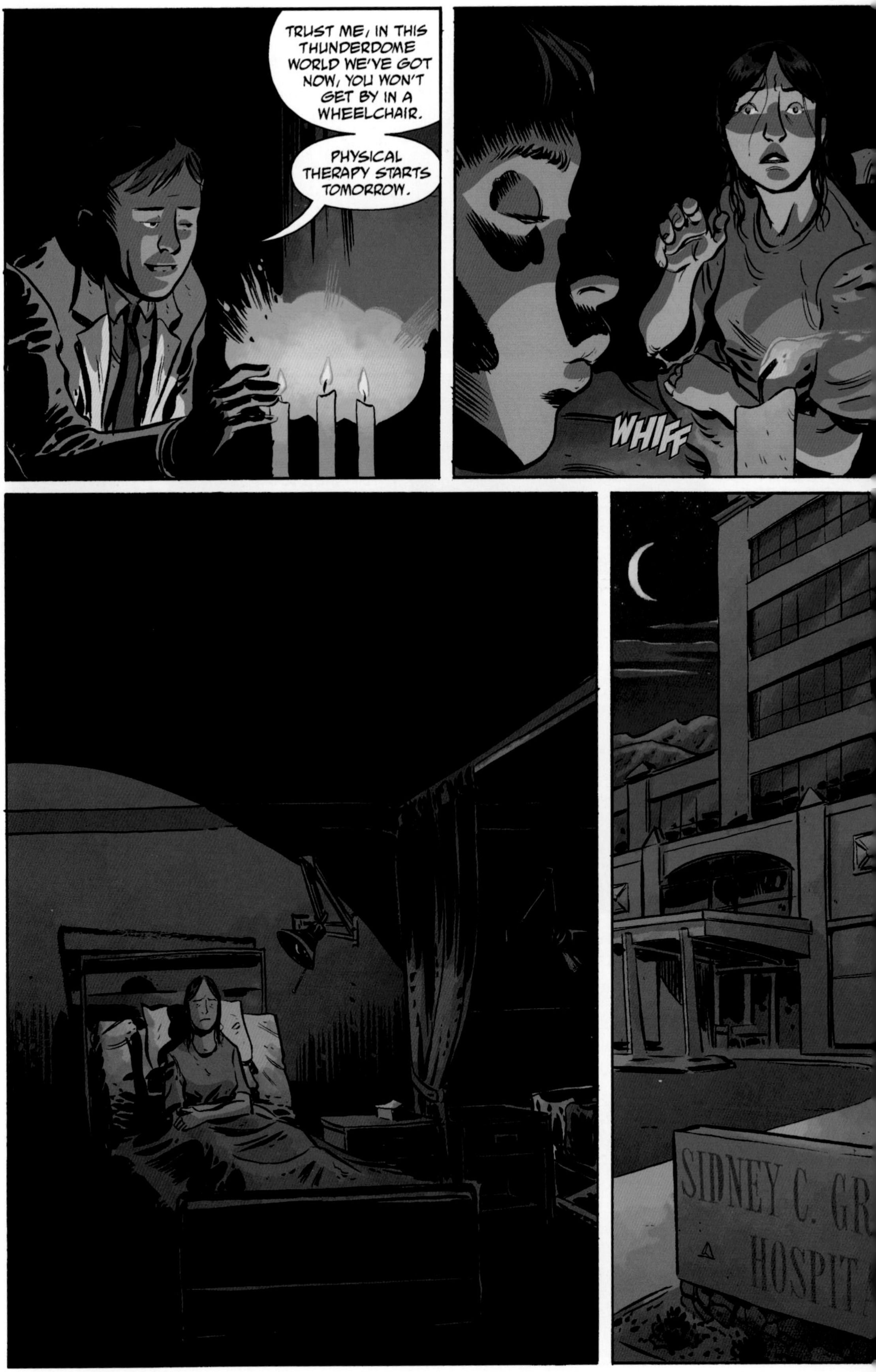
TRUST ME, IN THIS THUNDERDOME WORLD WE'VE GOT NOW, YOU WON'T GET BY IN A WHEELCHAIR.
PHYSICAL THERAPY STARTS TOMORROW.
WHIFF
SIDNEY C. GR
HOSPIT

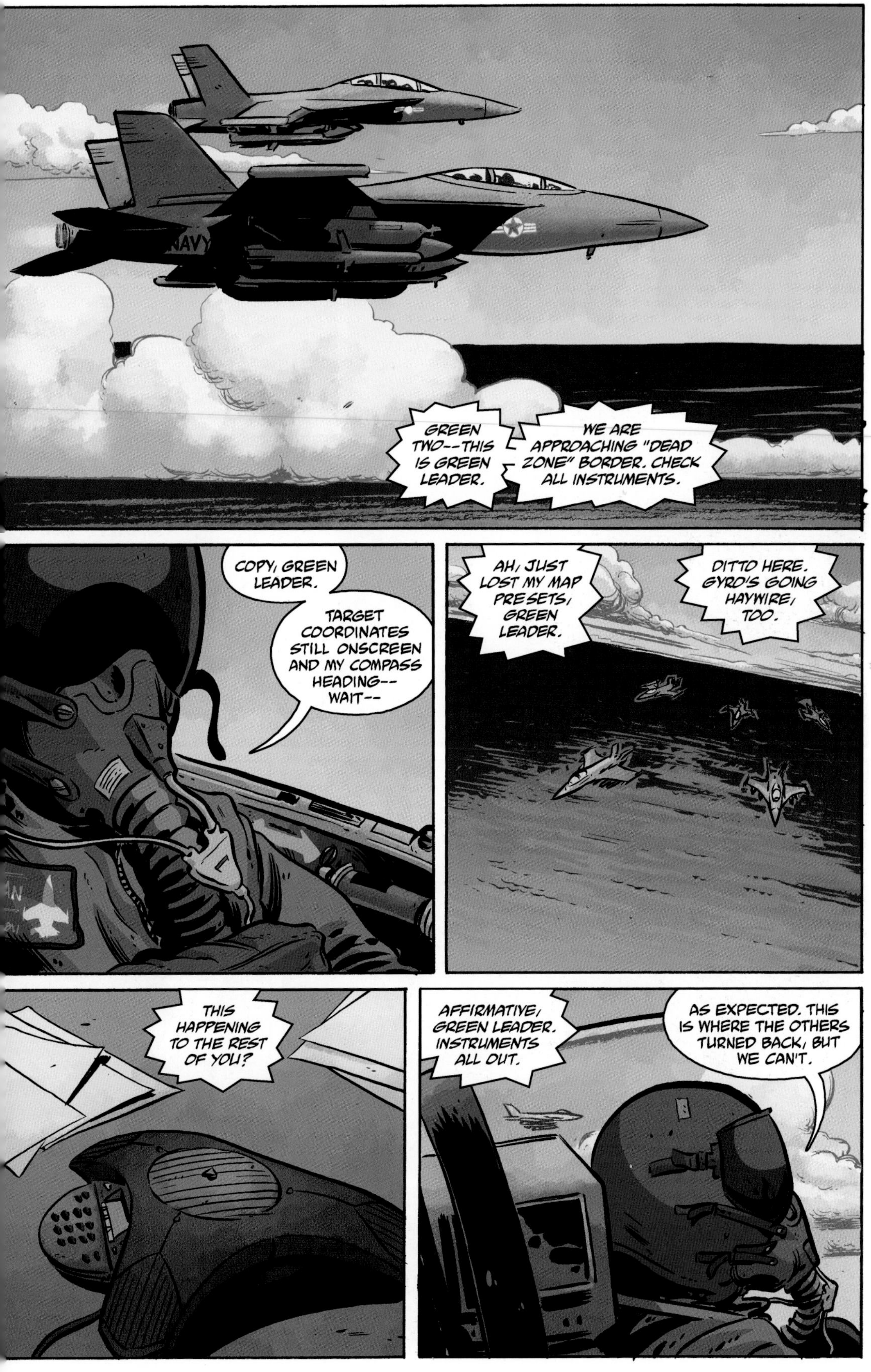
GREEN TWO--THIS IS GREEN LEADER.
WE ARE APPROACHING "DEAD ZONE" BORDER. CHECK ALL INSTRUMENTS.
COPY, GREEN LEADER.
TARGET COORDINATES STILL ONSCREEN AND MY COMPASS HEADING--WAIT--
AH, JUST LOST MY MAP PRESETS, GREEN LEADER.
DITTO HERE. GYRO'S GOING HAYWIRE, TOO.
THIS HAPPENING TO THE REST OF YOU?
AFFIRMATIVE, GREEN LEADER. INSTRUMENTS ALL OUT.
AS EXPECTED. THIS IS WHERE THE OTHERS TURNED BACK, BUT WE CAN'T.
NAVY

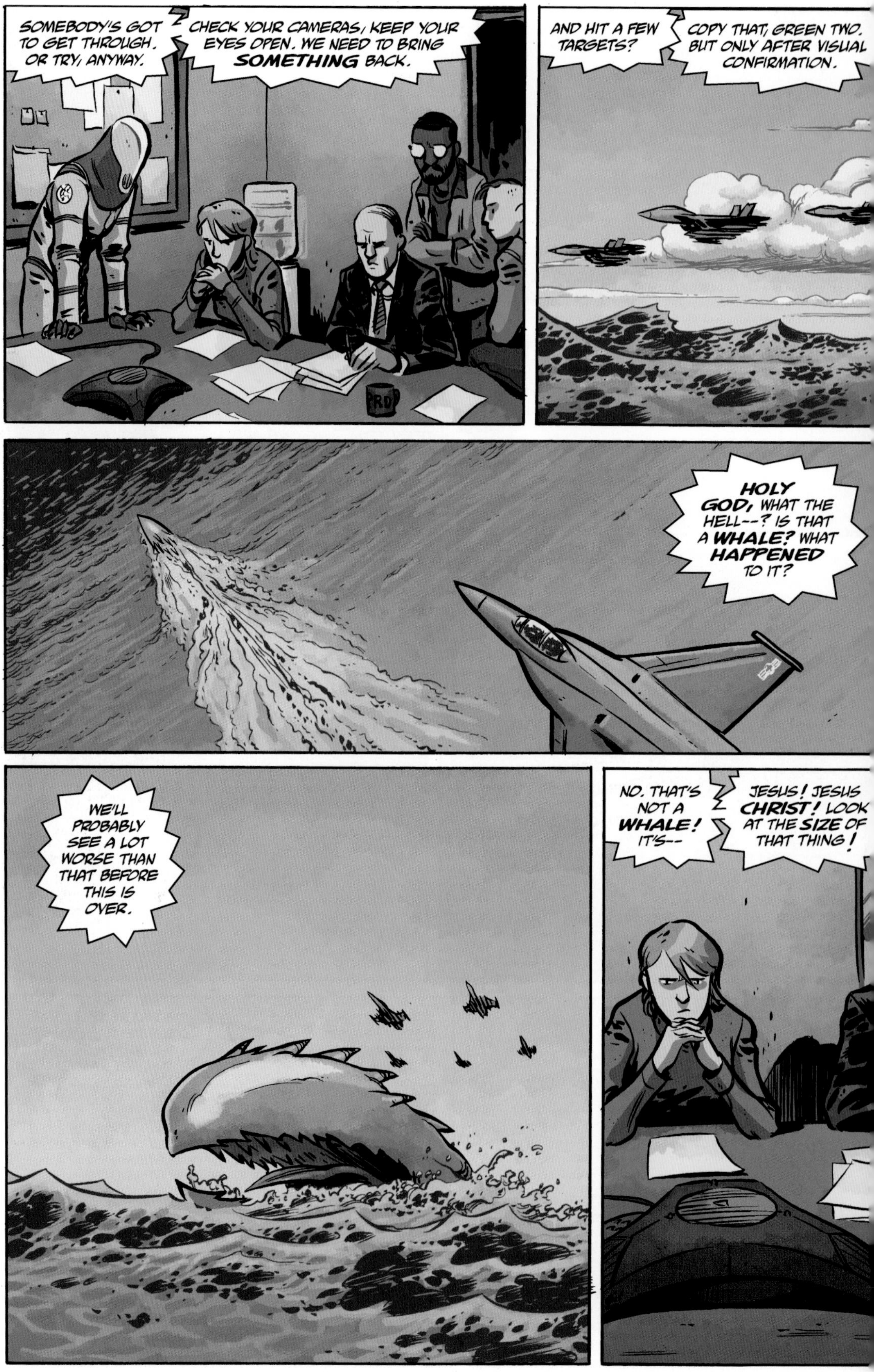
SOMEBODY'S GOT TO GET THROUGH. OR TRY, ANYWAY.
CHECK YOUR CAMERAS, KEEP YOUR EYES OPEN. WE NEED TO BRING SOMETHING BACK.
AND HIT A FEW TARGETS?
COPY THAT, GREEN TWO. BUT ONLY AFTER VISUAL CONFIRMATION.
HOLY GOD, WHAT THE HELL--? IS THAT A WHALE? WHAT HAPPENED TO IT?
WE'LL PROBABLY SEE A LOT WORSE THAN THAT BEFORE THIS IS OVER.
NO. THAT'S NOT A WHALE! IT'S--
JESUS! JESUS CHRIST! LOOK AT THE SIZE OF THAT THING!
PRD

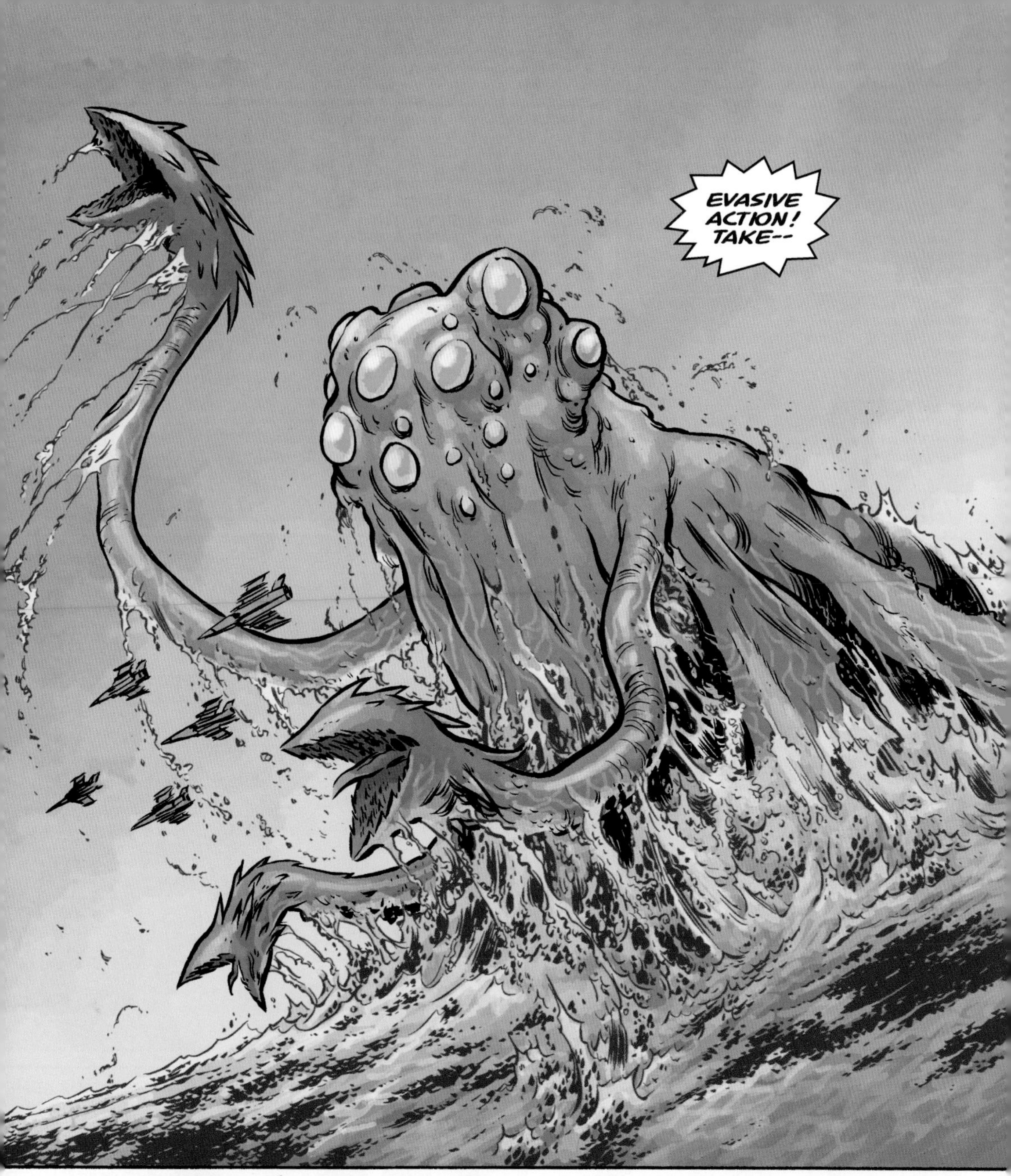
EVASIVE ACTION! TAKE--

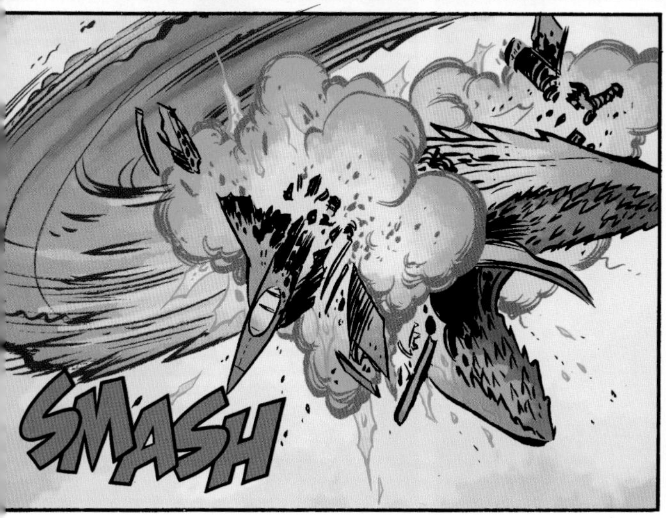
SMASH

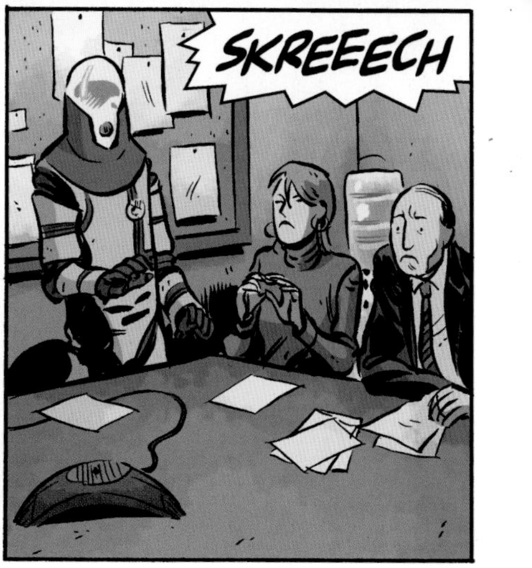
SKREEECH

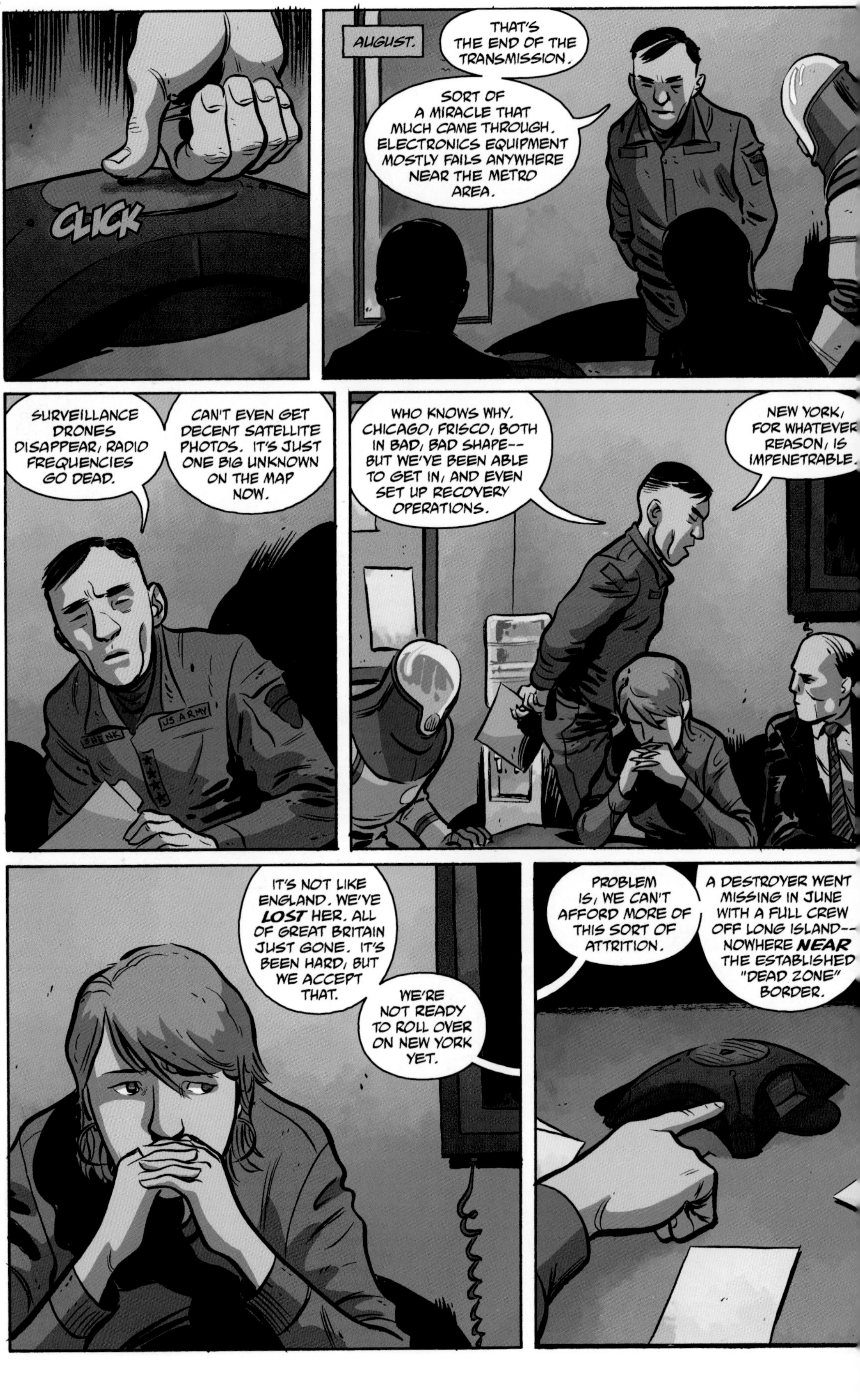
CLICK
AUGUST.
THAT'S THE END OF THE TRANSMISSION.
SORT OF A MIRACLE THAT MUCH CAME THROUGH. ELECTRONICS EQUIPMENT MOSTLY FAILS ANYWHERE NEAR THE METRO AREA.
SURVEILLANCE DRONES DISAPPEAR, RADIO FREQUENCIES GO DEAD.
CAN'T EVEN GET DECENT SATELLITE PHOTOS. IT'S JUST ONE BIG UNKNOWN ON THE MAP NOW.
SHENK
U.S. ARMY
WHO KNOWS WHY. CHICAGO, FRISCO, BOTH IN BAD, BAD SHAPE-- BUT WE'VE BEEN ABLE TO GET IN, AND EVEN SET UP RECOVERY OPERATIONS.
NEW YORK, FOR WHATEVER REASON, IS IMPENETRABLE.
IT'S NOT LIKE ENGLAND. WE'VE LOST HER. ALL OF GREAT BRITAIN JUST GONE. IT'S BEEN HARD, BUT WE ACCEPT THAT.
WE'RE NOT READY TO ROLL OVER ON NEW YORK YET.
PROBLEM IS, WE CAN'T AFFORD MORE OF THIS SORT OF ATTRITION.
A DESTROYER WENT MISSING IN JUNE WITH A FULL CREW OFF LONG ISLAND-- NOWHERE NEAR THE ESTABLISHED "DEAD ZONE" BORDER.

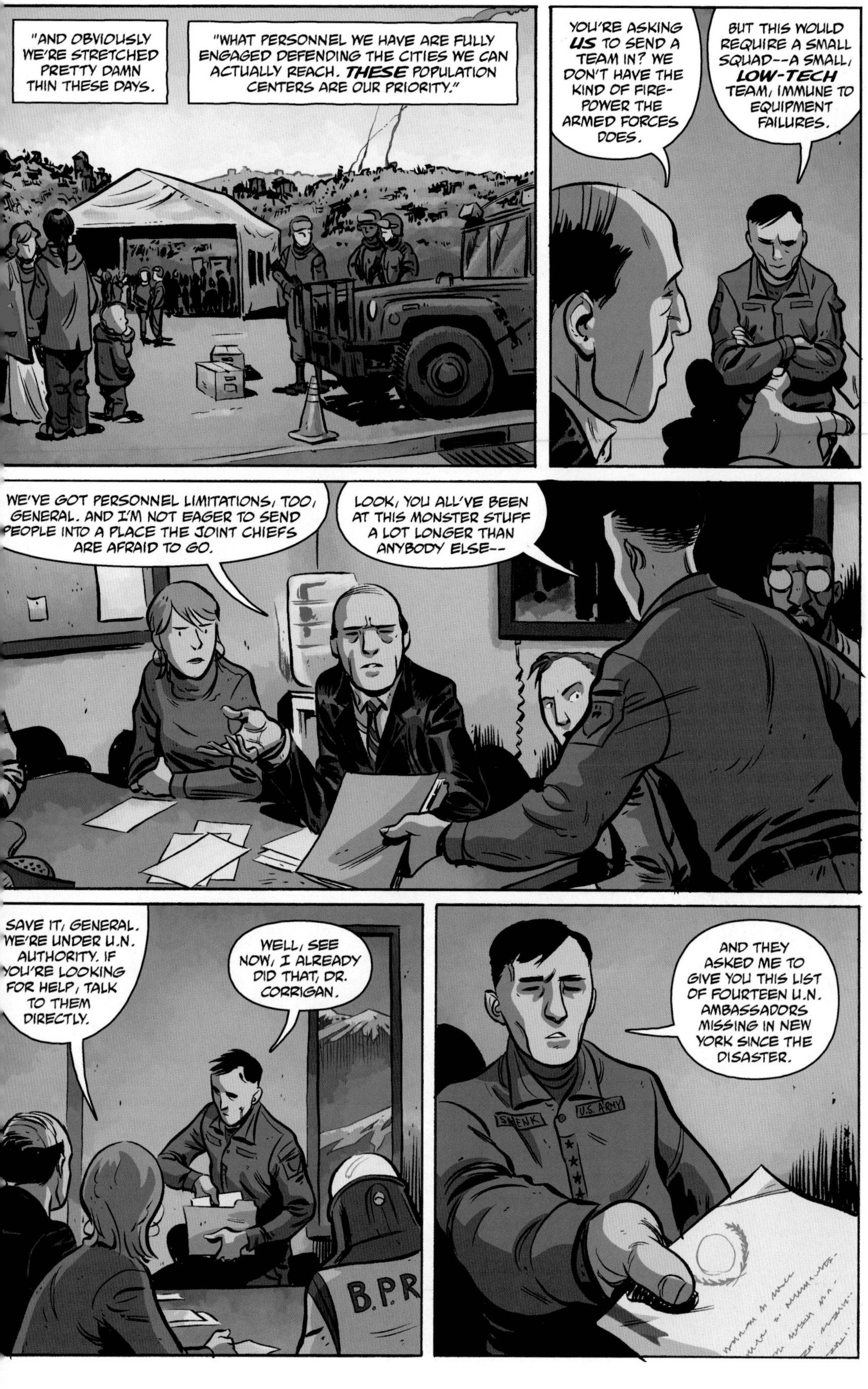
"AND OBVIOUSLY WE'RE STRETCHED PRETTY DAMN THIN THESE DAYS.
"WHAT PERSONNEL WE HAVE ARE FULLY ENGAGED DEFENDING THE CITIES WE CAN ACTUALLY REACH. *THESE* POPULATION CENTERS ARE OUR PRIORITY."
YOU'RE ASKING *US* TO SEND A TEAM IN? WE DON'T HAVE THE KIND OF FIRE-POWER THE ARMED FORCES DOES.
BUT THIS WOULD REQUIRE A SMALL SQUAD--A SMALL, *LOW-TECH* TEAM, IMMUNE TO EQUIPMENT FAILURES.
WE'VE GOT PERSONNEL LIMITATIONS, TOO, GENERAL. AND I'M NOT EAGER TO SEND PEOPLE INTO A PLACE THE JOINT CHIEFS ARE AFRAID TO GO.
LOOK, YOU ALL'VE BEEN AT THIS MONSTER STUFF A LOT LONGER THAN ANYBODY ELSE--
SAVE IT, GENERAL. WE'RE UNDER U.N. AUTHORITY. IF YOU'RE LOOKING FOR HELP, TALK TO THEM DIRECTLY.
WELL, SEE NOW, I ALREADY DID THAT, DR. CORRIGAN.
B.P.R
AND THEY ASKED ME TO GIVE YOU THIS LIST OF FOURTEEN U.N. AMBASSADORS MISSING IN NEW YORK SINCE THE DISASTER.
U.S. ARMY

--AND IF PEOPLE WANT TO THINK I'M CRAZY, THEN THEY CAN GO AHEAD.
BZZ BZZ
BZZ BZZ
BUT THEY ONLY THINK THAT BECAUSE I'M NOT TALKIN' ABOUT HEAVEN, OR HELL, OR KOLOB, OR ANY **OTHER** WORLD.
BZZ
blood taken
from San Francisco
months ago
vigorous
and my
BZZ
I'M TALKIN' ABOUT **THIS** WORLD. I'M TALKIN' ABOUT **NOW!** AND **THAT** MAKES ME CRAZY.
BZZ
BZZ
THE BIBLE? IT'S A NICE BOOK. LOTS OF STORIES IN HERE.
BUT IT'S NOT **OUR** BOOK!

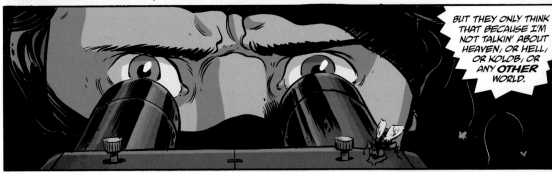

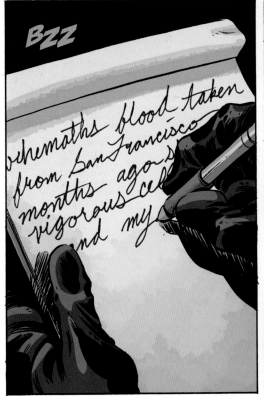

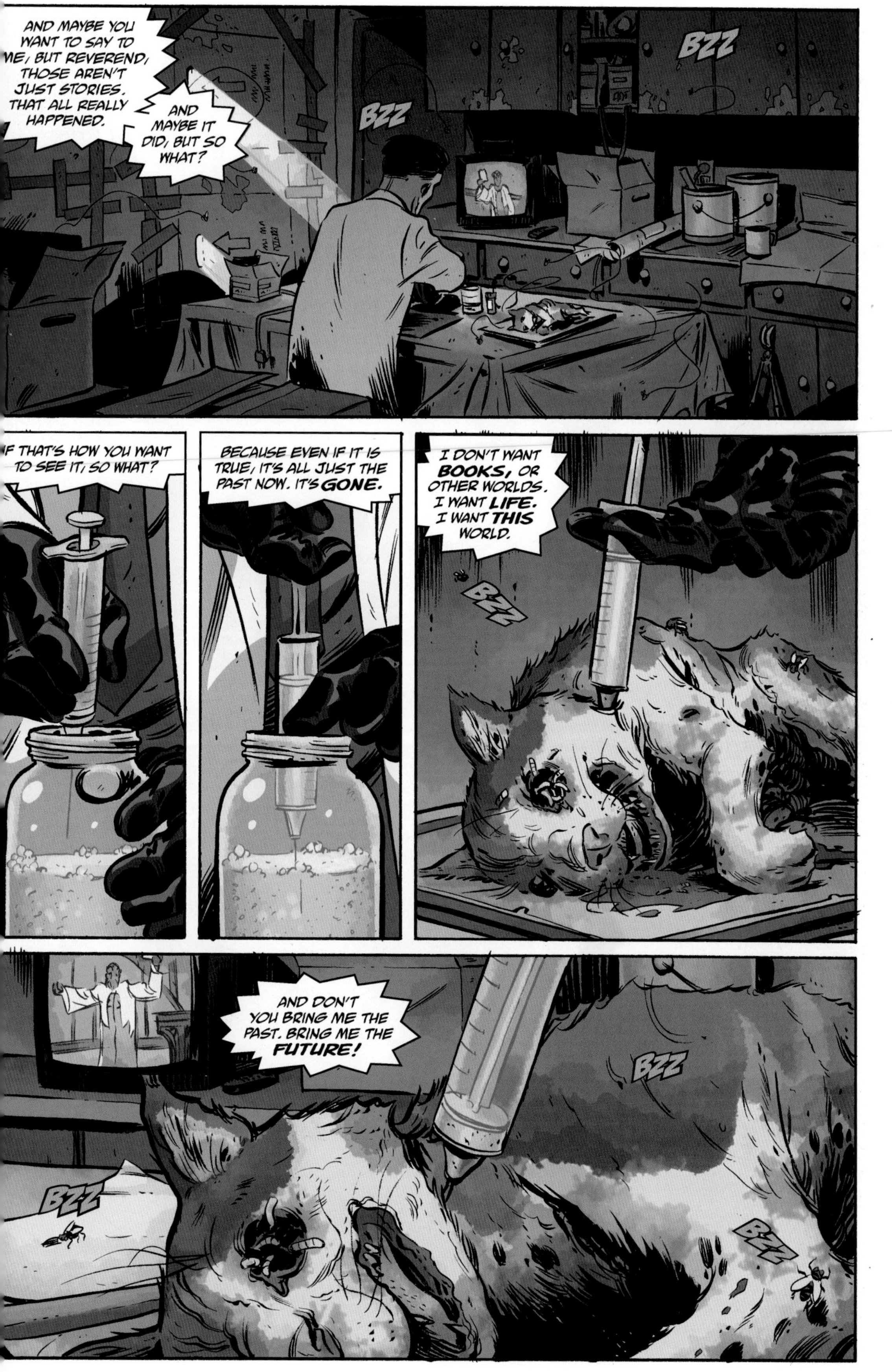
AND MAYBE YOU WANT TO SAY TO ME, BUT REVEREND, THOSE AREN'T JUST STORIES. THAT ALL REALLY HAPPENED.
AND MAYBE IT DID, BUT SO WHAT?
BZZ
BZZ
IF THAT'S HOW YOU WANT TO SEE IT, SO WHAT?
BECAUSE EVEN IF IT IS TRUE, IT'S ALL JUST THE PAST NOW. IT'S **GONE.**
I DON'T WANT **BOOKS,** OR OTHER WORLDS. I WANT **LIFE.** I WANT **THIS** WORLD.
BZZ
AND DON'T YOU BRING ME THE PAST. BRING ME THE **FUTURE!**
BZZ
BZZ
BZZ

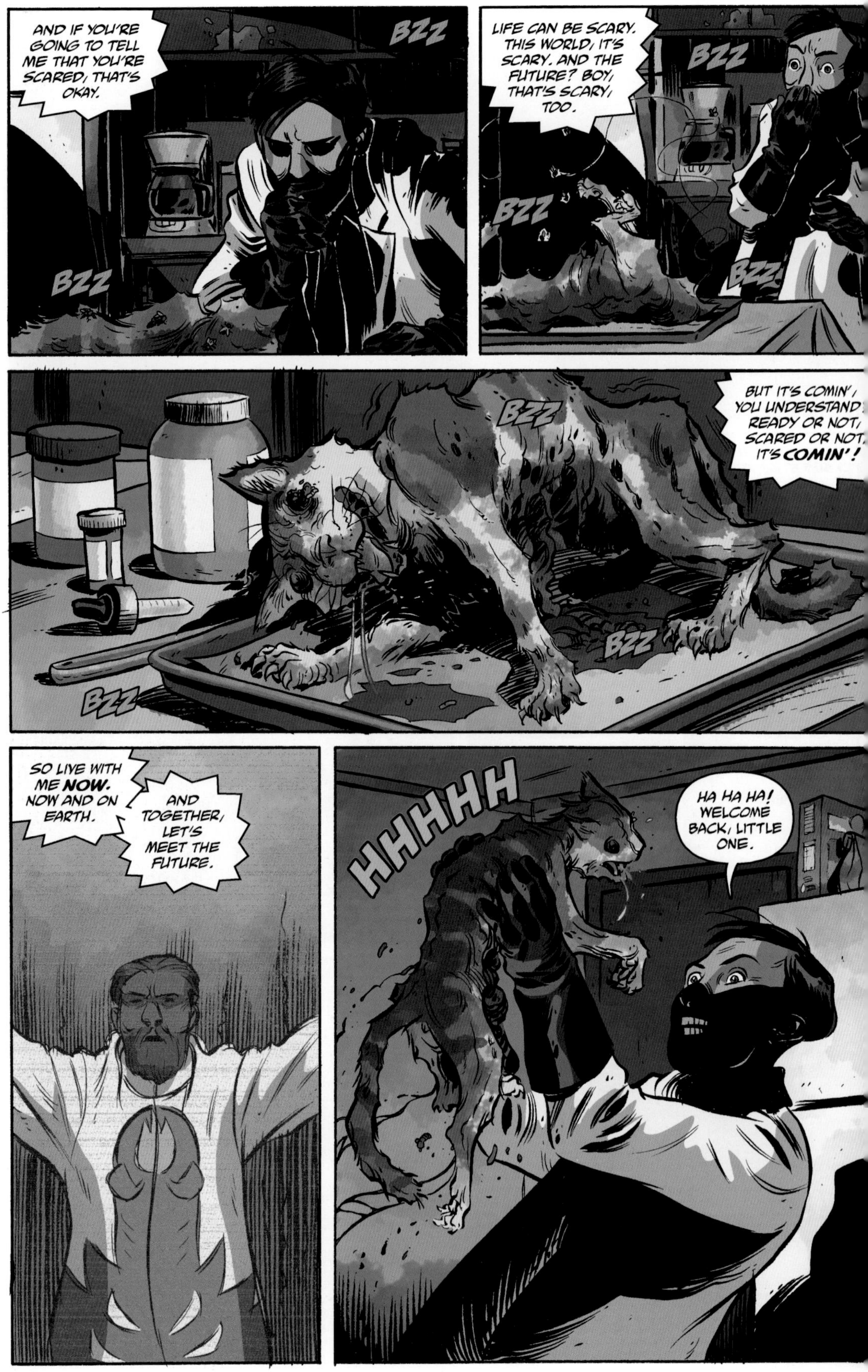
AND IF YOU'RE GOING TO TELL ME THAT YOU'RE SCARED, THAT'S OKAY.
BZZ
BZZ
LIFE CAN BE SCARY. THIS WORLD, IT'S SCARY. AND THE FUTURE? BOY, THAT'S SCARY, TOO.
BZZ
BZZ
BZZ
BUT IT'S COMIN', YOU UNDERSTAND? READY OR NOT, SCARED OR NOT, IT'S COMIN'!
BZZ
BZZ
BZZ
SO LIVE WITH ME NOW. NOW AND ON EARTH.
AND TOGETHER, LET'S MEET THE FUTURE.
HHHHHH
HA HA HA! WELCOME BACK, LITTLE ONE.

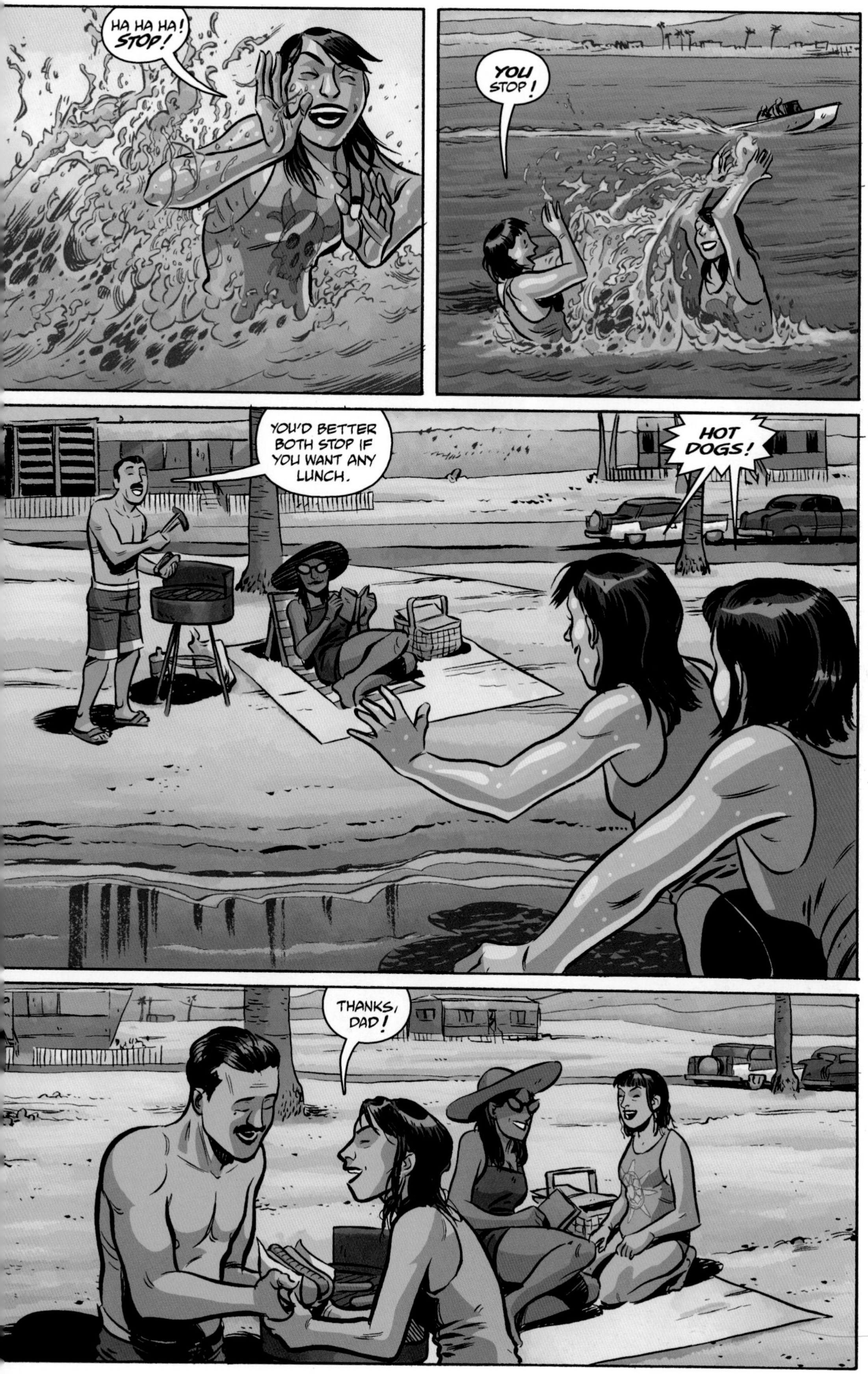
HA HA HA! STOP!
YOU STOP!
YOU'D BETTER BOTH STOP IF YOU WANT ANY LUNCH.
HOT DOGS!
THANKS, DAD!

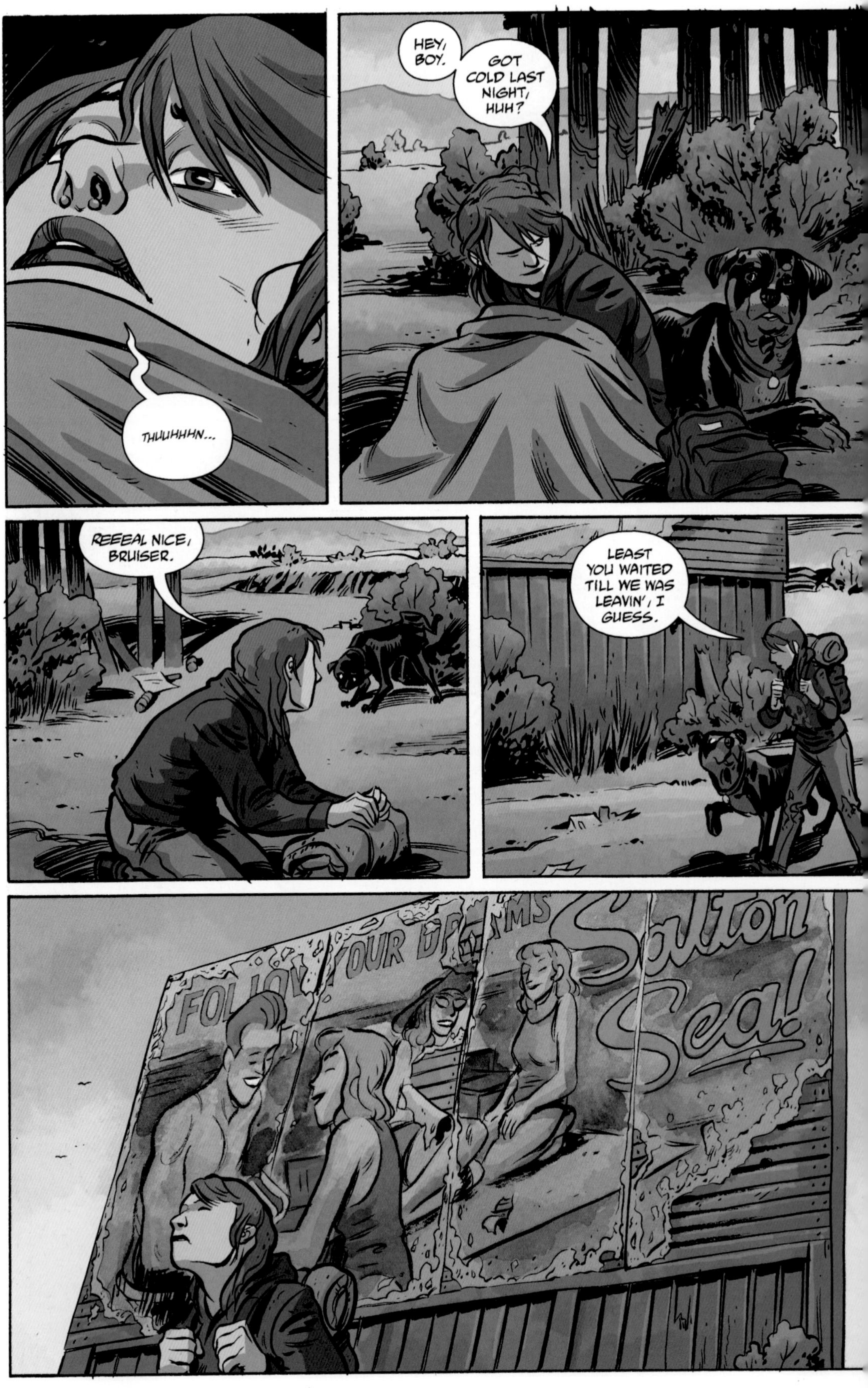
THUUHHHN...
HEY, BOY.
GOT COLD LAST NIGHT, HUH?
REEEAL NICE, BRUISER.
LEAST YOU WAITED TILL WE WAS LEAVIN', I GUESS.
FOLLOW YOUR DR MS
Salton Sea!

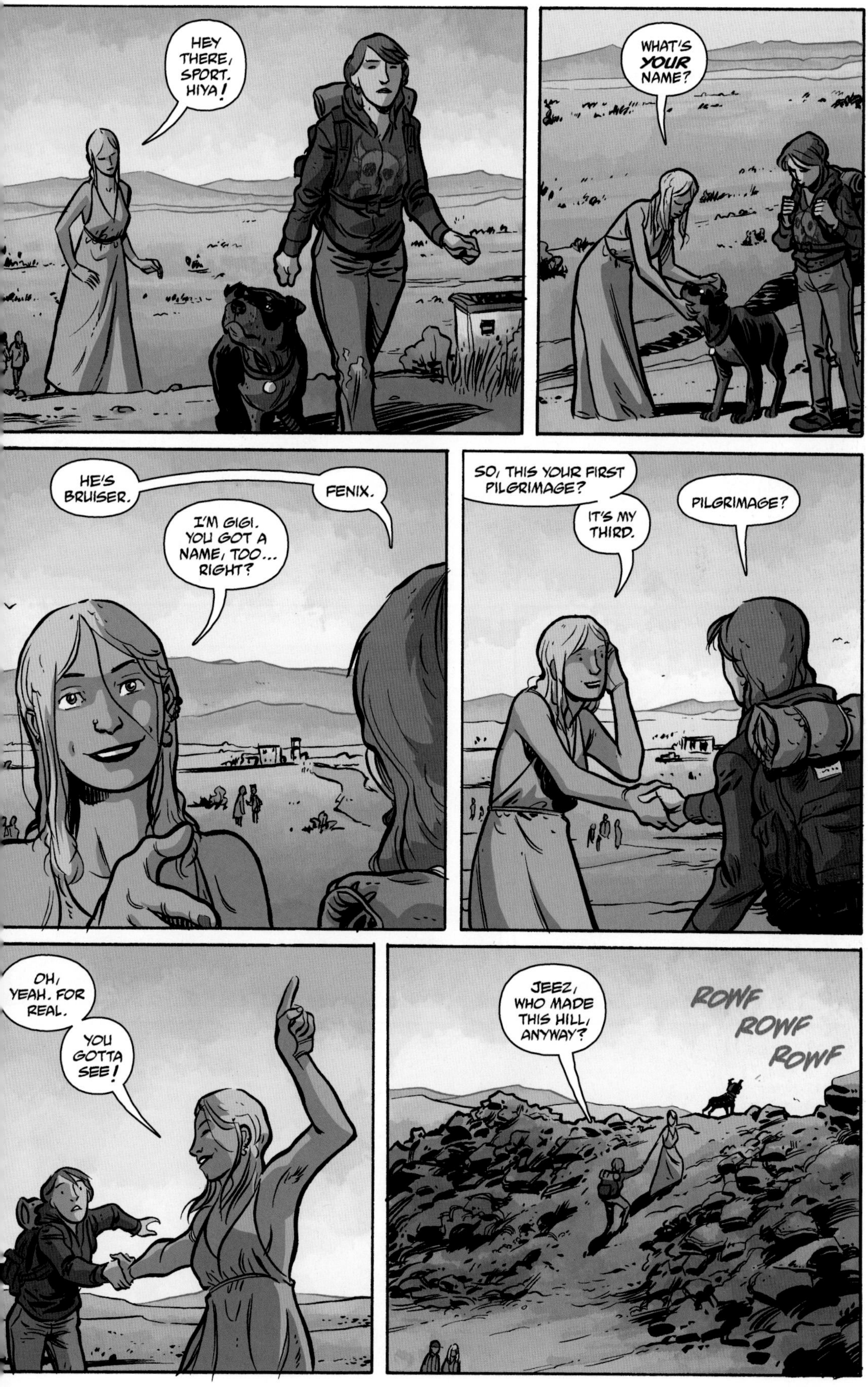
HEY THERE, SPORT. HIYA!
WHAT'S YOUR NAME?
HE'S BRUISER.
FENIX.
I'M GIGI. YOU GOT A NAME, TOO... RIGHT?
SO, THIS YOUR FIRST PILGRIMAGE?
IT'S MY THIRD.
PILGRIMAGE?
OH, YEAH. FOR REAL.
YOU GOTTA SEE!
JEEZ, WHO MADE THIS HILL, ANYWAY?
ROWF ROWF ROWF

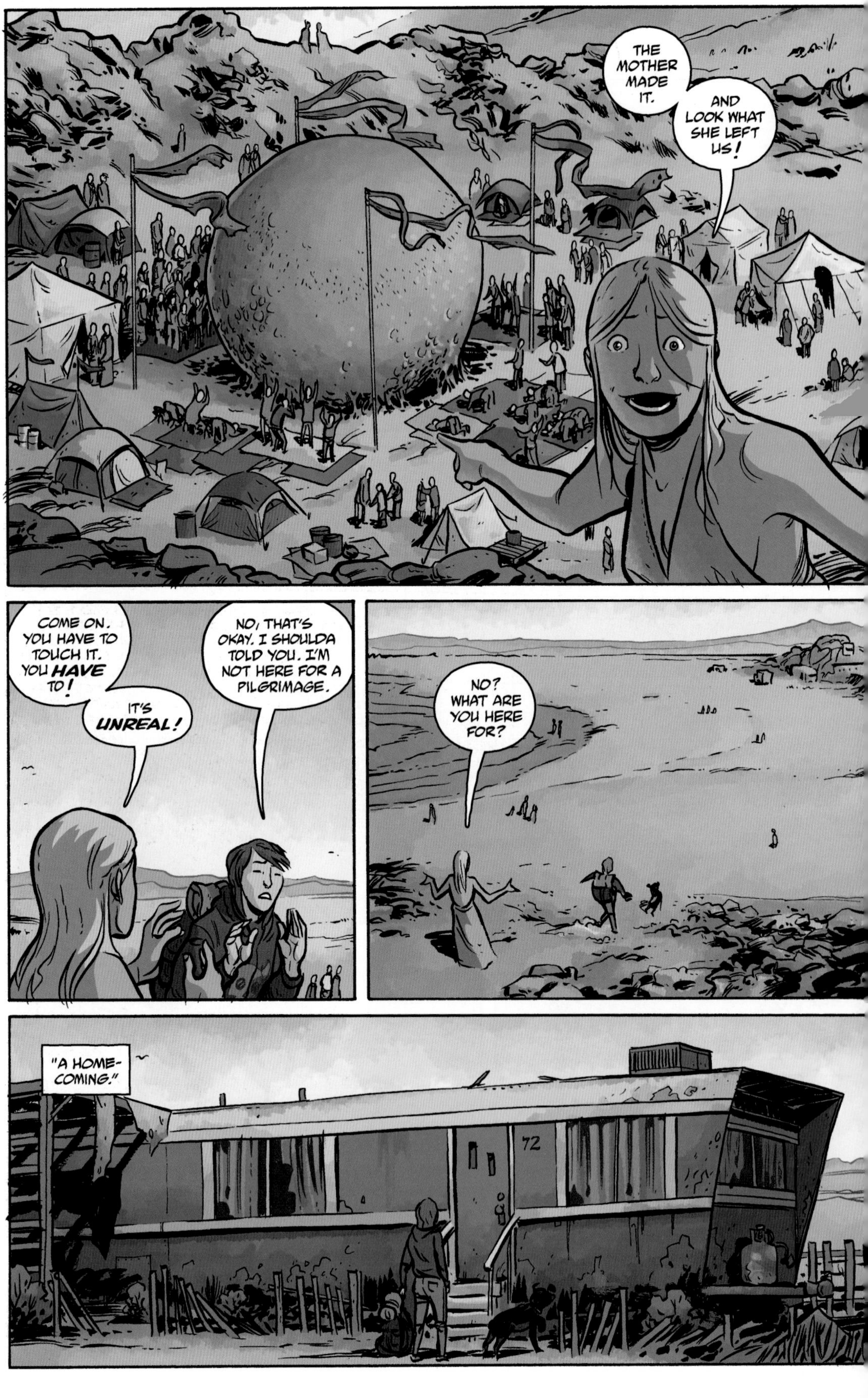
THE MOTHER MADE IT.
AND LOOK WHAT SHE LEFT US!
COME ON. YOU HAVE TO TOUCH IT. YOU HAVE TO!
IT'S UNREAL!
NO, THAT'S OKAY. I SHOULDA TOLD YOU. I'M NOT HERE FOR A PILGRIMAGE.
NO? WHAT ARE YOU HERE FOR?
"A HOME-COMING."
72

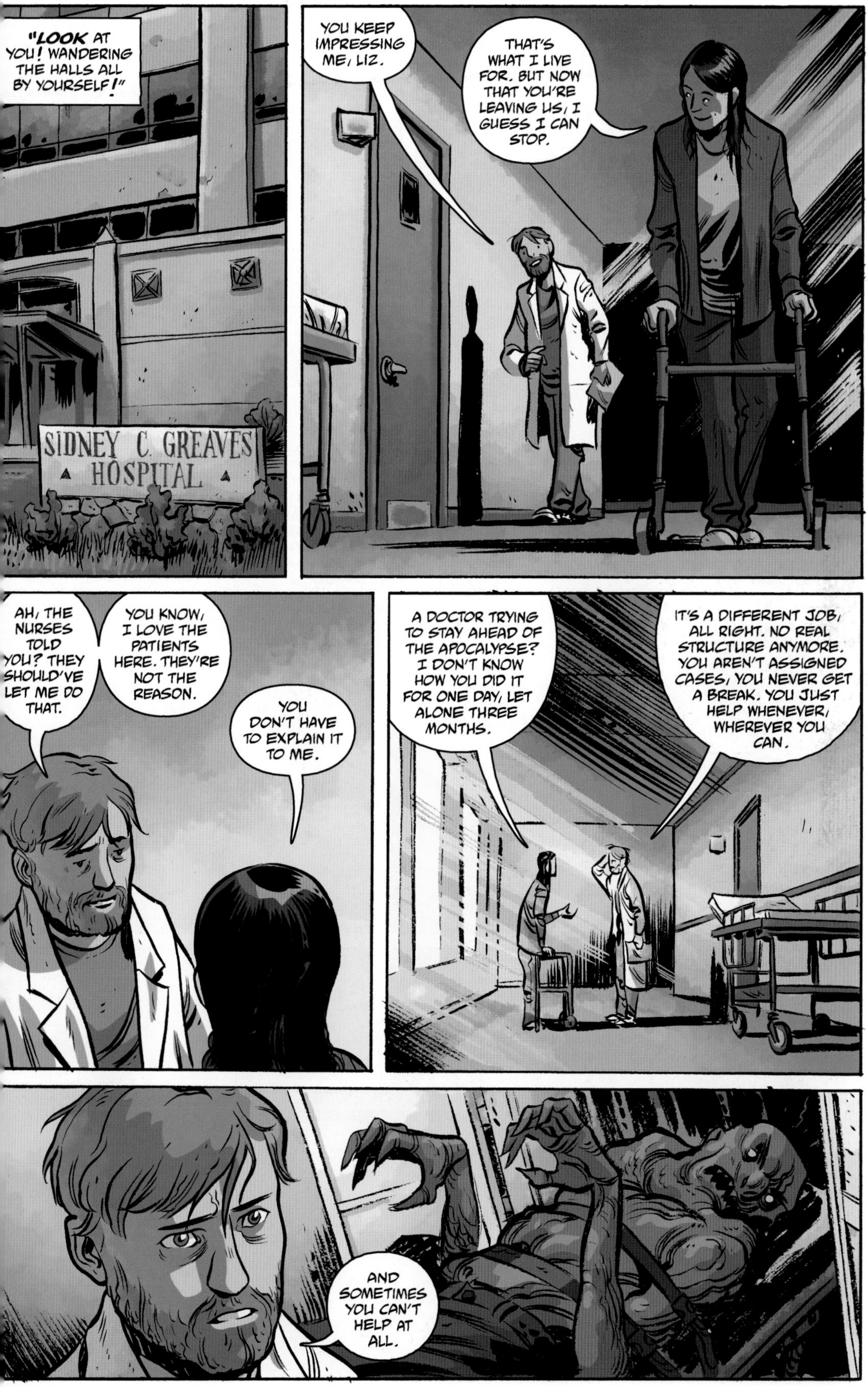
"LOOK AT YOU! WANDERING THE HALLS ALL BY YOURSELF!"
SIDNEY C. GREAVES HOSPITAL
YOU KEEP IMPRESSING ME, LIZ.
THAT'S WHAT I LIVE FOR. BUT NOW THAT YOU'RE LEAVING US, I GUESS I CAN STOP.
AH, THE NURSES TOLD YOU? THEY SHOULD'VE LET ME DO THAT.
YOU KNOW, I LOVE THE PATIENTS HERE. THEY'RE NOT THE REASON.
YOU DON'T HAVE TO EXPLAIN IT TO ME.
A DOCTOR TRYING TO STAY AHEAD OF THE APOCALYPSE? I DON'T KNOW HOW YOU DID IT FOR ONE DAY, LET ALONE THREE MONTHS.
IT'S A DIFFERENT JOB, ALL RIGHT. NO REAL STRUCTURE ANYMORE. YOU AREN'T ASSIGNED CASES, YOU NEVER GET A BREAK. YOU JUST HELP WHENEVER, WHEREVER YOU CAN.
AND SOMETIMES YOU CAN'T HELP AT ALL.

AGAIN, NO EXPLANATION NECESSARY.

BUT I *WAS* THINKING THE WAY YOU'VE BEEN STALKING ME ALL THIS TIME IT WAS LEADING UP TO A DINNER DATE EVENTUALLY.

I'LL MAKE A SPECIAL TRIP FOR THAT--THAT IS, IF YOU DON'T FALL IN LOVE WITH MY REPLACEMENT.

BUT ACTUALLY, THERE'S A REASON I WAS LOOKING FOR YOU TODAY.

YOU'VE GOT A NEW ROOM-MATE.

AND? I MEAN, I'VE HAD LOTS OF 'EM.

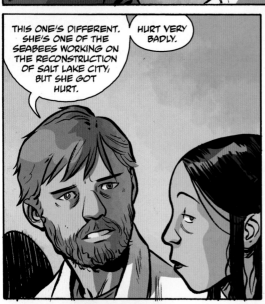

THIS ONE'S DIFFERENT. SHE'S ONE OF THE SEABEES WORKING ON THE RECONSTRUCTION OF SALT LAKE CITY, BUT SHE GOT HURT.

HURT VERY BADLY.

HER SPIRITS ARE LOW, AND I FELT THAT IF SHE COULD BE AROUND SOMEBODY WHO CAME THROUGH THE FIRE AND IS DOING AS WELL AS YOU...

SO NOW I'M YOUR CHEERLEADER? BOY, THAT BETTER BE *SOME* DINNER.

HEY, WHO LET YOU IN HERE?

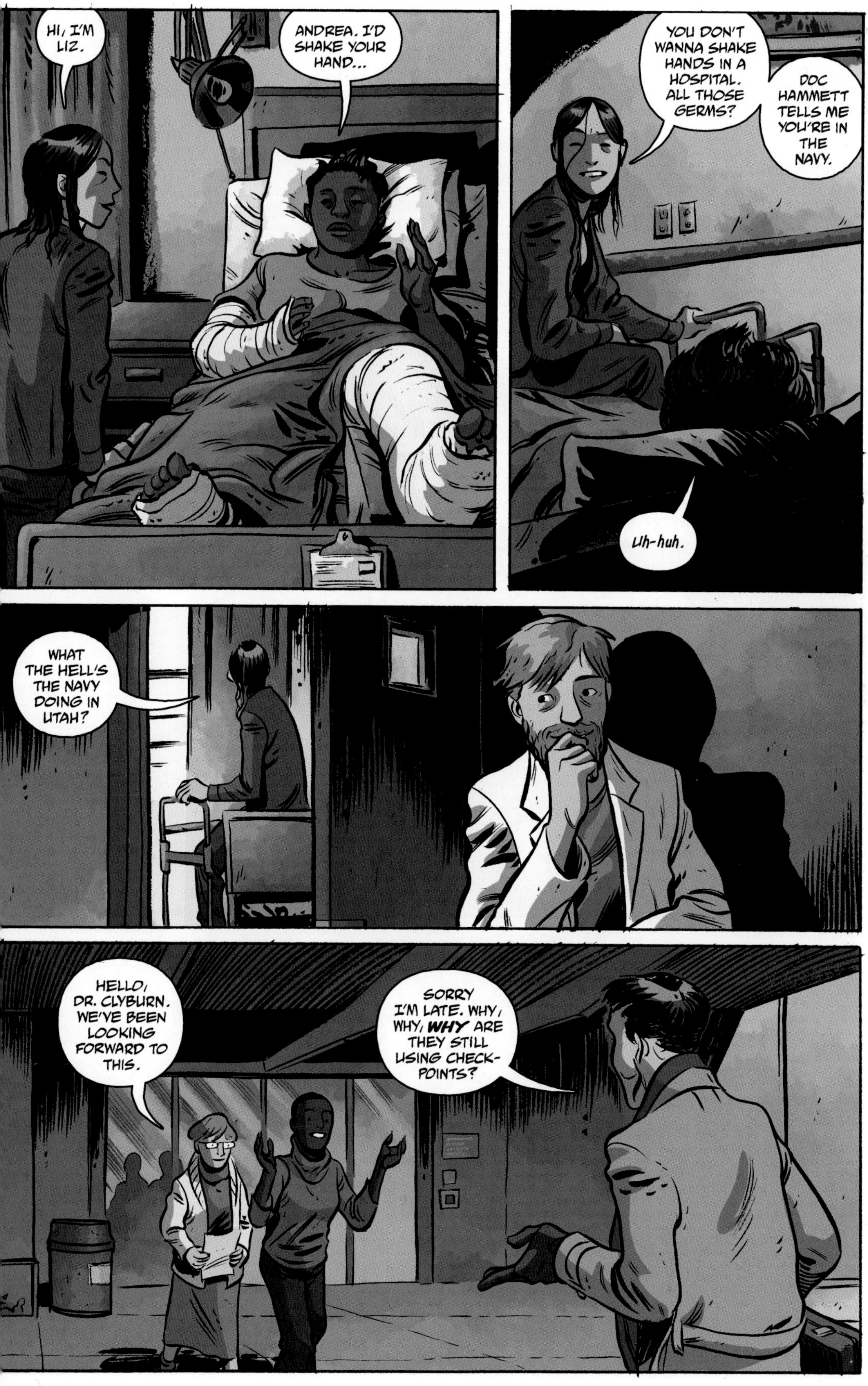

HI, I'M LIZ.
ANDREA. I'D SHAKE YOUR HAND...
YOU DON'T WANNA SHAKE HANDS IN A HOSPITAL. ALL THOSE GERMS?
DOC HAMMETT TELLS ME YOU'RE IN THE NAVY.
Uh-huh.
WHAT THE HELL'S THE NAVY DOING IN UTAH?
HELLO, DR. CLYBURN. WE'VE BEEN LOOKING FORWARD TO THIS.
SORRY I'M LATE. WHY, WHY, **WHY** ARE THEY STILL USING CHECK-POINTS?

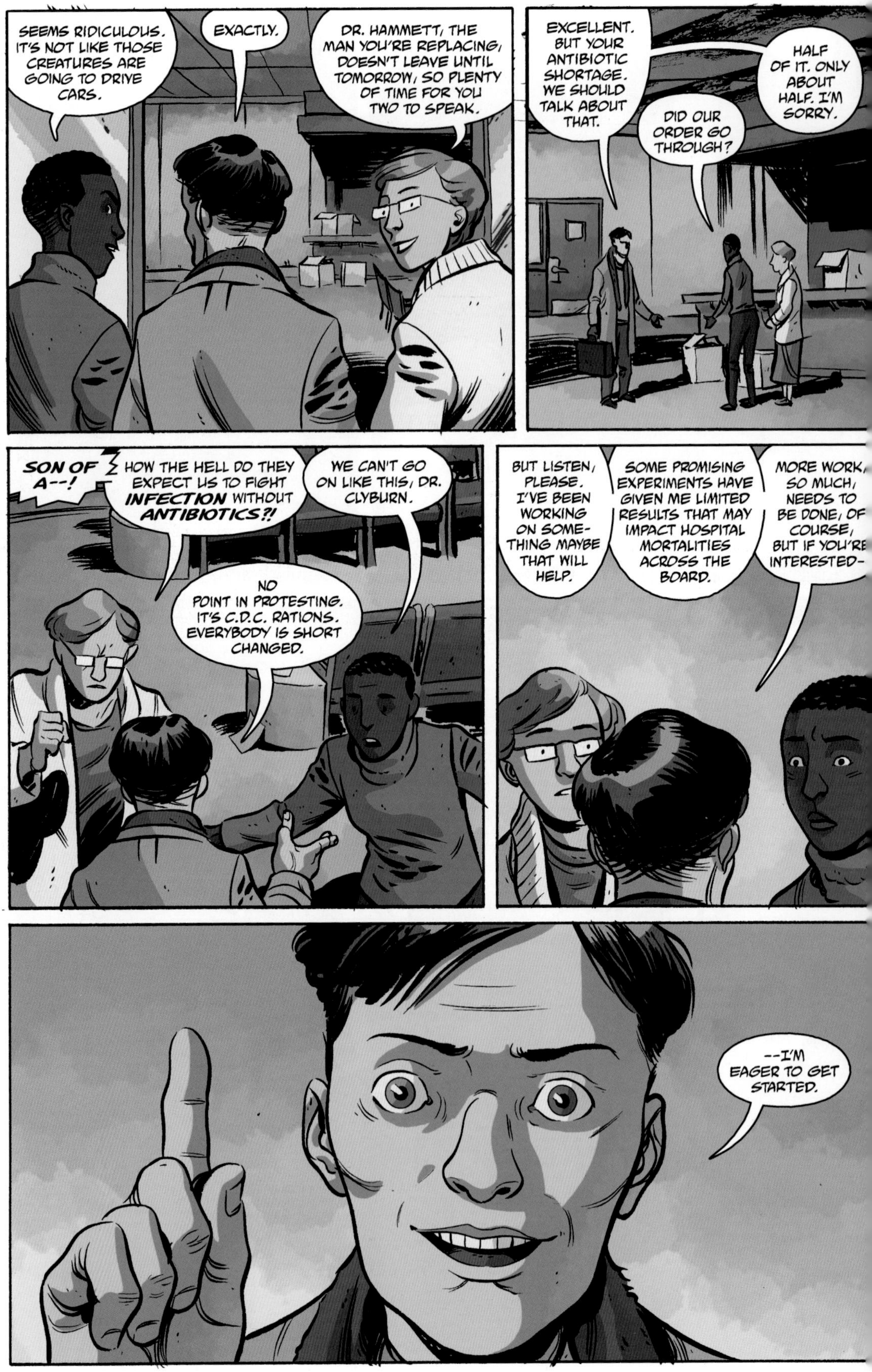
SEEMS RIDICULOUS. IT'S NOT LIKE THOSE CREATURES ARE GOING TO DRIVE CARS.
EXACTLY.
DR. HAMMETT, THE MAN YOU'RE REPLACING, DOESN'T LEAVE UNTIL TOMORROW, SO PLENTY OF TIME FOR YOU TWO TO SPEAK.
EXCELLENT. BUT YOUR ANTIBIOTIC SHORTAGE. WE SHOULD TALK ABOUT THAT.
DID OUR ORDER GO THROUGH?
HALF OF IT. ONLY ABOUT HALF. I'M SORRY.
SON OF A--!
HOW THE HELL DO THEY EXPECT US TO FIGHT INFECTION WITHOUT ANTIBIOTICS?!
WE CAN'T GO ON LIKE THIS, DR. CLYBURN.
NO POINT IN PROTESTING. IT'S C.D.C. RATIONS. EVERYBODY IS SHORT CHANGED.
BUT LISTEN, PLEASE. I'VE BEEN WORKING ON SOME-THING MAYBE THAT WILL HELP.
SOME PROMISING EXPERIMENTS HAVE GIVEN ME LIMITED RESULTS THAT MAY IMPACT HOSPITAL MORTALITIES ACROSS THE BOARD.
MORE WORK, SO MUCH, NEEDS TO BE DONE, OF COURSE, BUT IF YOU'RE INTERESTED-
--I'M EAGER TO GET STARTED.

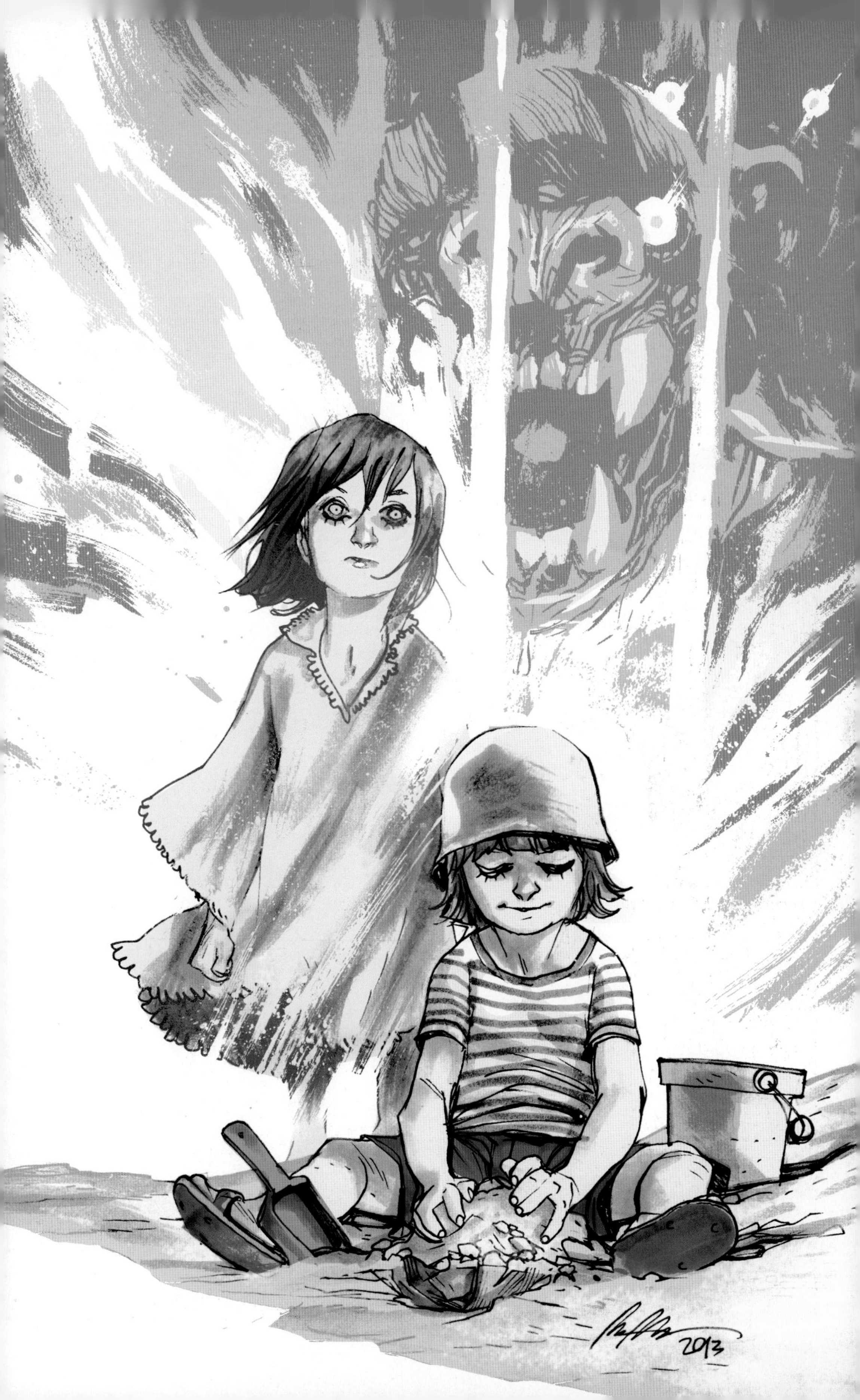
2013

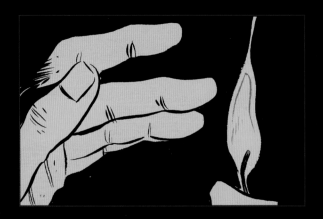

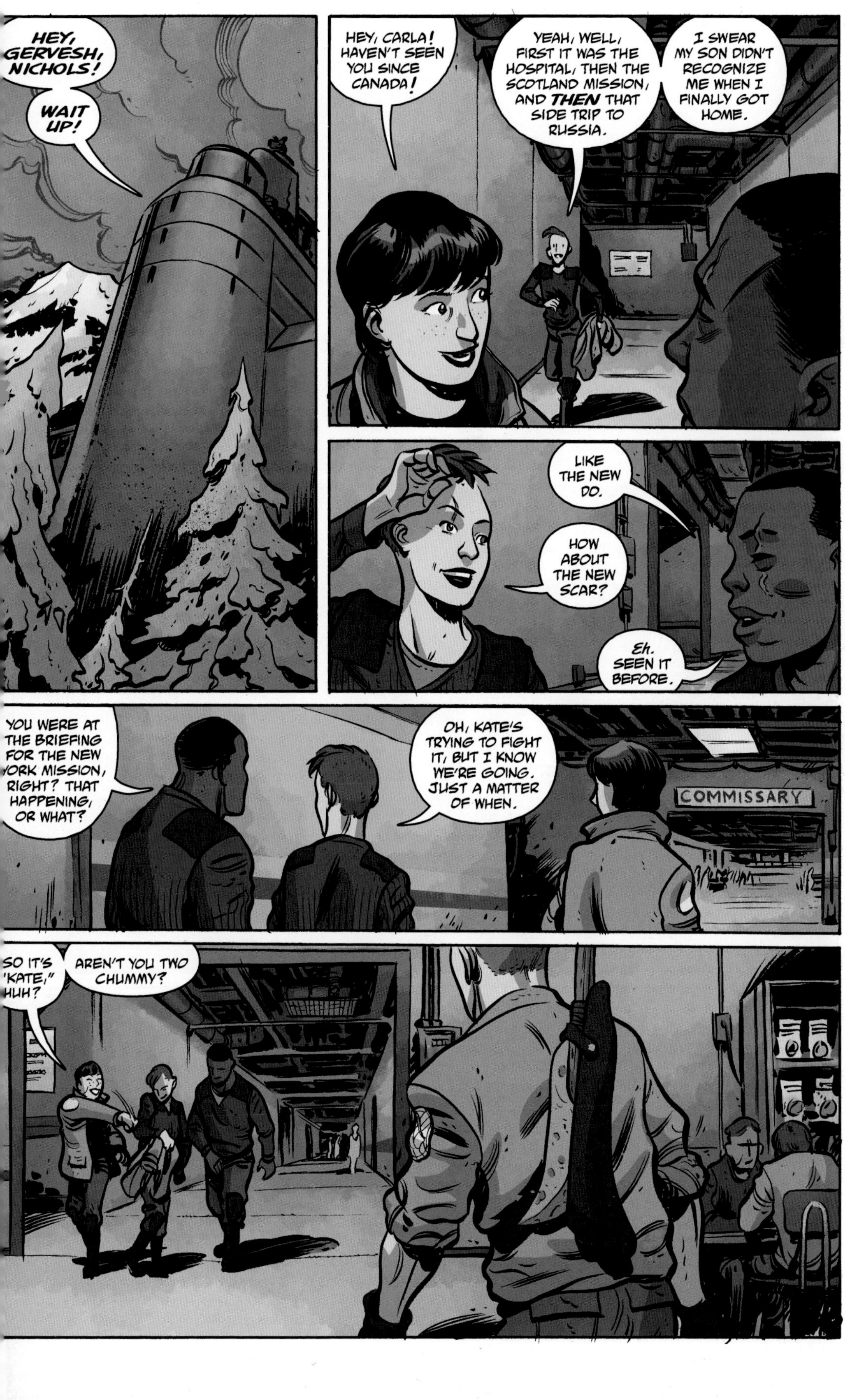
HEY, GERVESH, NICHOLS!
WAIT UP!
HEY, CARLA! HAVEN'T SEEN YOU SINCE CANADA!
YEAH, WELL, FIRST IT WAS THE HOSPITAL, THEN THE SCOTLAND MISSION, AND THEN THAT SIDE TRIP TO RUSSIA.
I SWEAR MY SON DIDN'T RECOGNIZE ME WHEN I FINALLY GOT HOME.
LIKE THE NEW DO.
HOW ABOUT THE NEW SCAR?
Eh. SEEN IT BEFORE.
YOU WERE AT THE BRIEFING FOR THE NEW YORK MISSION, RIGHT? THAT HAPPENING, OR WHAT?
OH, KATE'S TRYING TO FIGHT IT, BUT I KNOW WE'RE GOING. JUST A MATTER OF WHEN.
COMMISSARY
SO IT'S "KATE," HUH?
AREN'T YOU TWO CHUMMY?

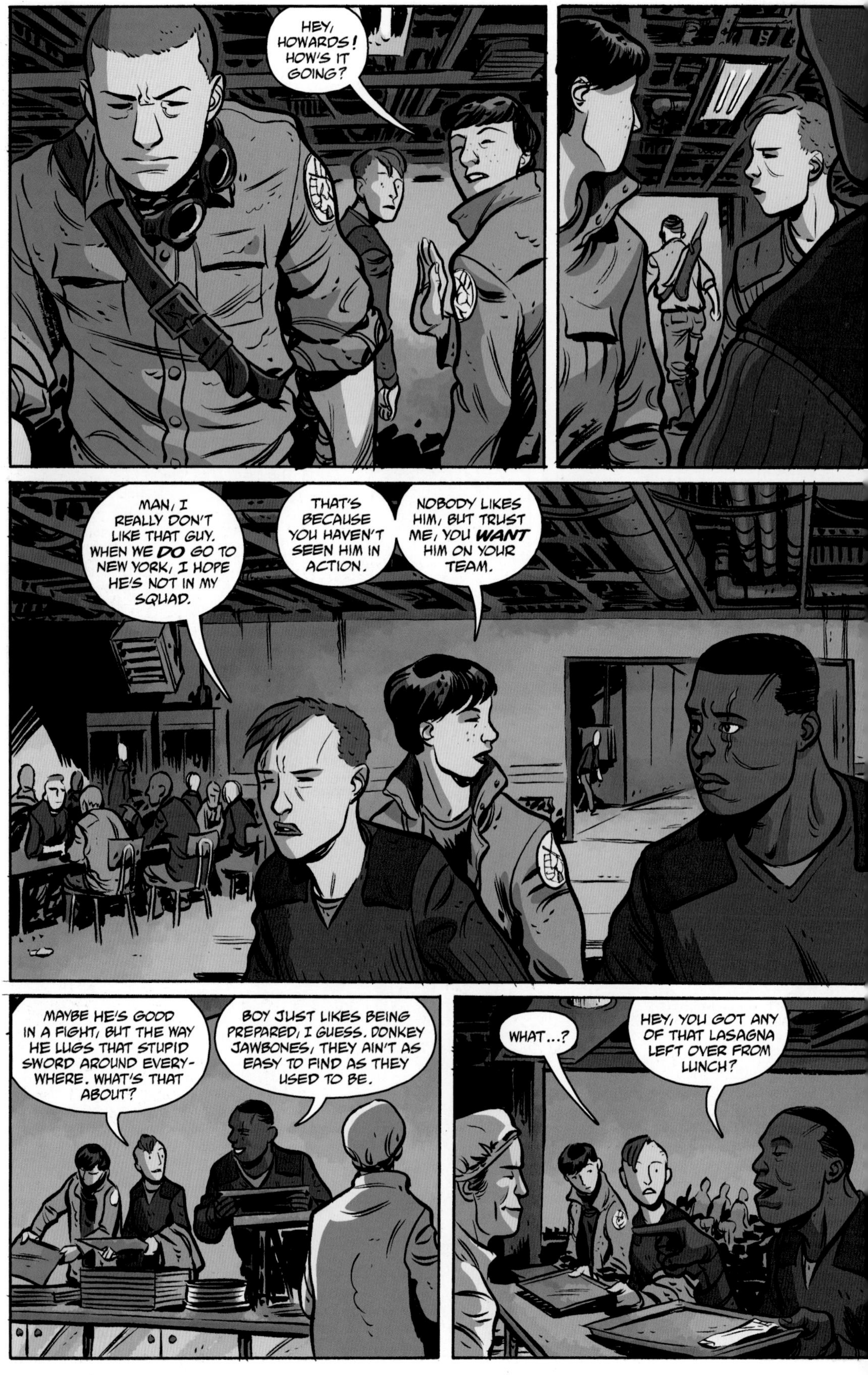

HEY, HOWARDS! HOW'S IT GOING?
MAN, I REALLY DON'T LIKE THAT GUY. WHEN WE DO GO TO NEW YORK, I HOPE HE'S NOT IN MY SQUAD.
THAT'S BECAUSE YOU HAVEN'T SEEN HIM IN ACTION.
NOBODY LIKES HIM, BUT TRUST ME, YOU WANT HIM ON YOUR TEAM.
MAYBE HE'S GOOD IN A FIGHT, BUT THE WAY HE LUGS THAT STUPID SWORD AROUND EVERY-WHERE. WHAT'S THAT ABOUT?
BOY JUST LIKES BEING PREPARED, I GUESS. DONKEY JAWBONES, THEY AIN'T AS EASY TO FIND AS THEY USED TO BE.
WHAT...?
HEY, YOU GOT ANY OF THAT LASAGNA LEFT OVER FROM LUNCH?

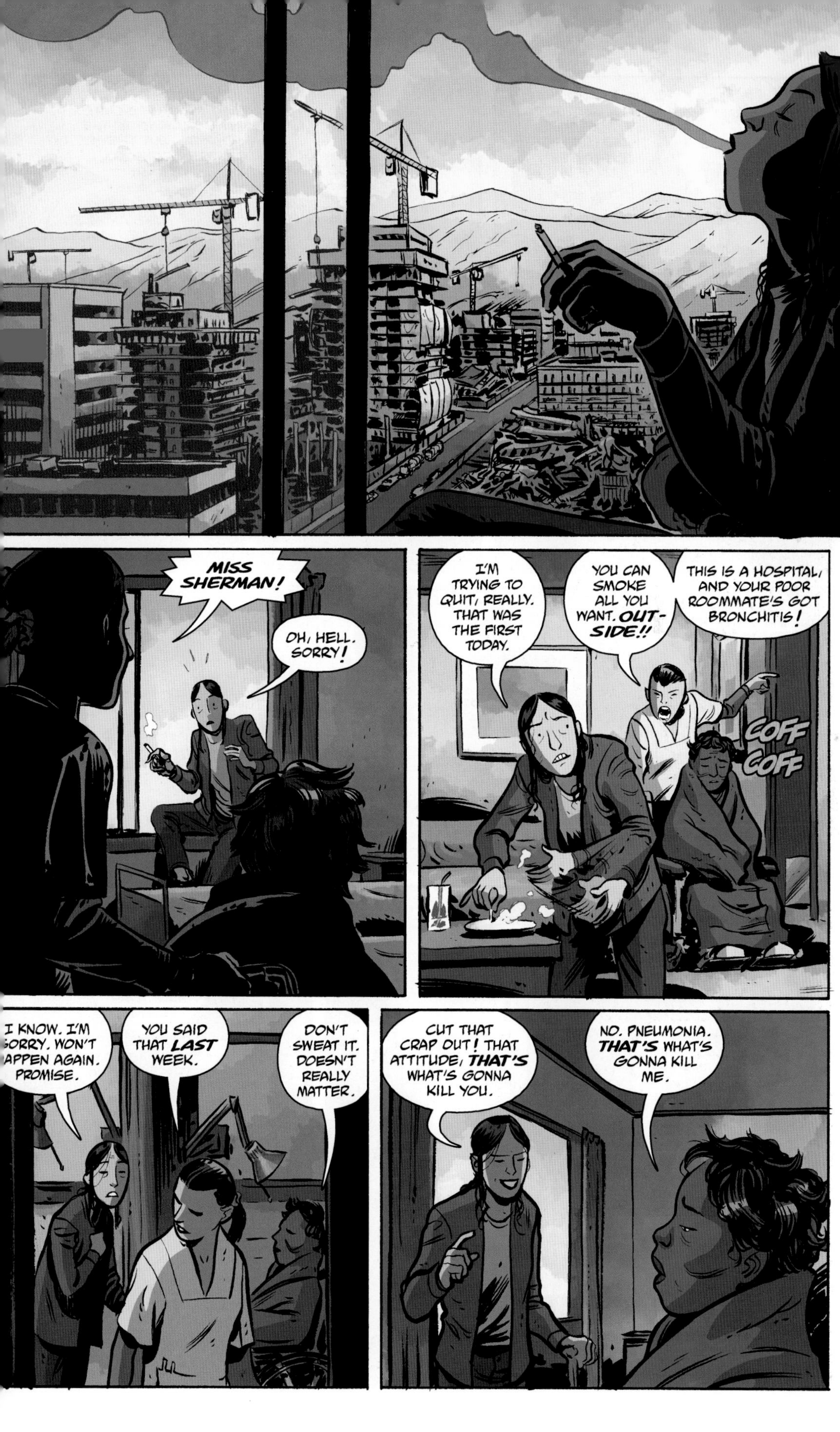
MISS SHERMAN!
OH, HELL. SORRY!
I'M TRYING TO QUIT, REALLY. THAT WAS THE FIRST TODAY.
YOU CAN SMOKE ALL YOU WANT. OUT-SIDE!!
THIS IS A HOSPITAL, AND YOUR POOR ROOMMATE'S GOT BRONCHITIS!
COFF COFF
I KNOW. I'M SORRY. WON'T HAPPEN AGAIN. PROMISE.
YOU SAID THAT LAST WEEK.
DON'T SWEAT IT. DOESN'T REALLY MATTER.
CUT THAT CRAP OUT! THAT ATTITUDE, THAT'S WHAT'S GONNA KILL YOU.
NO. PNEUMONIA. THAT'S WHAT'S GONNA KILL ME.

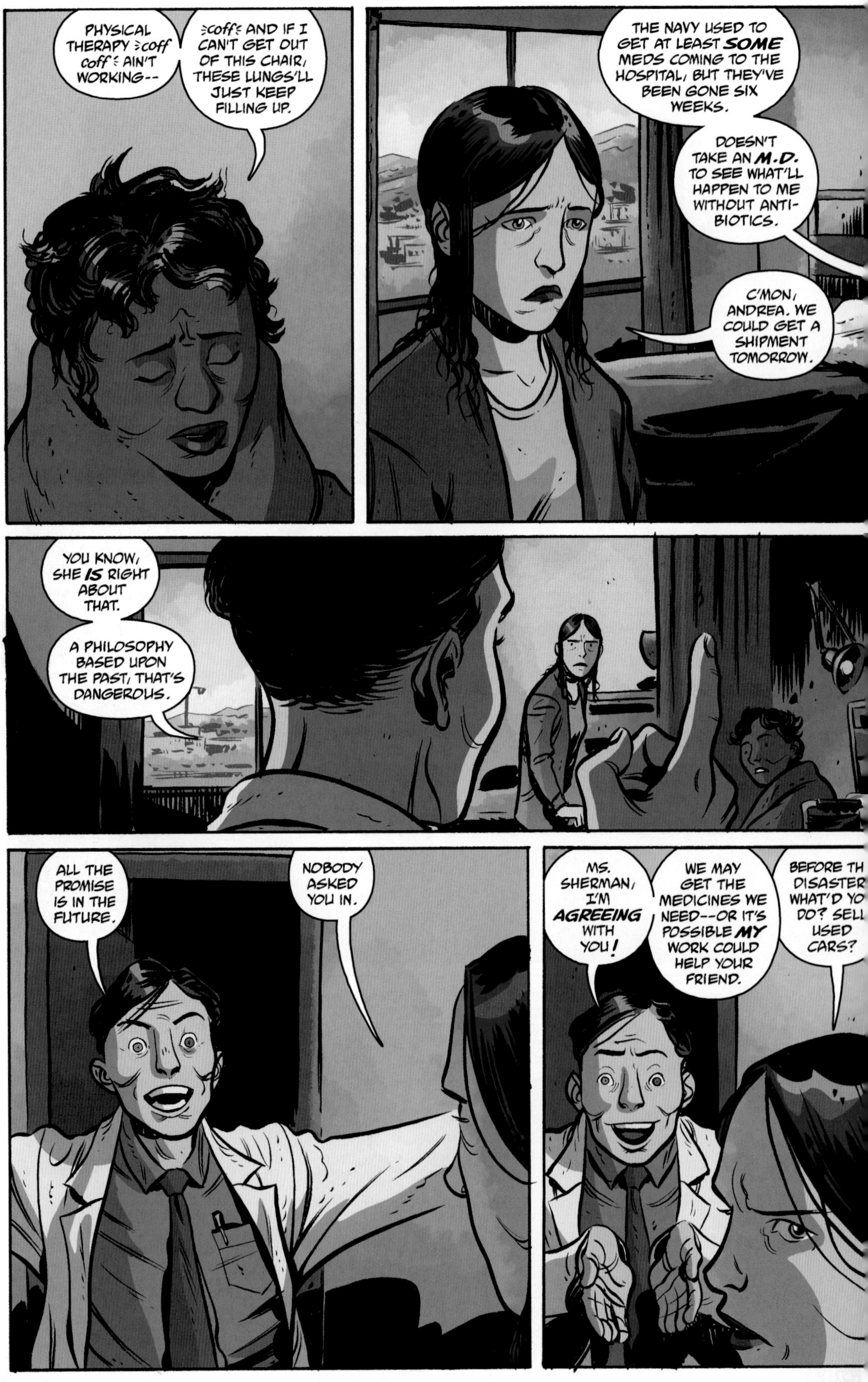
PHYSICAL THERAPY ⪾coff coff⪿ AIN'T WORKING--
⪾coff⪿ AND IF I CAN'T GET OUT OF THIS CHAIR, THESE LUNGS'LL JUST KEEP FILLING UP.
THE NAVY USED TO GET AT LEAST SOME MEDS COMING TO THE HOSPITAL, BUT THEY'VE BEEN GONE SIX WEEKS.
DOESN'T TAKE AN M.D. TO SEE WHAT'LL HAPPEN TO ME WITHOUT ANTI-BIOTICS.
C'MON, ANDREA. WE COULD GET A SHIPMENT TOMORROW.
YOU KNOW, SHE IS RIGHT ABOUT THAT.
A PHILOSOPHY BASED UPON THE PAST, THAT'S DANGEROUS.
ALL THE PROMISE IS IN THE FUTURE.
NOBODY ASKED YOU IN.
MS. SHERMAN, I'M AGREEING WITH YOU!
WE MAY GET THE MEDICINES WE NEED--OR IT'S POSSIBLE MY WORK COULD HELP YOUR FRIEND.
BEFORE TH DISASTER WHAT'D YO DO? SELL USED CARS?

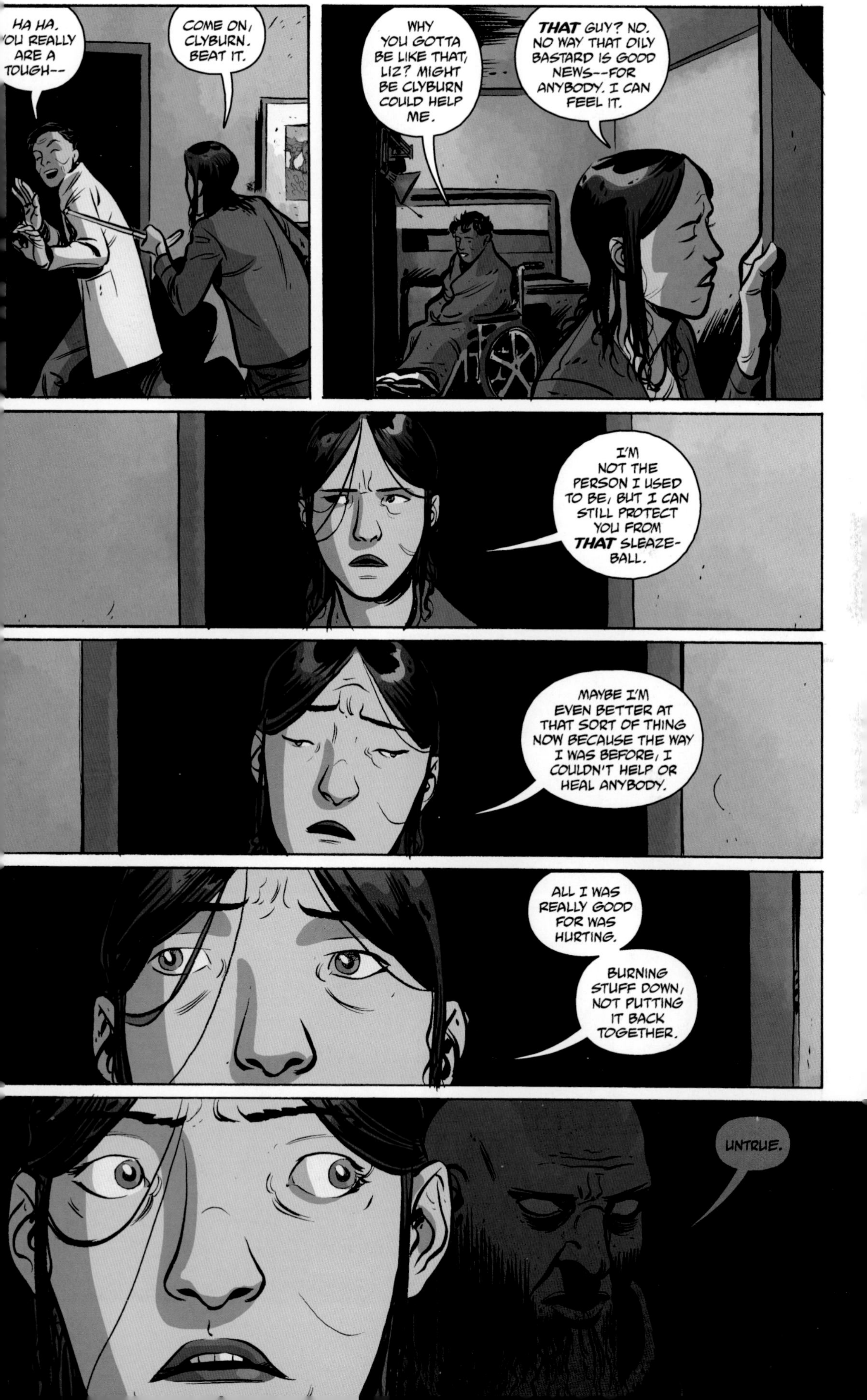
HA HA. YOU REALLY ARE A TOUGH--
COME ON, CLYBURN. BEAT IT.
WHY YOU GOTTA BE LIKE THAT, LIZ? MIGHT BE CLYBURN COULD HELP ME.
THAT GUY? NO. NO WAY THAT OILY BASTARD IS GOOD NEWS--FOR ANYBODY. I CAN FEEL IT.
I'M NOT THE PERSON I USED TO BE, BUT I CAN STILL PROTECT YOU FROM THAT SLEAZE-BALL.
MAYBE I'M EVEN BETTER AT THAT SORT OF THING NOW BECAUSE THE WAY I WAS BEFORE, I COULDN'T HELP OR HEAL ANYBODY.
ALL I WAS REALLY GOOD FOR WAS HURTING.
BURNING STUFF DOWN, NOT PUTTING IT BACK TOGETHER.
UNTRUE.

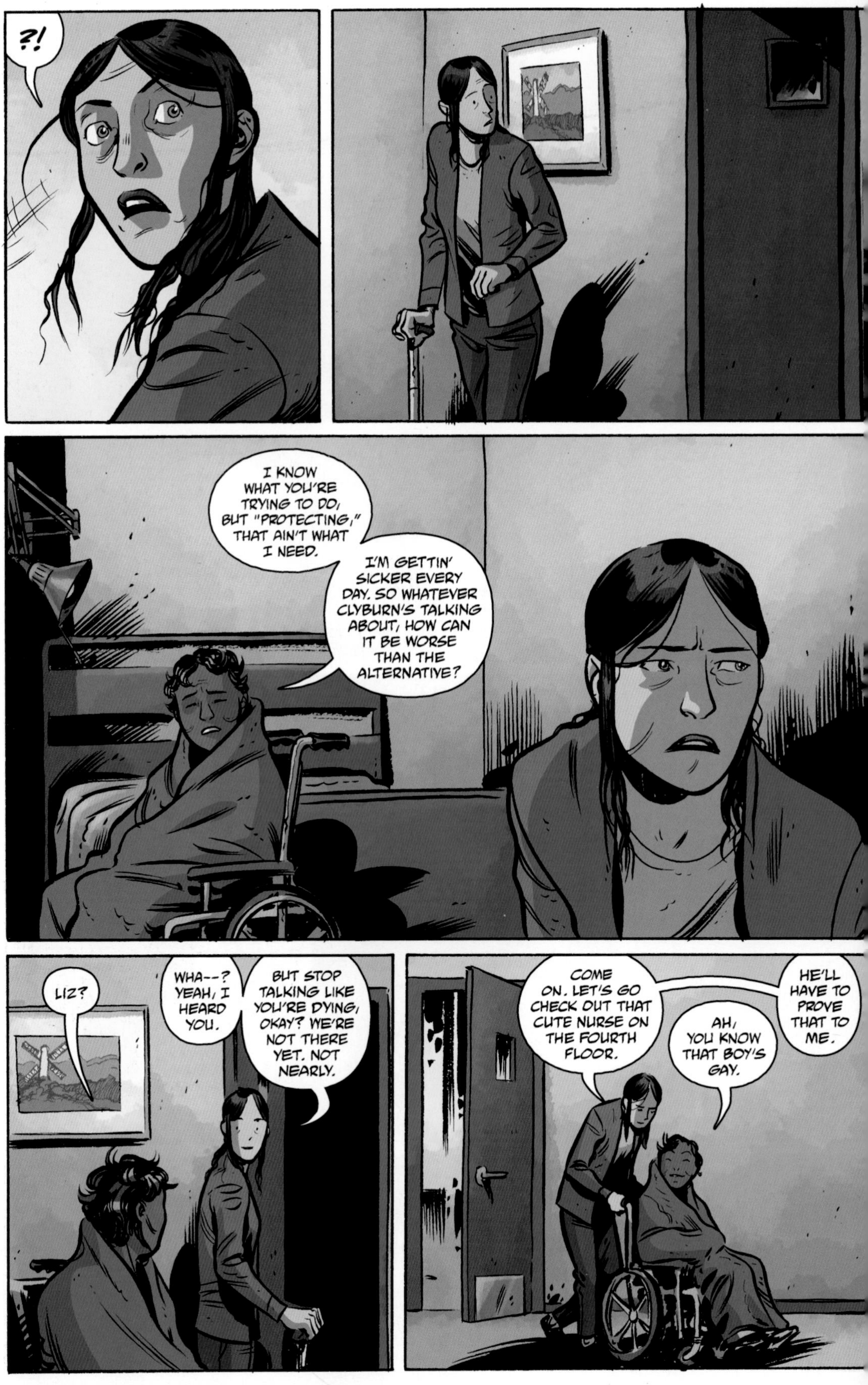
?!
I KNOW WHAT YOU'RE TRYING TO DO, BUT "PROTECTING," THAT AIN'T WHAT I NEED.
I'M GETTIN' SICKER EVERY DAY. SO WHATEVER CLYBURN'S TALKING ABOUT, HOW CAN IT BE WORSE THAN THE ALTERNATIVE?
LIZ?
WHA--? YEAH, I HEARD YOU.
BUT STOP TALKING LIKE YOU'RE DYING, OKAY? WE'RE NOT THERE YET. NOT NEARLY.
COME ON. LET'S GO CHECK OUT THAT CUTE NURSE ON THE FOURTH FLOOR.
AH, YOU KNOW THAT BOY'S GAY.
HE'LL HAVE TO PROVE THAT TO ME.

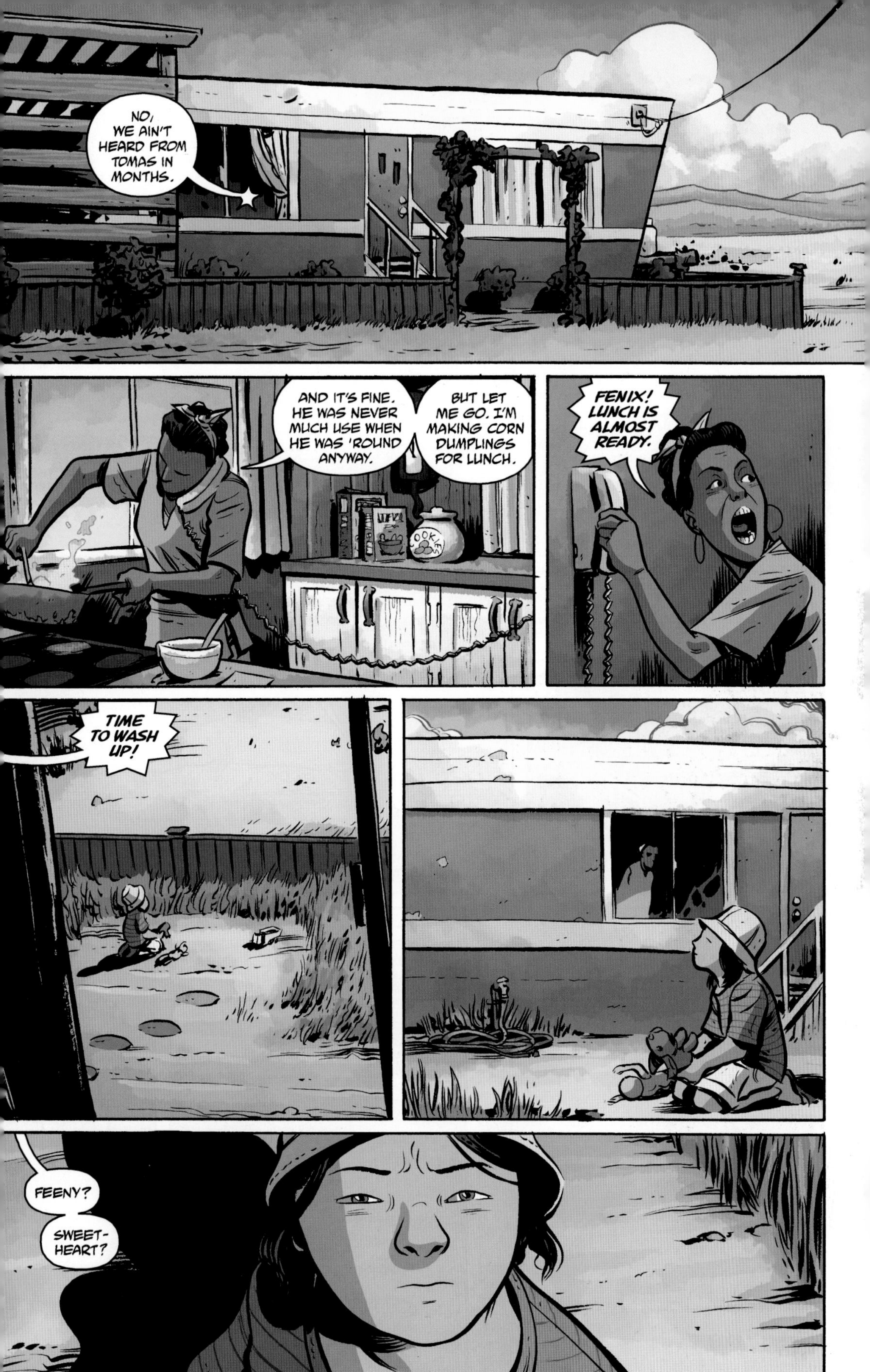
NO, WE AIN'T HEARD FROM TOMAS IN MONTHS.
AND IT'S FINE. HE WAS NEVER MUCH USE WHEN HE WAS 'ROUND ANYWAY.
BUT LET ME GO. I'M MAKING CORN DUMPLINGS FOR LUNCH.
COOKIES
FENIX! LUNCH IS ALMOST READY.
TIME TO WASH UP!
FEENY?
SWEET-HEART?

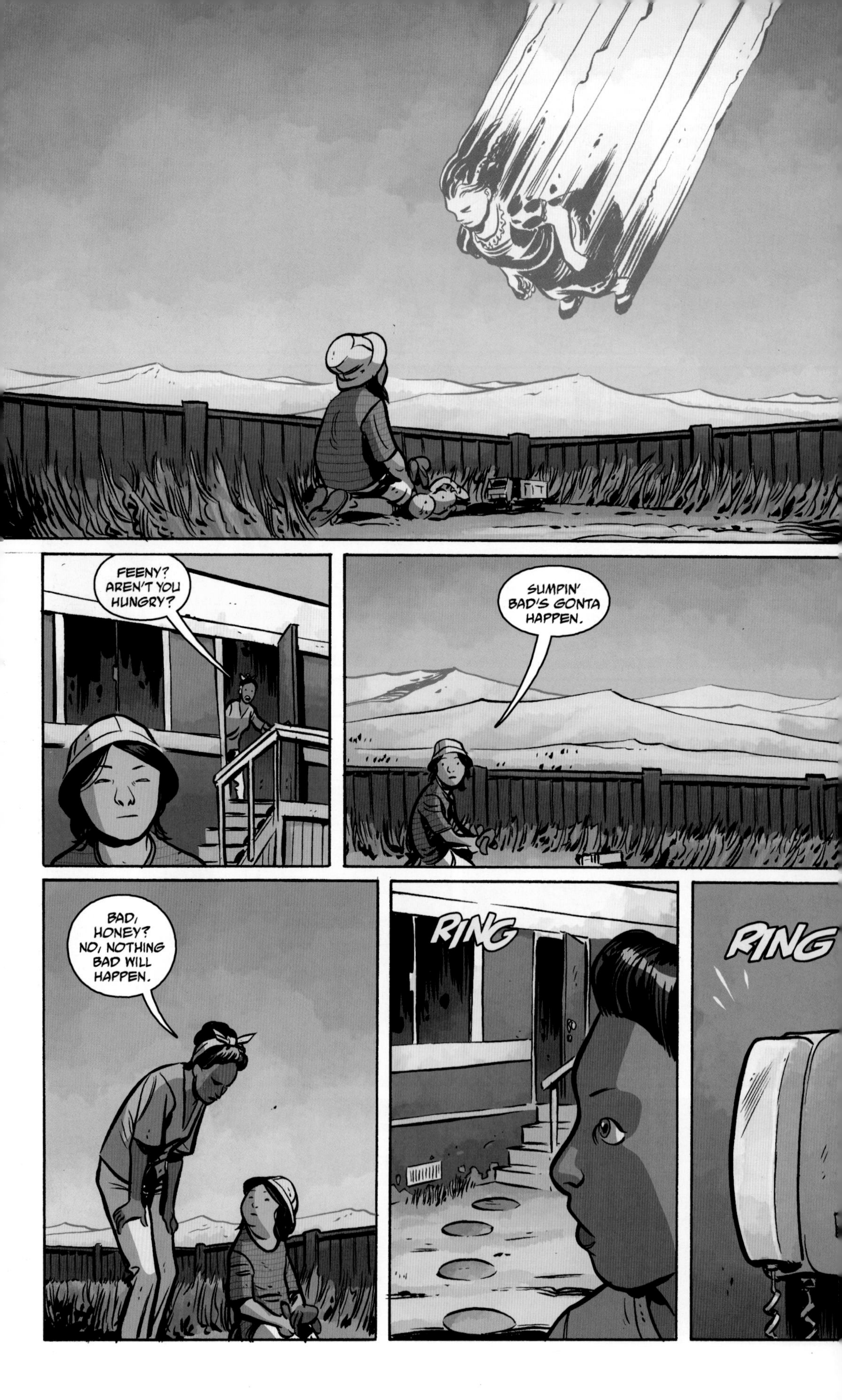
FEENY? AREN'T YOU HUNGRY?
SUMPIN' BAD'S GONTA HAPPEN.
BAD, HONEY? NO, NOTHING BAD WILL HAPPEN.
RING
RING

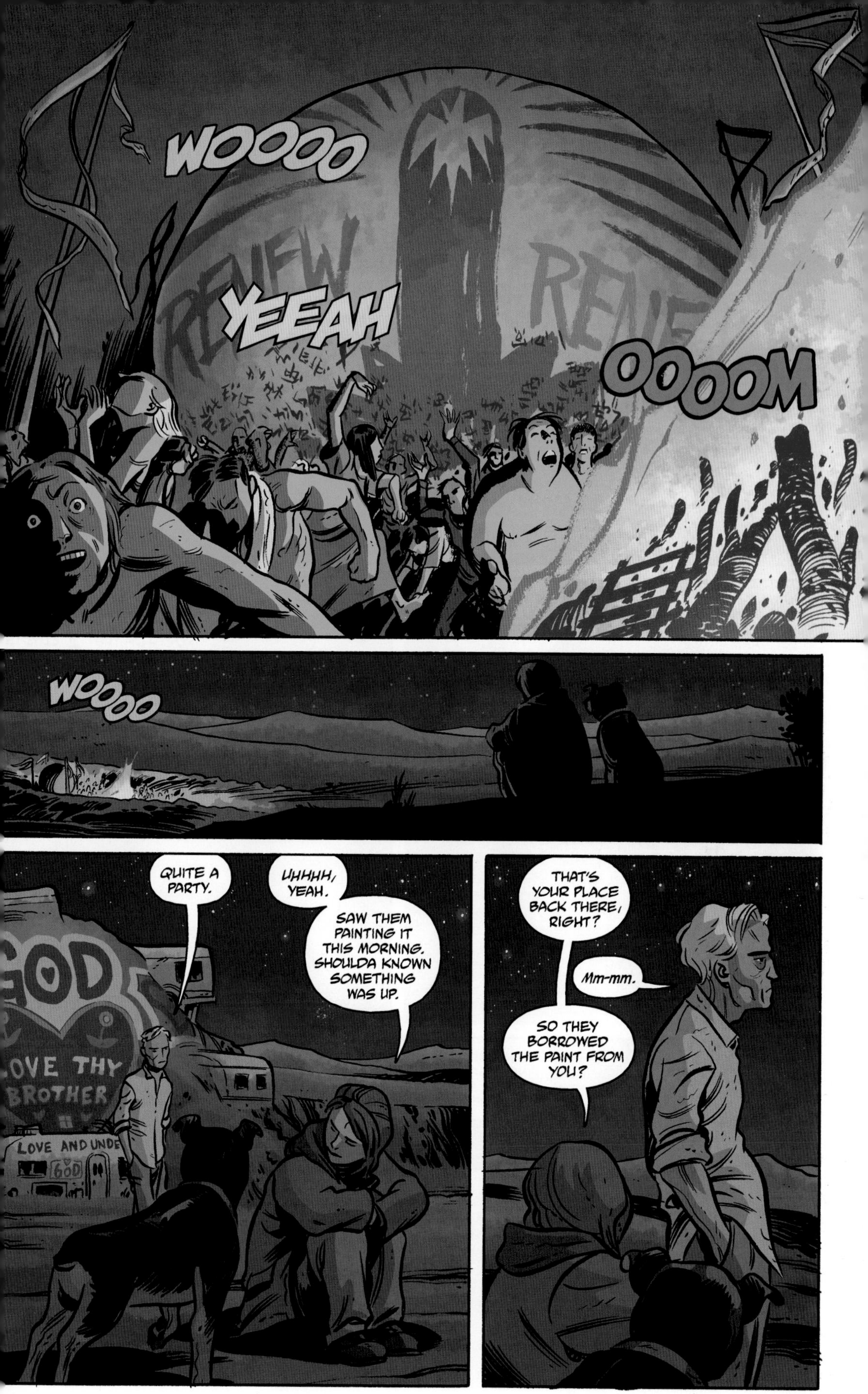
WOOOO
RENEW
YEEAH
RENE
OOOOM
WOOOO
QUITE A PARTY.
UHHHH, YEAH.
SAW THEM PAINTING IT THIS MORNING. SHOULDA KNOWN SOMETHING WAS UP.
GOD
OVE THY BROTHER
LOVE AND UNDE
GOD
THAT'S YOUR PLACE BACK THERE, RIGHT?
Mm-mm.
SO THEY BORROWED THE PAINT FROM YOU?

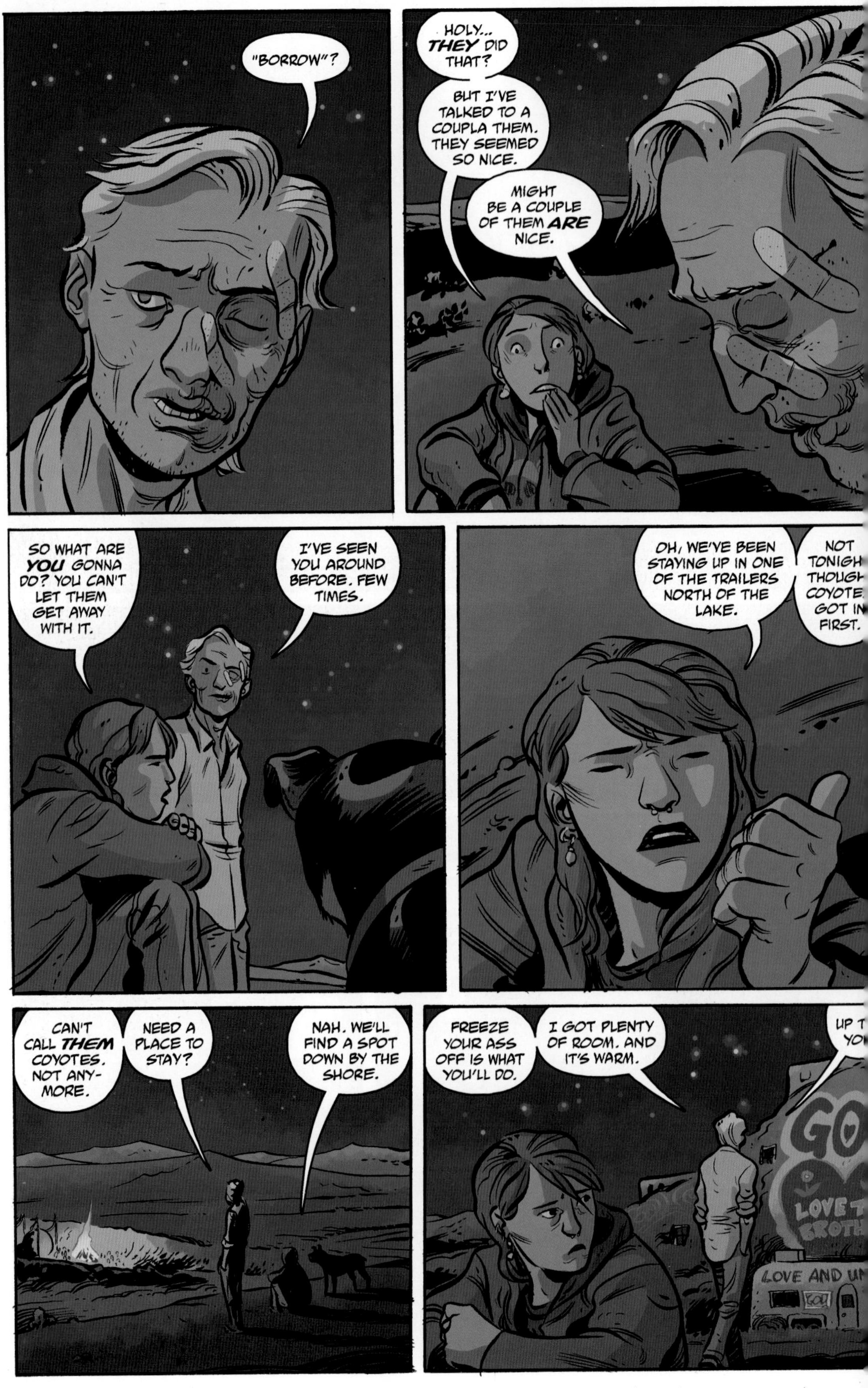
"BORROW"?
HOLY... THEY DID THAT?
BUT I'VE TALKED TO A COUPLA THEM. THEY SEEMED SO NICE.
MIGHT BE A COUPLE OF THEM ARE NICE.
SO WHAT ARE YOU GONNA DO? YOU CAN'T LET THEM GET AWAY WITH IT.
I'VE SEEN YOU AROUND BEFORE. FEW TIMES.
OH, WE'VE BEEN STAYING UP IN ONE OF THE TRAILERS NORTH OF THE LAKE.
NOT TONIGH THOUGH COYOTE GOT IN FIRST.
CAN'T CALL THEM COYOTES. NOT ANY-MORE.
NEED A PLACE TO STAY?
NAH. WE'LL FIND A SPOT DOWN BY THE SHORE.
FREEZE YOUR ASS OFF IS WHAT YOU'LL DO.
I GOT PLENTY OF ROOM. AND IT'S WARM.
LOVE AND UN

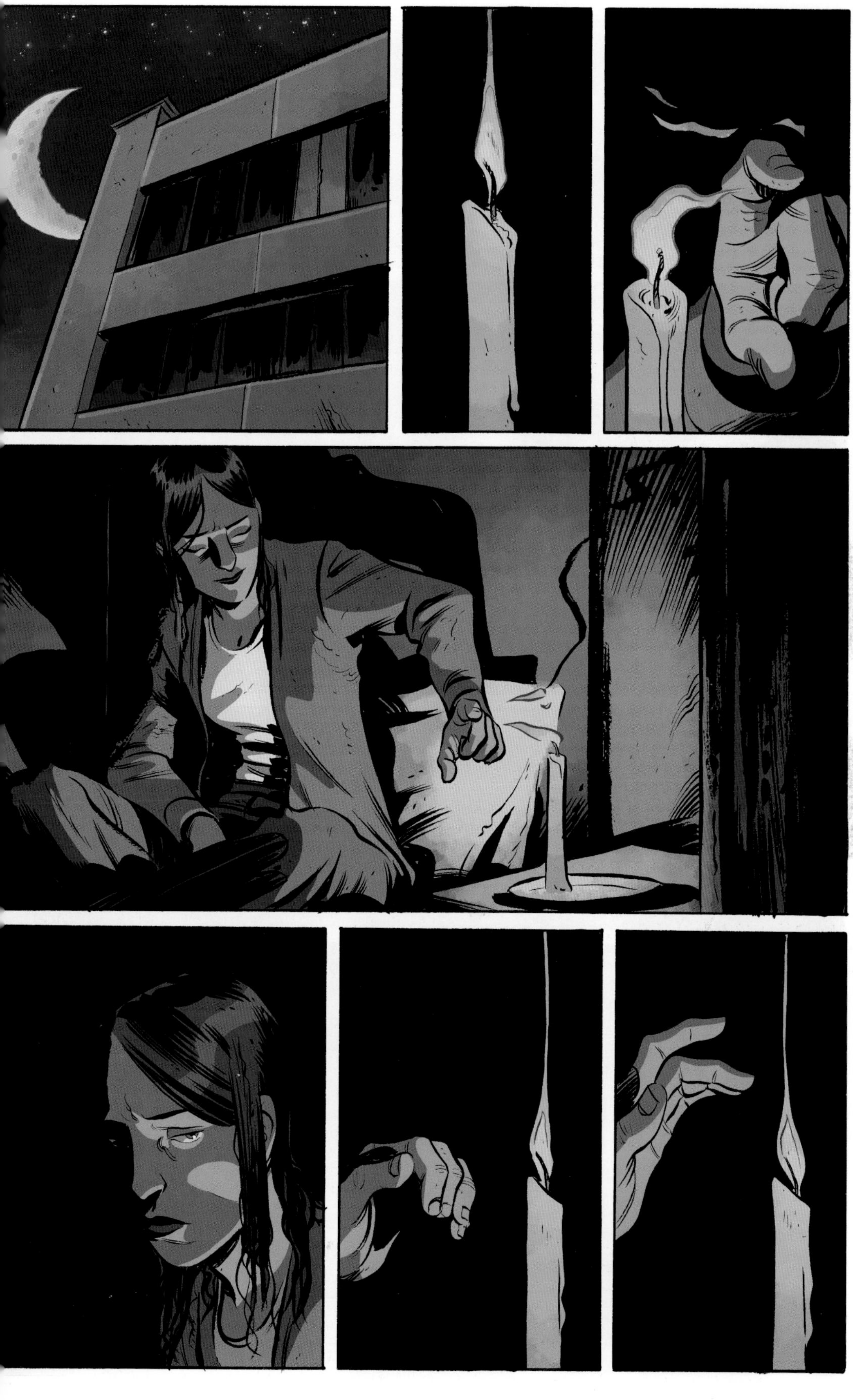

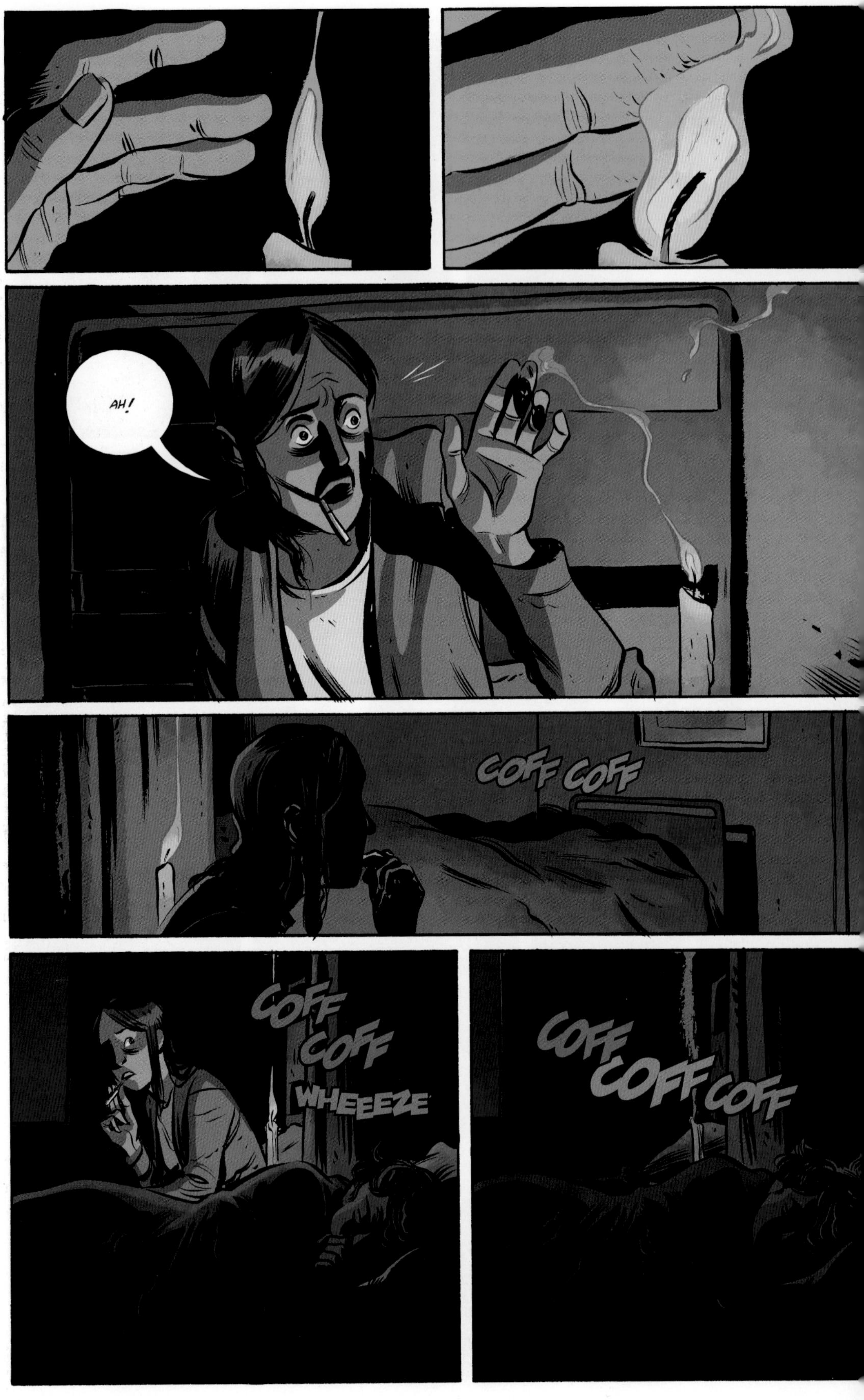
AH!
COFF COFF
COFF
COFF
WHEEEZE
COFF COFF COFF

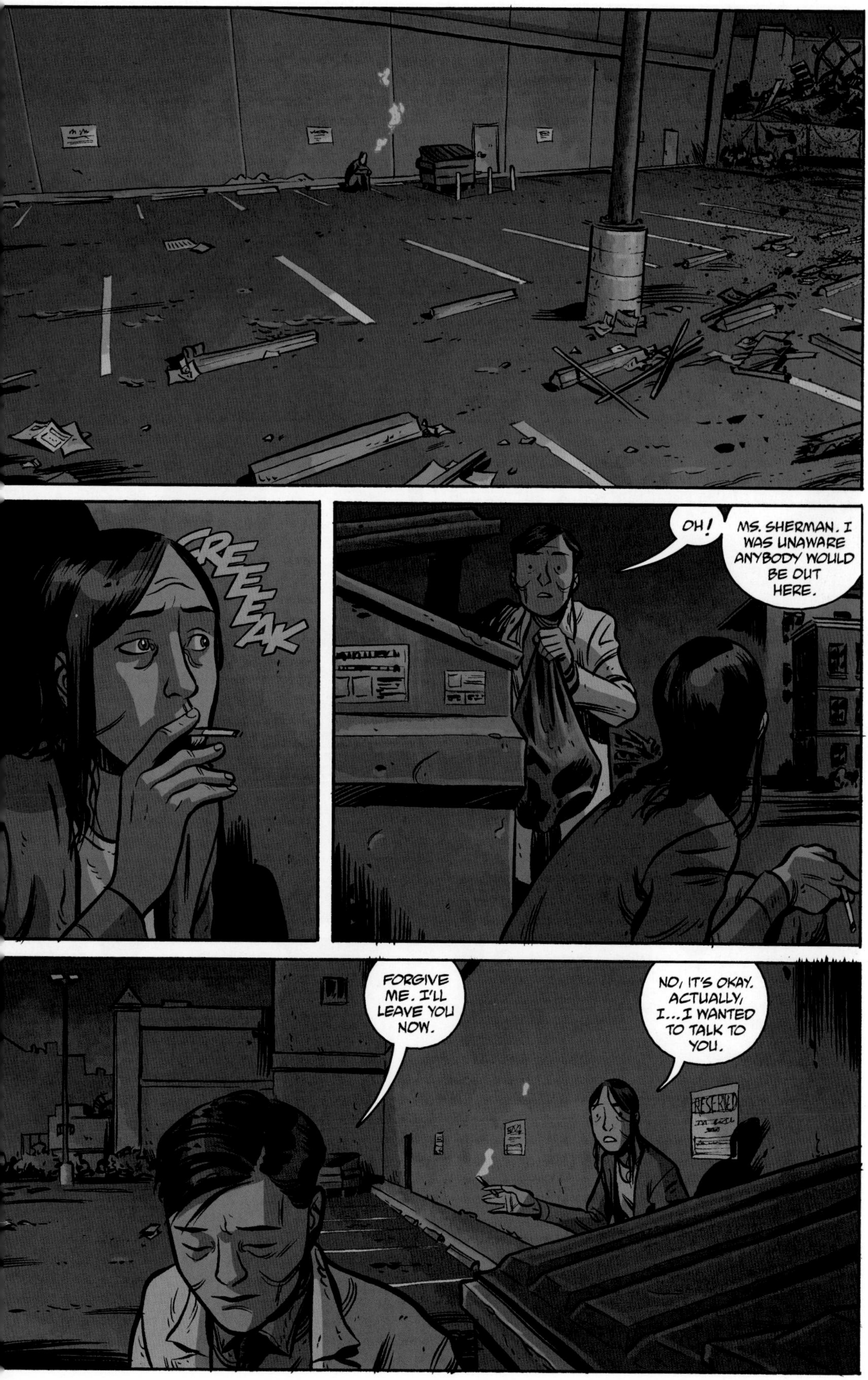
OH!
MS. SHERMAN. I WAS UNAWARE ANYBODY WOULD BE OUT HERE.
FORGIVE ME. I'LL LEAVE YOU NOW.
NO, IT'S OKAY. ACTUALLY, I...I WANTED TO TALK TO YOU.
RESERVED

UM, PERHAPS TOMORROW WOULD BE BETTER.

RELAX, I'M NOT GONNA HURT YOU.

BESIDES, IT'LL BE EASIER TO ADMIT MY MISTAKE WITH NOBODY ELSE AROUND.

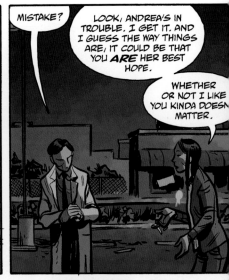

MISTAKE?

LOOK, ANDREA'S IN TROUBLE. I GET IT. AND I GUESS THE WAY THINGS ARE, IT COULD BE THAT YOU *ARE* HER BEST HOPE.

WHETHER OR NOT I LIKE YOU KINDA DOESN'T MATTER.

SHE'S SCARED, AND I WANT TO TAKE THAT AWAY, BUT I CAN'T. ALL I CAN BE RIGHT NOW FOR HER IS A FRIEND.

GOTTA LEARN HOW TO DO A BETTER JOB OF THAT.

IT'S NOT A BAD THING, MS. SHERMAN. A FRIEND IS ALL MOST OF US CAN BE.

NOT ME. I USED TO BE MORE. I WAS--

AH, WH CARE WHAT WAS

I UNDERSTAND. THE PAST IS HARD TO RELEASE. IT'S FAMILIAR. WE'VE *LIVED* IT, AFTER ALL.

CHANGE IS DIFFICULT. THE FUTURE, SO DIFFICULT, BECAUSE WE *DON'T* KNOW IT. BUT IT *IS* COMING.

THANK YOU, MS. SHERMAN. IN THE MORNING I'LL DROP IN. WE'LL ALL TALK MORE THEN.

CAN'T SLEE EITHER? HEL I DIDN'T REALIZE TH PUT YOU DO UP IN THE BASEMEN

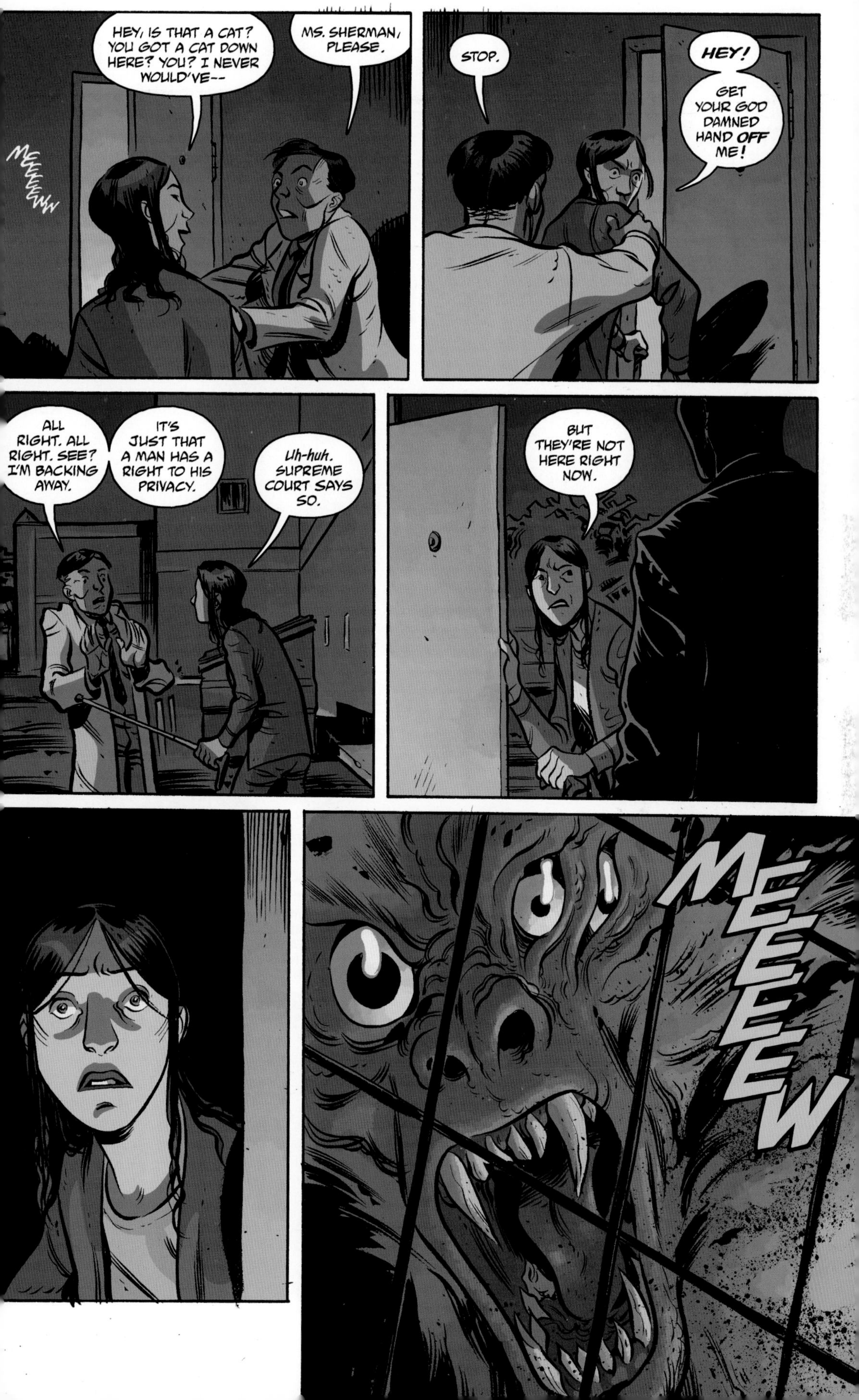

HEY, IS THAT A CAT? YOU GOT A CAT DOWN HERE? YOU? I NEVER WOULD'VE--
MS. SHERMAN, PLEASE.
MEEEEEW
STOP.
HEY!
GET YOUR GOD DAMNED HAND OFF ME!
ALL RIGHT. ALL RIGHT. SEE? I'M BACKING AWAY.
IT'S JUST THAT A MAN HAS A RIGHT TO HIS PRIVACY.
Uh-huh. SUPREME COURT SAYS SO.
BUT THEY'RE NOT HERE RIGHT NOW.
MEEEEEW

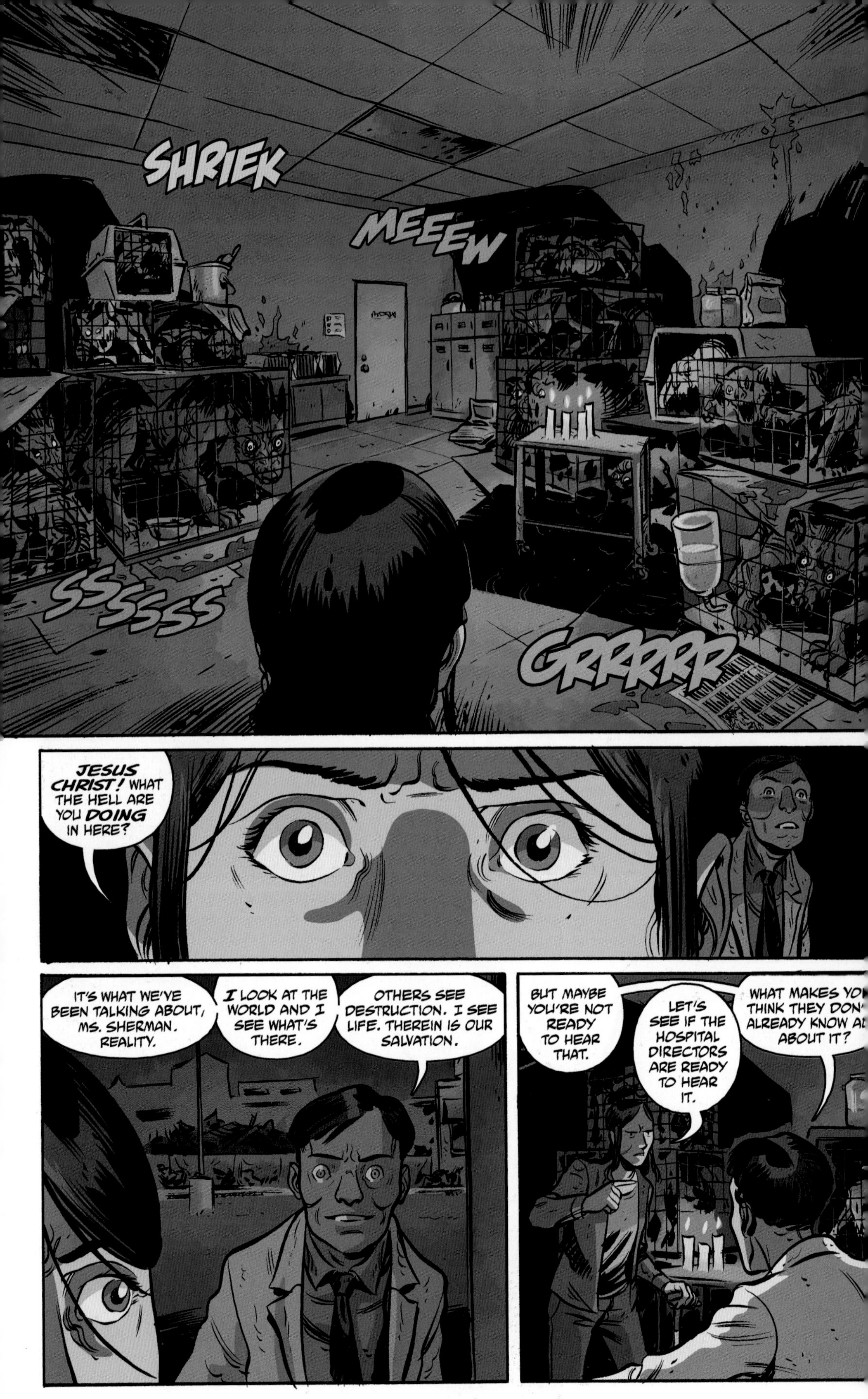
SHRIEK
MEEEW
SSSSSSS
GRRRRR
JESUS CHRIST! WHAT THE HELL ARE YOU DOING IN HERE?
IT'S WHAT WE'VE BEEN TALKING ABOUT, MS. SHERMAN. REALITY.
I LOOK AT THE WORLD AND I SEE WHAT'S THERE.
OTHERS SEE DESTRUCTION. I SEE LIFE. THEREIN IS OUR SALVATION.
BUT MAYBE YOU'RE NOT READY TO HEAR THAT.
LET'S SEE IF THE HOSPITAL DIRECTORS ARE READY TO HEAR IT.
WHAT MAKES YO
THINK THEY DON'
ALREADY KNOW AL
ABOUT IT?

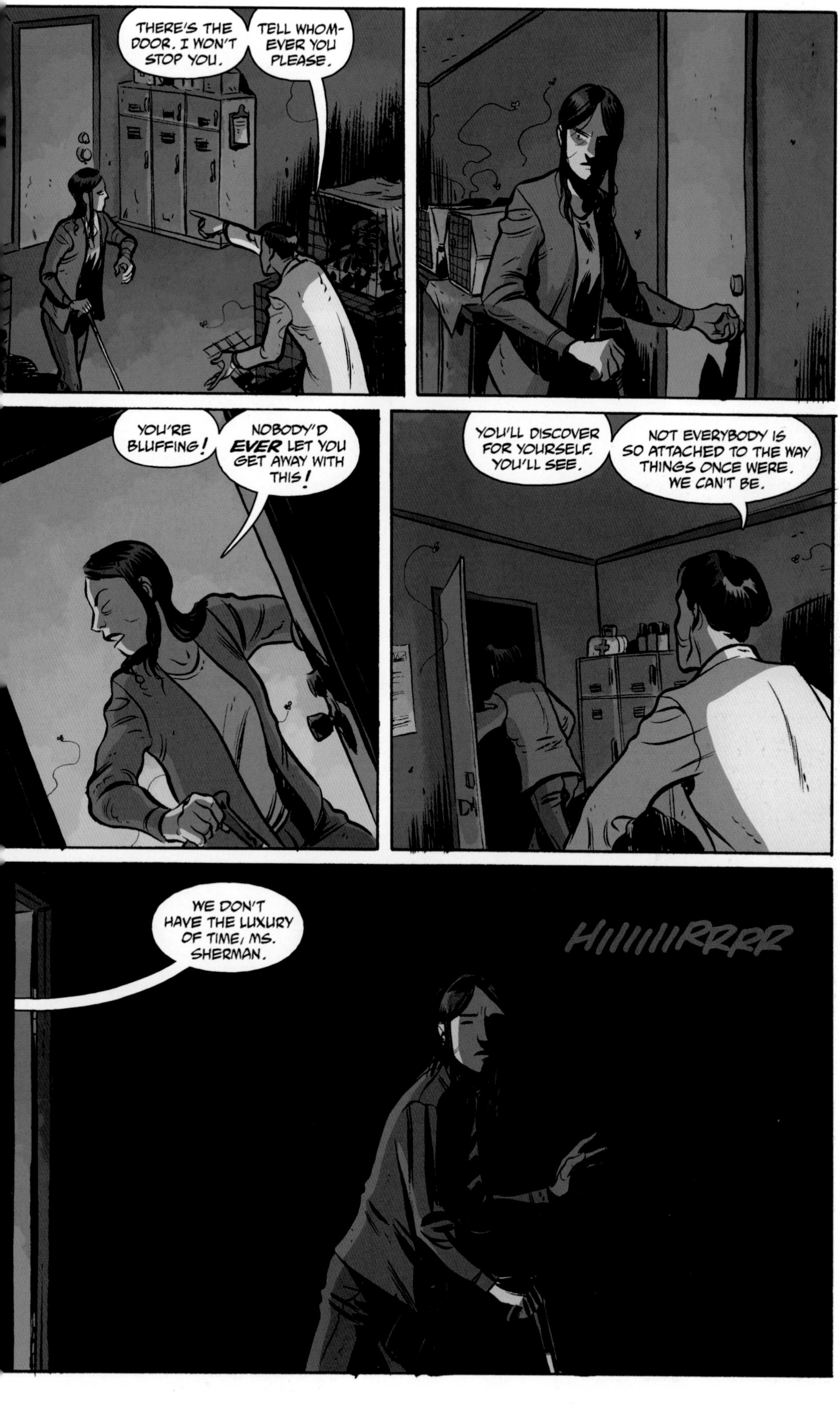
THERE'S THE DOOR. I WON'T STOP YOU.
TELL WHOMEVER YOU PLEASE.
YOU'RE BLUFFING!
NOBODY'D EVER LET YOU GET AWAY WITH THIS!
YOU'LL DISCOVER FOR YOURSELF. YOU'LL SEE.
NOT EVERYBODY IS SO ATTACHED TO THE WAY THINGS ONCE WERE. WE CAN'T BE.
WE DON'T HAVE THE LUXURY OF TIME, MS. SHERMAN.
HIIIIIIRRRR

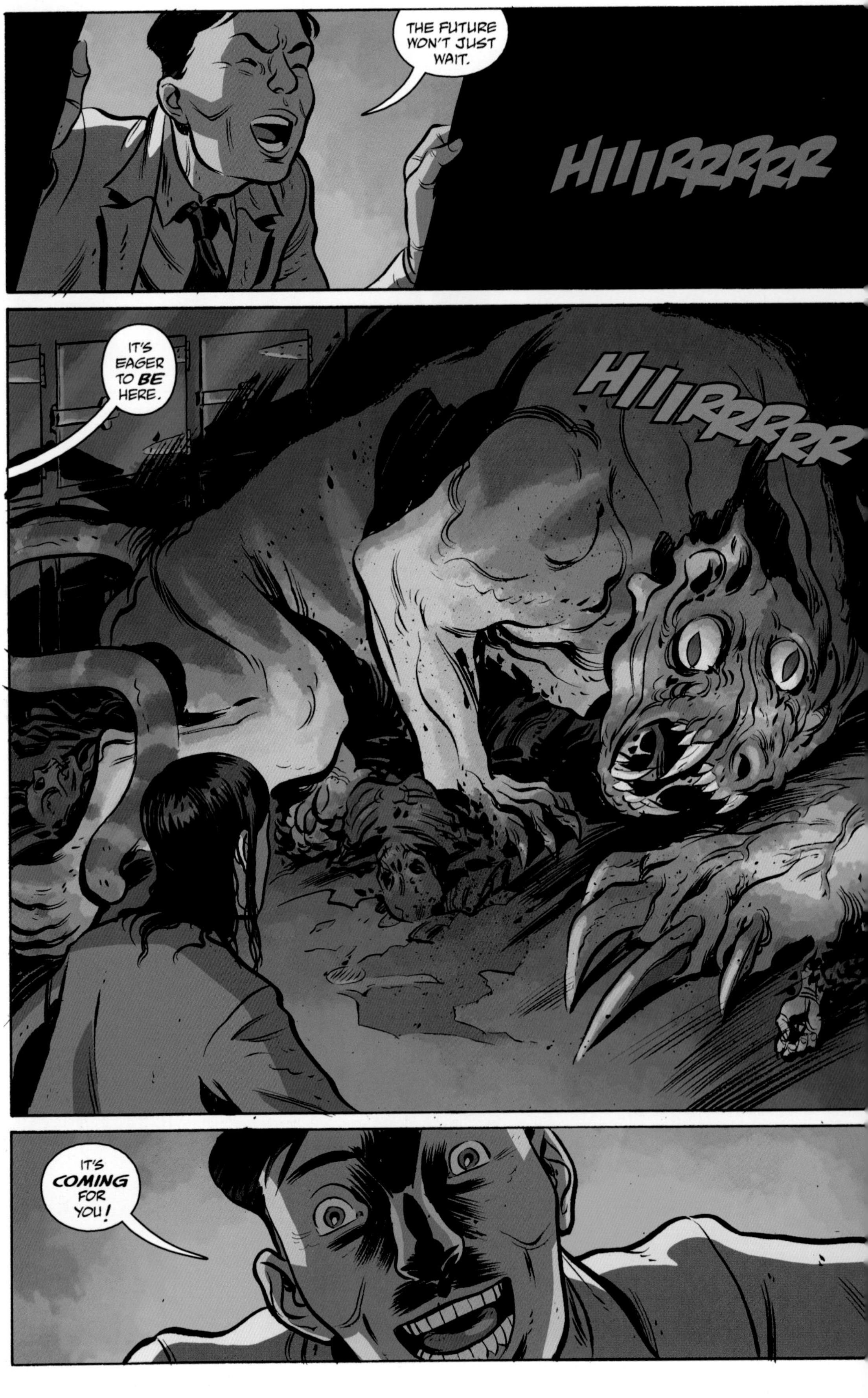
THE FUTURE WON'T JUST WAIT.
HIIIRRRRRR
IT'S EAGER TO BE HERE.
HIIIRRRRRR
IT'S COMING FOR YOU!

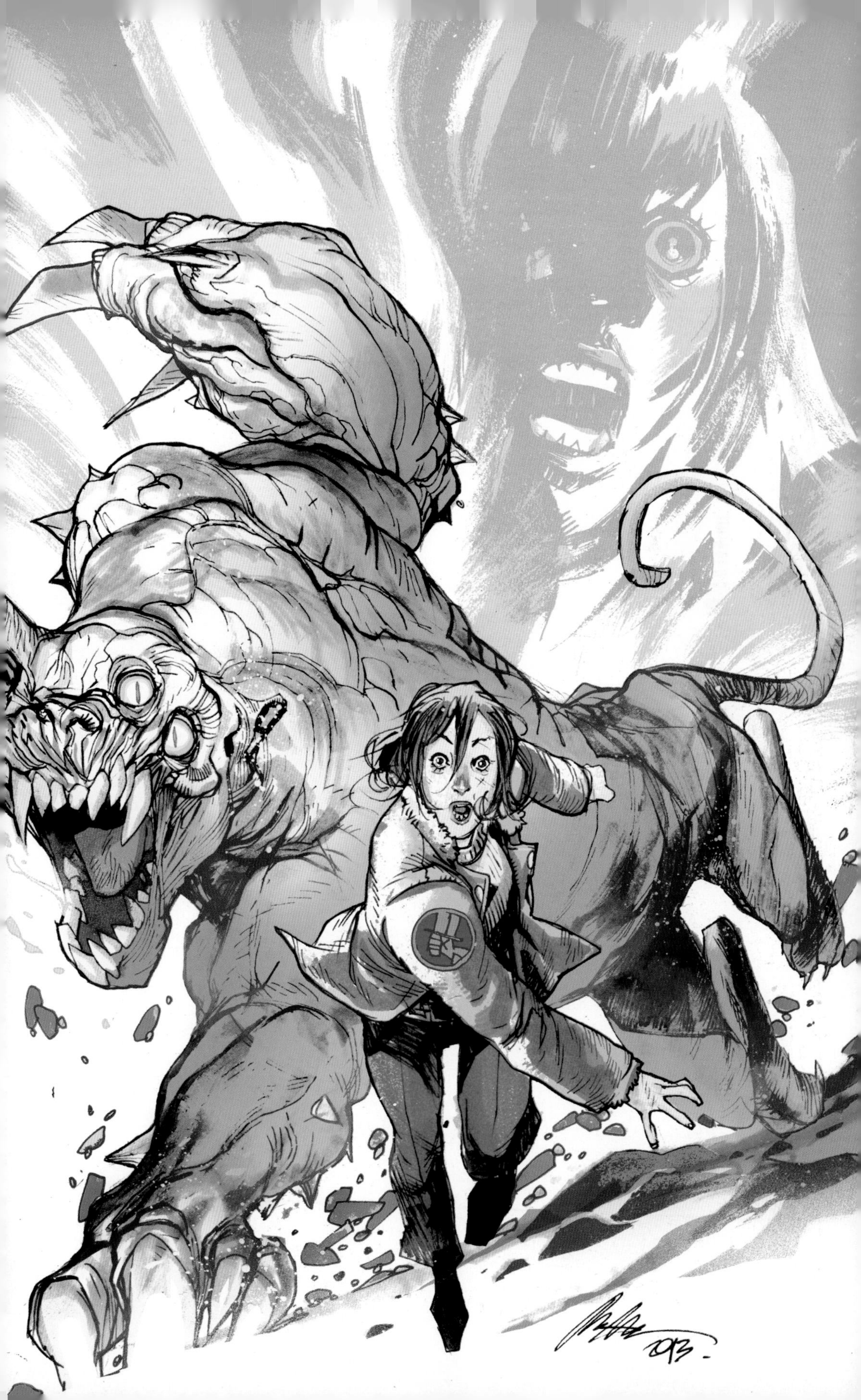

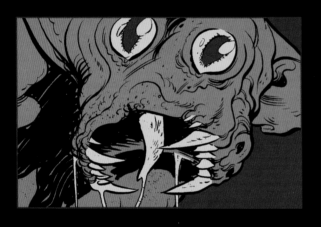

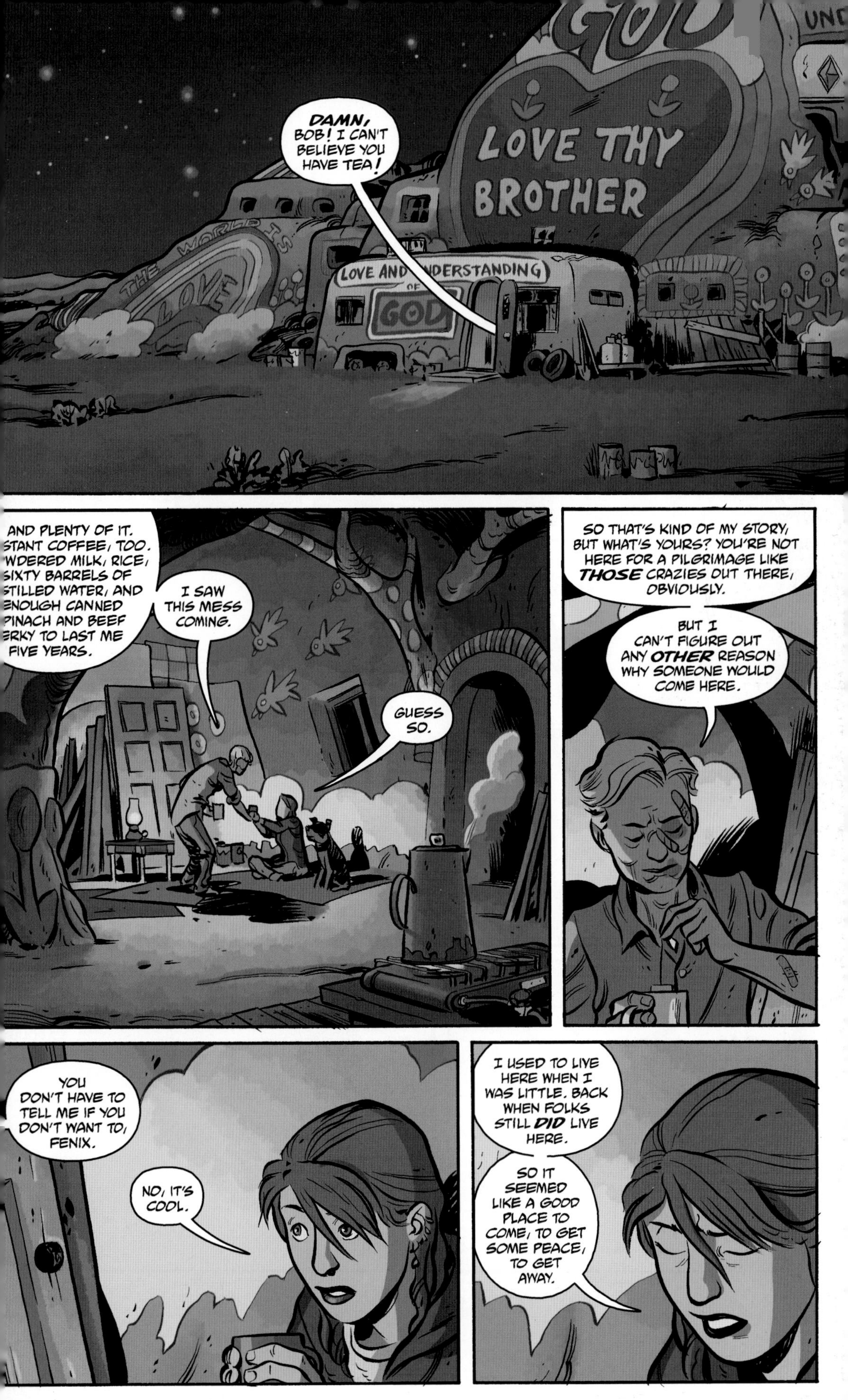
GOD
LOVE THY BROTHER
THE WORLD IS LOVE
LOVE AND UNDERSTANDING OF GOD
DAMN, BOB! I CAN'T BELIEVE YOU HAVE TEA!
AND PLENTY OF IT. STANT COFFEE, TOO. WDERED MILK, RICE, SIXTY BARRELS OF STILLED WATER, AND ENOUGH CANNED PINACH AND BEEF ERKY TO LAST ME FIVE YEARS.
I SAW THIS MESS COMING.
GUESS SO.
SO THAT'S KIND OF MY STORY, BUT WHAT'S YOURS? YOU'RE NOT HERE FOR A PILGRIMAGE LIKE THOSE CRAZIES OUT THERE, OBVIOUSLY.
BUT I CAN'T FIGURE OUT ANY OTHER REASON WHY SOMEONE WOULD COME HERE.
YOU DON'T HAVE TO TELL ME IF YOU DON'T WANT TO, FENIX.
NO, IT'S COOL.
I USED TO LIVE HERE WHEN I WAS LITTLE. BACK WHEN FOLKS STILL DID LIVE HERE.
SO IT SEEMED LIKE A GOOD PLACE TO COME, TO GET SOME PEACE, TO GET AWAY.

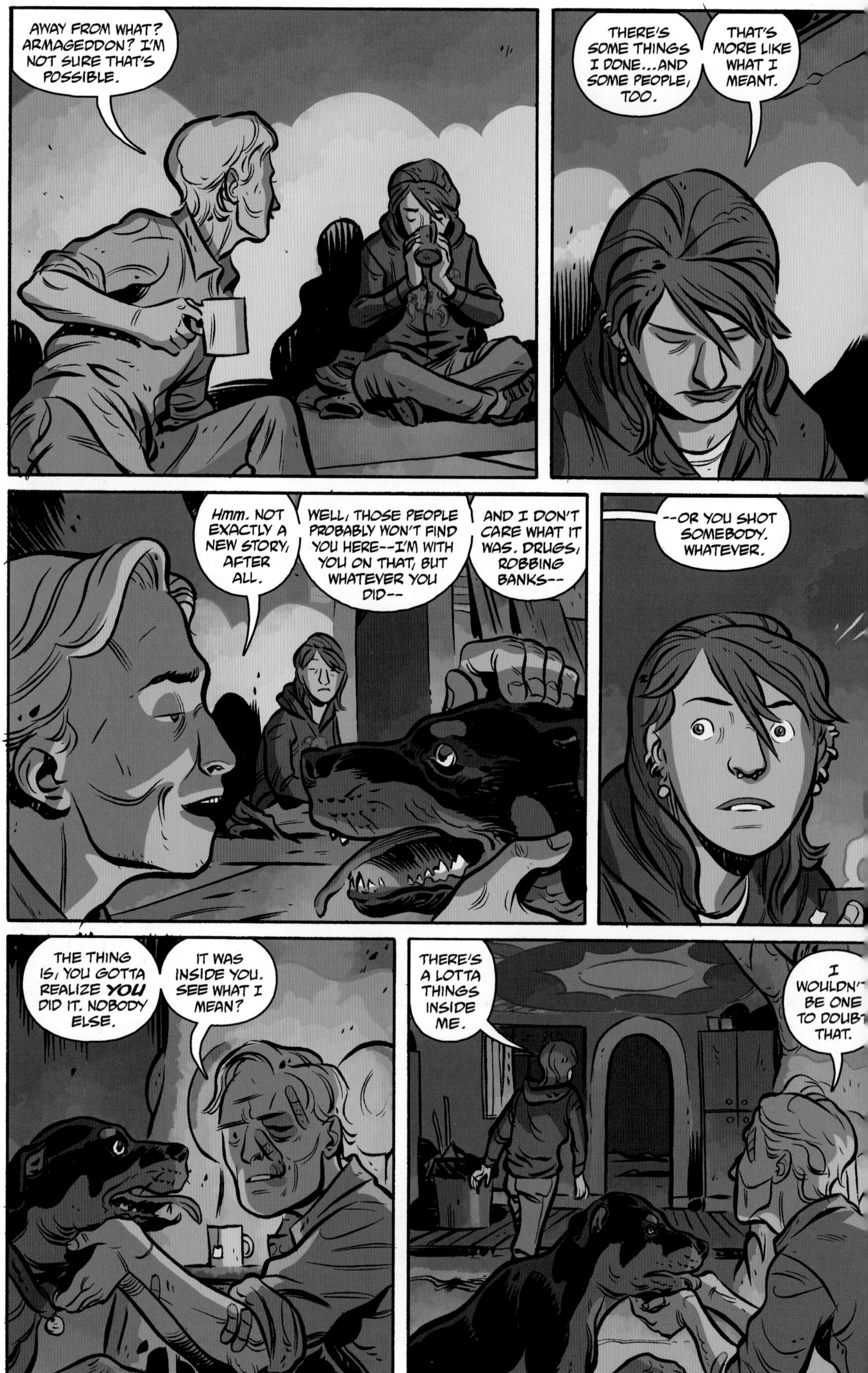
AWAY FROM WHAT? ARMAGEDDON? I'M NOT SURE THAT'S POSSIBLE.
THERE'S SOME THINGS I DONE...AND SOME PEOPLE, TOO.
THAT'S MORE LIKE WHAT I MEANT.
Hmm. NOT EXACTLY A NEW STORY, AFTER ALL.
WELL, THOSE PEOPLE PROBABLY WON'T FIND YOU HERE--I'M WITH YOU ON THAT, BUT WHATEVER YOU DID--
AND I DON'T CARE WHAT IT WAS. DRUGS, ROBBING BANKS--
--OR YOU SHOT SOMEBODY. WHATEVER.
THE THING IS, YOU GOTTA REALIZE ***YOU*** DID IT. NOBODY ELSE.
IT WAS INSIDE YOU. SEE WHAT I MEAN?
THERE'S A LOTTA THINGS INSIDE ME.
I WOULDN'T BE ONE TO DOUBT THAT.

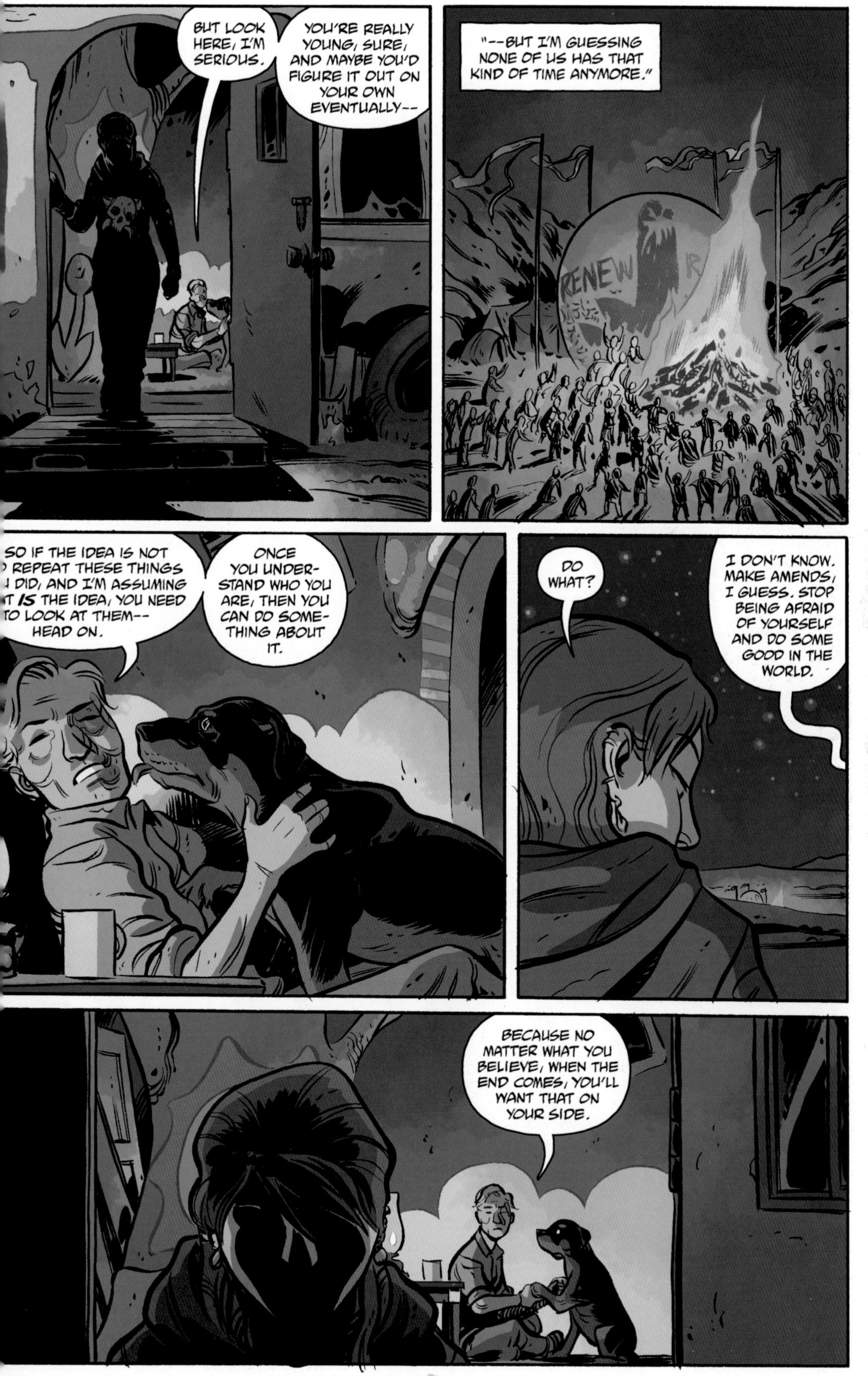
BUT LOOK HERE, I'M SERIOUS.
YOU'RE REALLY YOUNG, SURE, AND MAYBE YOU'D FIGURE IT OUT ON YOUR OWN EVENTUALLY--
"--BUT I'M GUESSING NONE OF US HAS THAT KIND OF TIME ANYMORE."
RENEW
SO IF THE IDEA IS NOT TO REPEAT THESE THINGS YOU DID, AND I'M ASSUMING THAT *IS* THE IDEA, YOU NEED TO LOOK AT THEM-- HEAD ON.
ONCE YOU UNDERSTAND WHO YOU ARE, THEN YOU CAN DO SOMETHING ABOUT IT.
DO WHAT?
I DON'T KNOW. MAKE AMENDS, I GUESS. STOP BEING AFRAID OF YOURSELF AND DO SOME GOOD IN THE WORLD.
BECAUSE NO MATTER WHAT YOU BELIEVE, WHEN THE END COMES, YOU'LL WANT THAT ON YOUR SIDE.

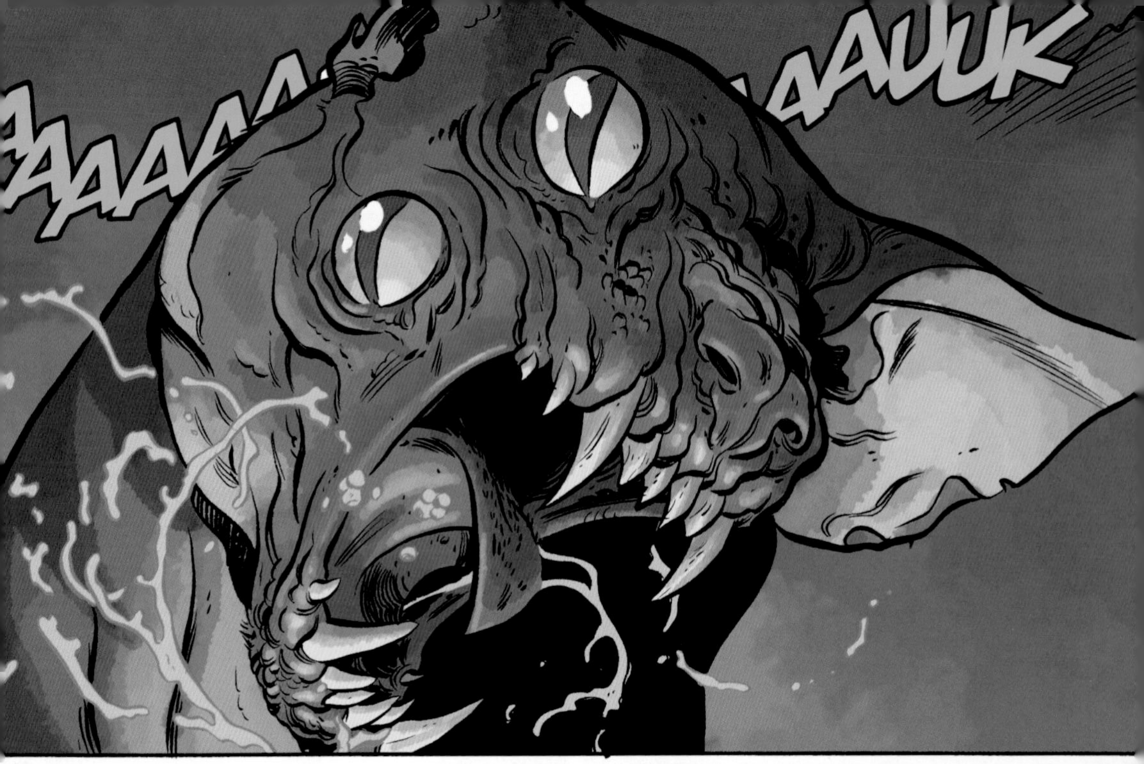
AAAAAA
AAAUUK

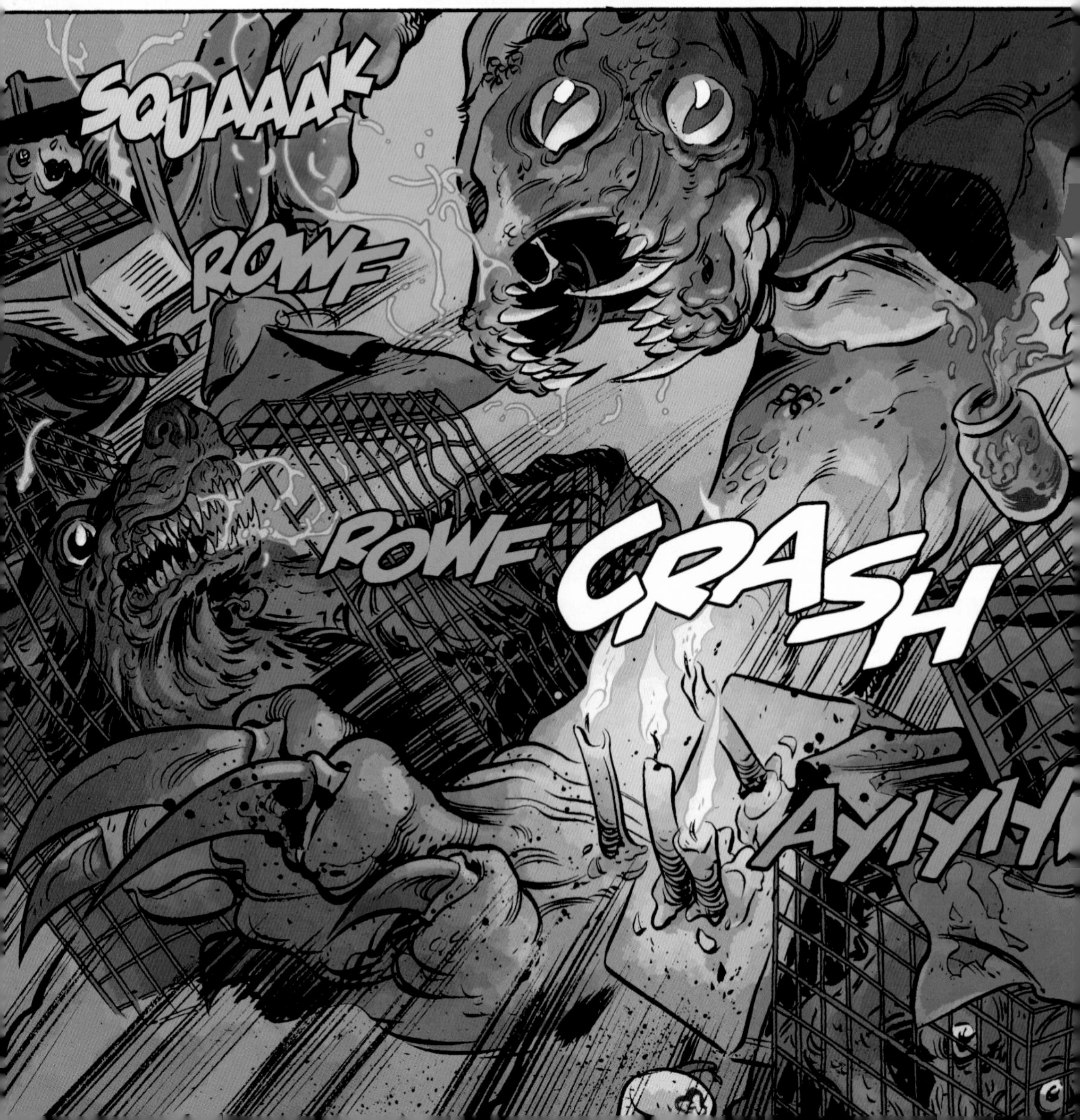
SQUAAAK
ROWF
ROWF
CRASH
AYYYY

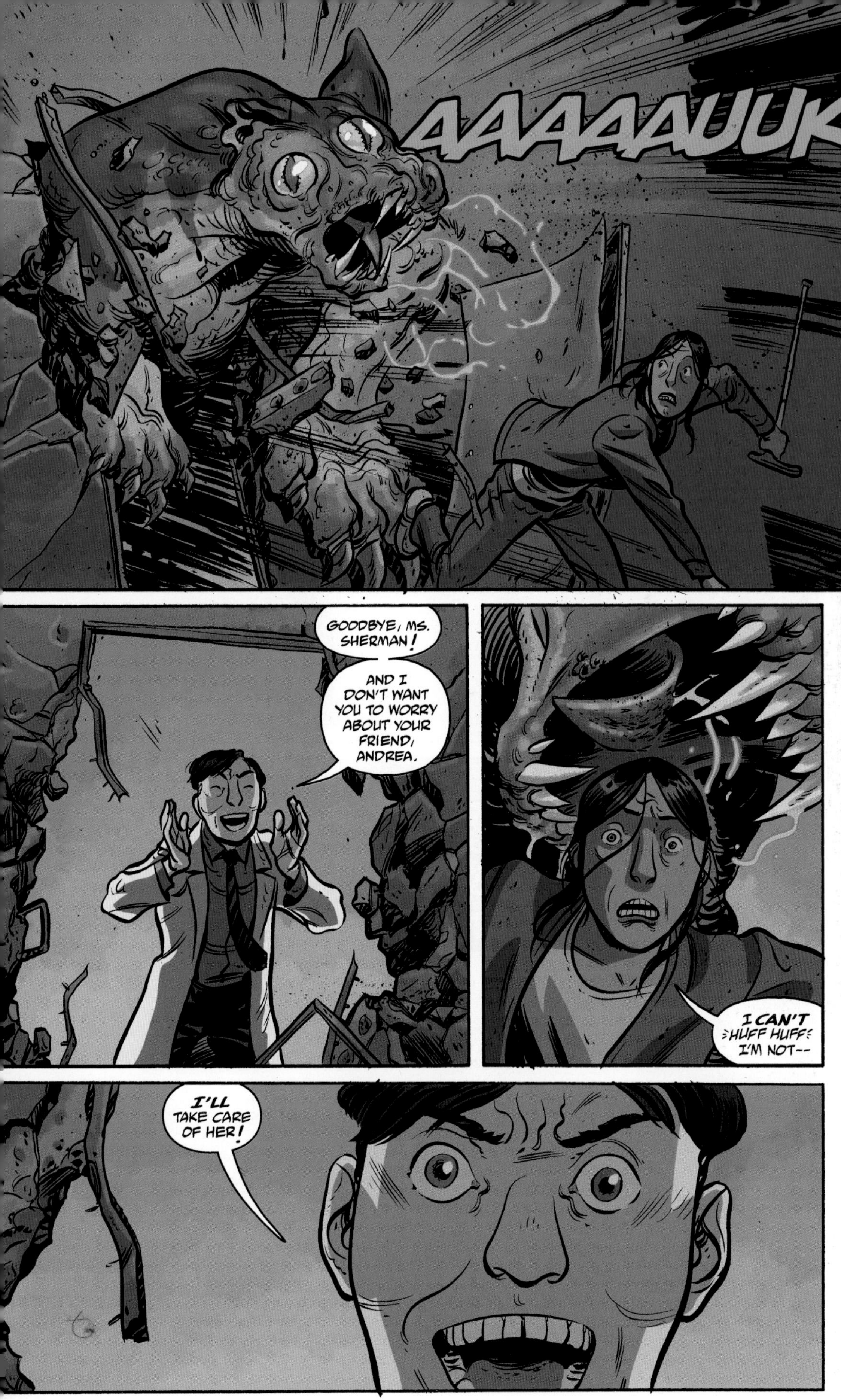
AAAAAUUK
GOODBYE, MS. SHERMAN!
AND I DON'T WANT YOU TO WORRY ABOUT YOUR FRIEND, ANDREA.
I CAN'T HUFF HUFF I'M NOT--
I'LL TAKE CARE OF HER!

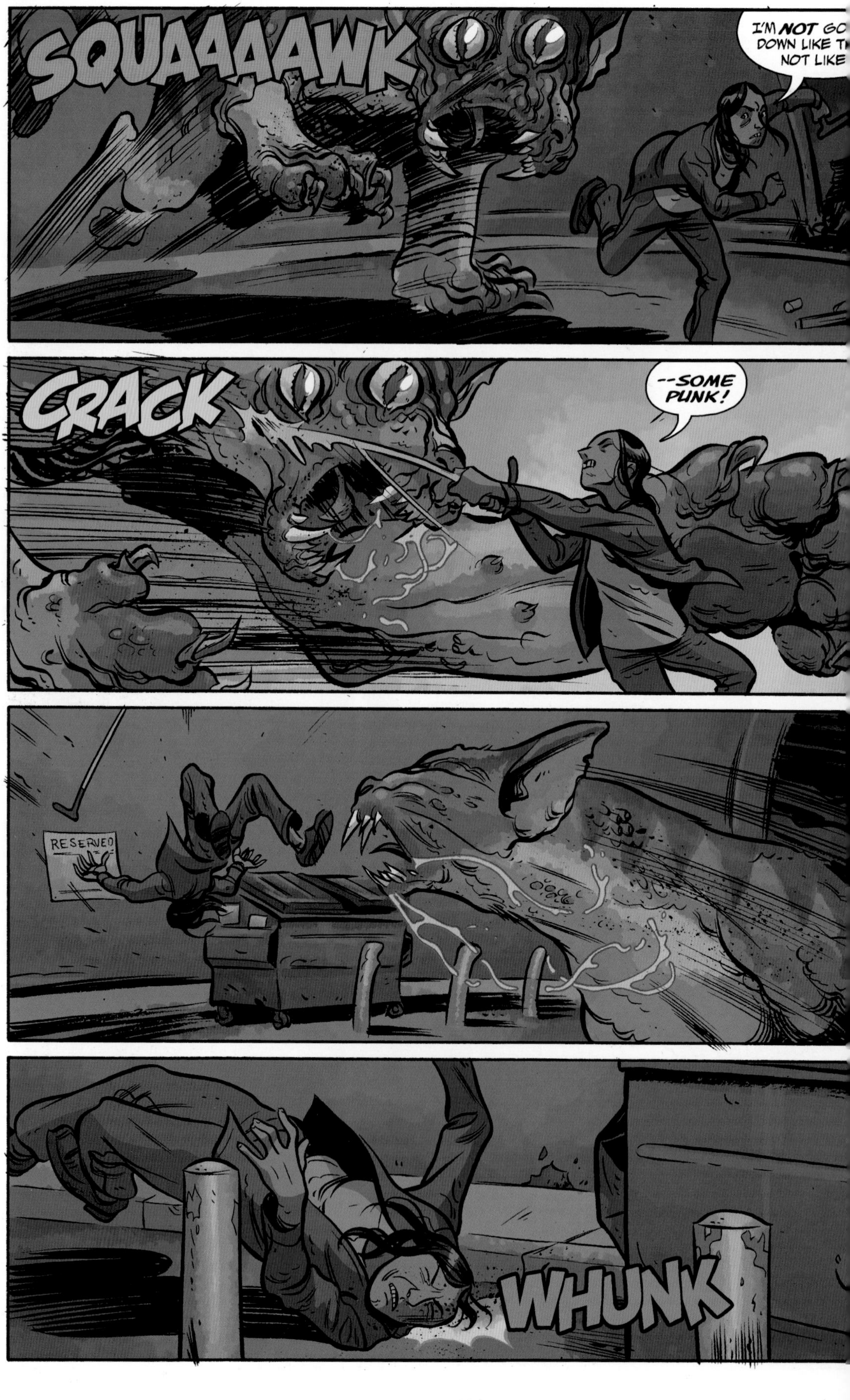
SQUAAAAAWK
I'M NOT GO
DOWN LIKE TH
NOT LIKE
CRACK
--SOME PUNK!
RESERVED
WHUNK

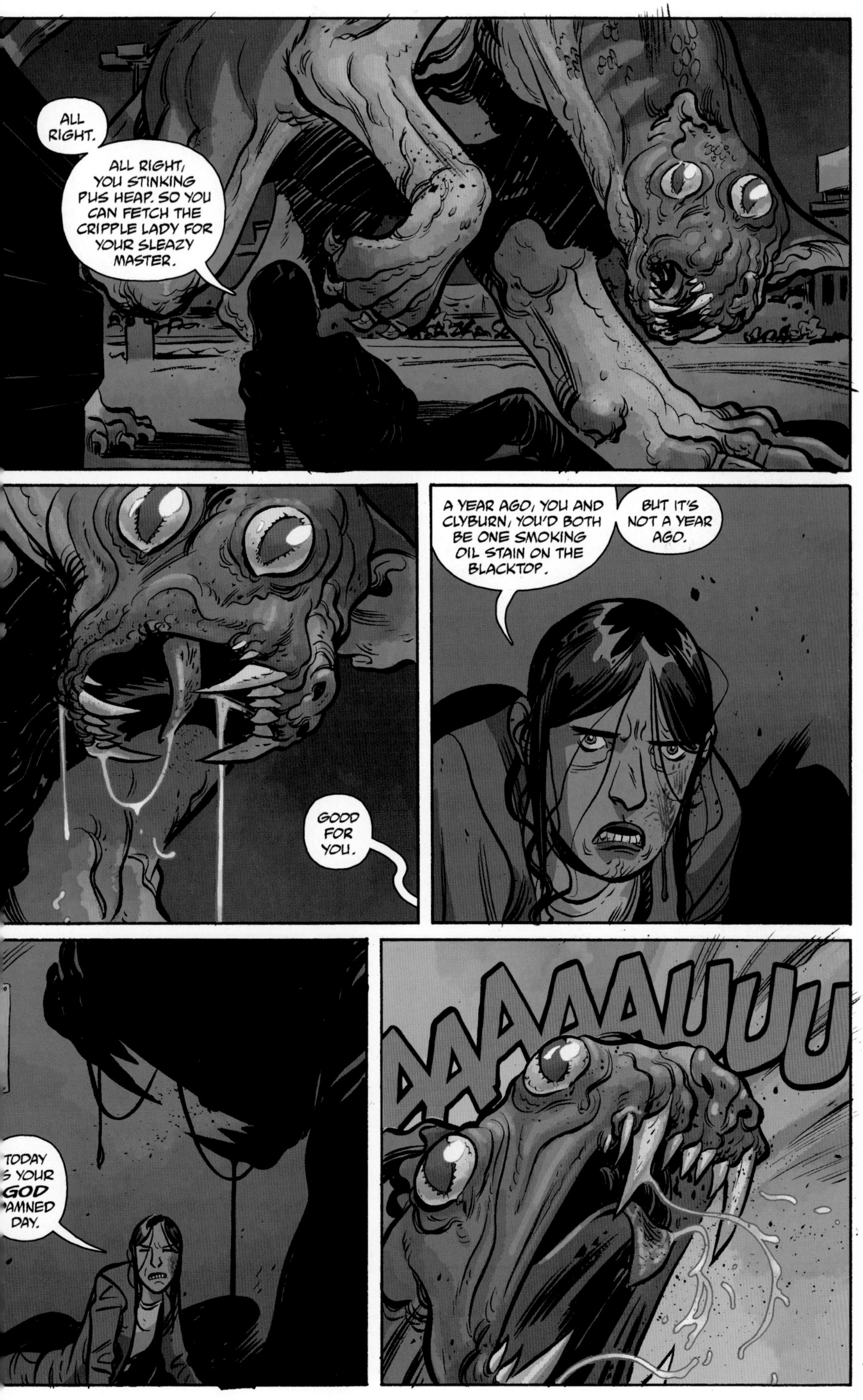
ALL RIGHT.
ALL RIGHT, YOU STINKING PUS HEAP. SO YOU CAN FETCH THE CRIPPLE LADY FOR YOUR SLEAZY MASTER.
A YEAR AGO, YOU AND CLYBURN, YOU'D BOTH BE ONE SMOKING OIL STAIN ON THE BLACKTOP.
BUT IT'S NOT A YEAR AGO.
GOOD FOR YOU.
TODAY
S YOUR
GOD
AMNED
DAY.
AAAAAUUU

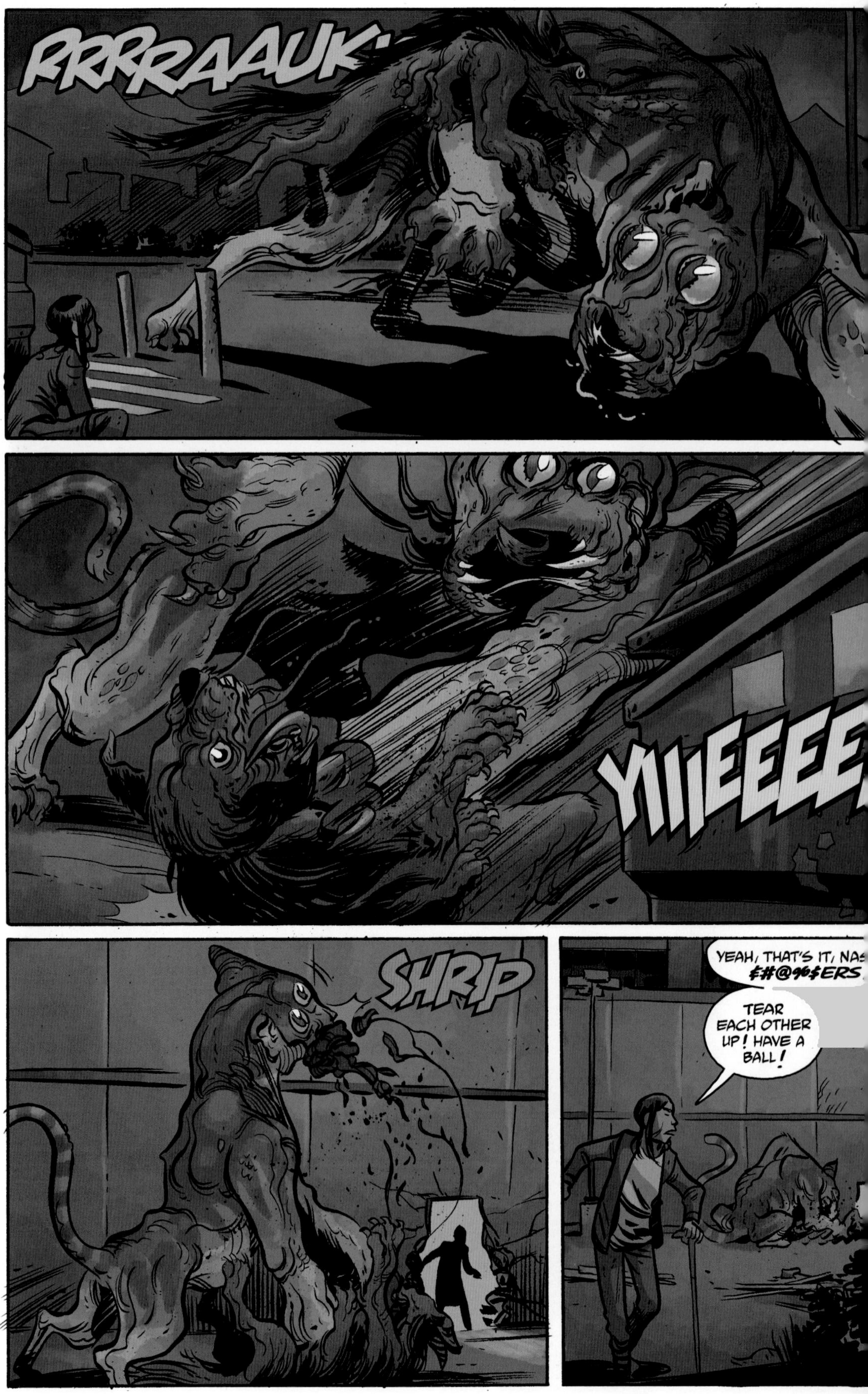
RRRRAAUK
YIIEEEE
SHRIP
YEAH, THAT'S IT,
£#@%$ERS
TEAR EACH OTHER UP! HAVE A BALL!

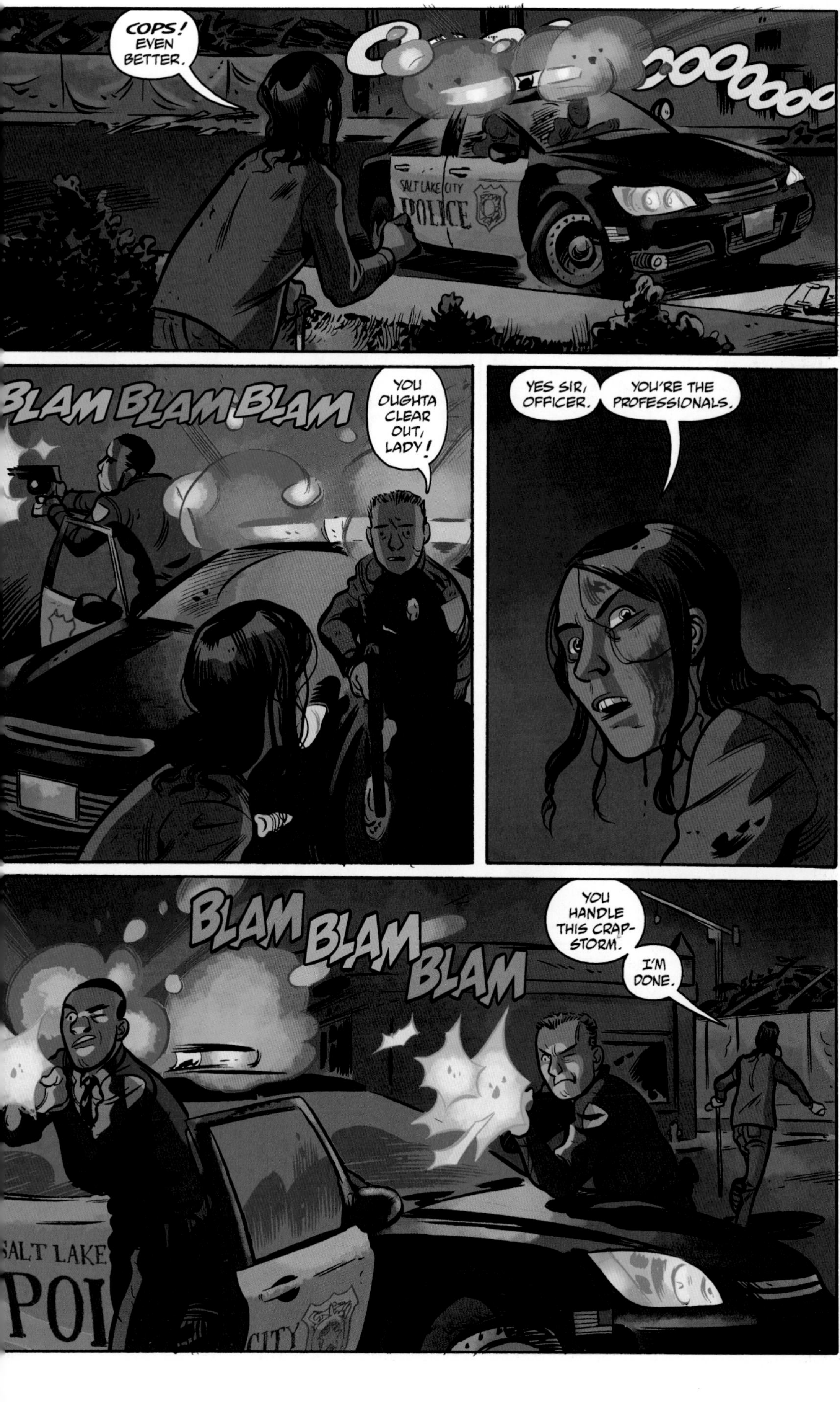
COPS! EVEN BETTER.
SALT LAKE CITY POLICE
BLAM BLAM BLAM
YOU OUGHTA CLEAR OUT, LADY!
YES SIR, OFFICER.
YOU'RE THE PROFESSIONALS.
BLAM BLAM BLAM
YOU HANDLE THIS CRAP-STORM.
I'M DONE.
SALT LAKE
POI
CITY

DNA Test Repo

D.A.T
DNA ANALYTICS TECH.

CASE 17427	MOTHER	CHILD
NAME		
DATE		
TEST NO.		

I DON'T GET IT. WHAT IS THIS?

TWO DIFFERENT D.N.A. RESULTS, **BOTH** TAKEN FROM YOUR DAUGHTER, FENIX.

THERE'S NO MISTAKE. I TOOK THE SAMPLES MYSELF.

NO. THAT AIN'T POSSIBLE... RIGHT?

NORMALLY, NO, BUT YOUR SOCIAL WORKER'S SUSPICIONS OF PUBLIC-ASSISTANCE FRAUD FORCED ME TO LOOK AT THE **ABNORMAL.**

SEE, HERE THE THING GENETIC TESTING DIFFERS FR STATE TO STATE.

"HERE IN CALIFORNIA, WE USE A CHEEK SWAB. IT'S RELIABLE AND MUCH EASIER TO ADMINISTER TO A CHILD. BUT BACK WHEN YOU WERE IN UTAH, THEY WERE STILL DRAWING BLOOD."

SO I REPEATED BOTH TESTS--SWAB AND BLOOD DRAW--AND, AS I SAID, THEY SHOWED TWO DISTINCT GENETIC FINGERPRINTS.

TWO SEPARATE PARTS OF THE BODY, TWO DIFFERENT RESULTS.

SO WHAT'S ALL THAT MEAN?

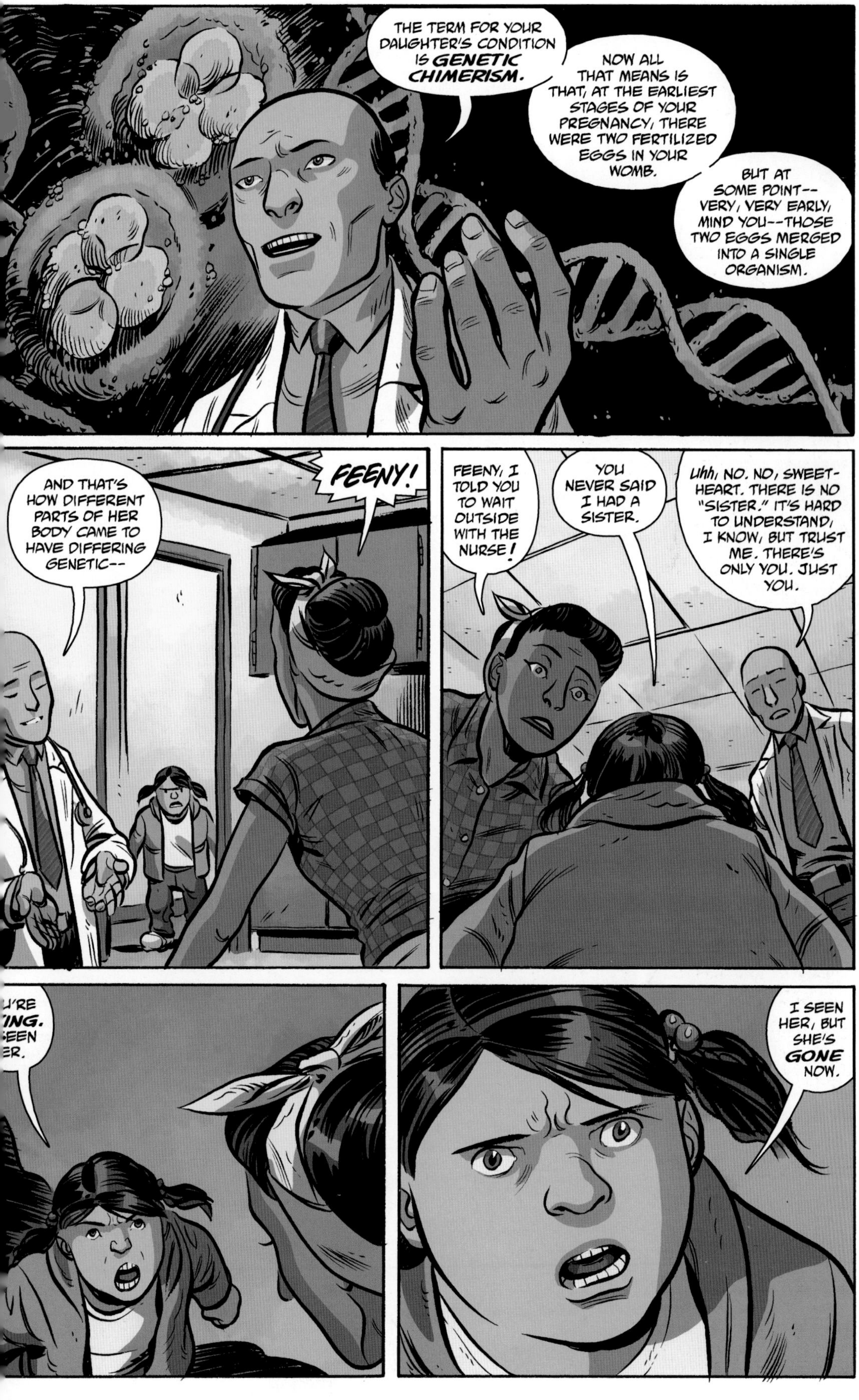
THE TERM FOR YOUR DAUGHTER'S CONDITION IS GENETIC CHIMERISM.
NOW ALL THAT MEANS IS THAT, AT THE EARLIEST STAGES OF YOUR PREGNANCY, THERE WERE TWO FERTILIZED EGGS IN YOUR WOMB.
BUT AT SOME POINT-- VERY, VERY EARLY, MIND YOU--THOSE TWO EGGS MERGED INTO A SINGLE ORGANISM.
AND THAT'S HOW DIFFERENT PARTS OF HER BODY CAME TO HAVE DIFFERING GENETIC--
FEENY!
FEENY, I TOLD YOU TO WAIT OUTSIDE WITH THE NURSE!
YOU NEVER SAID I HAD A SISTER.
Uhh, NO. NO, SWEET-HEART. THERE IS NO "SISTER." IT'S HARD TO UNDERSTAND, I KNOW, BUT TRUST ME. THERE'S ONLY YOU. JUST YOU.
I SEEN HER, BUT SHE'S GONE NOW.

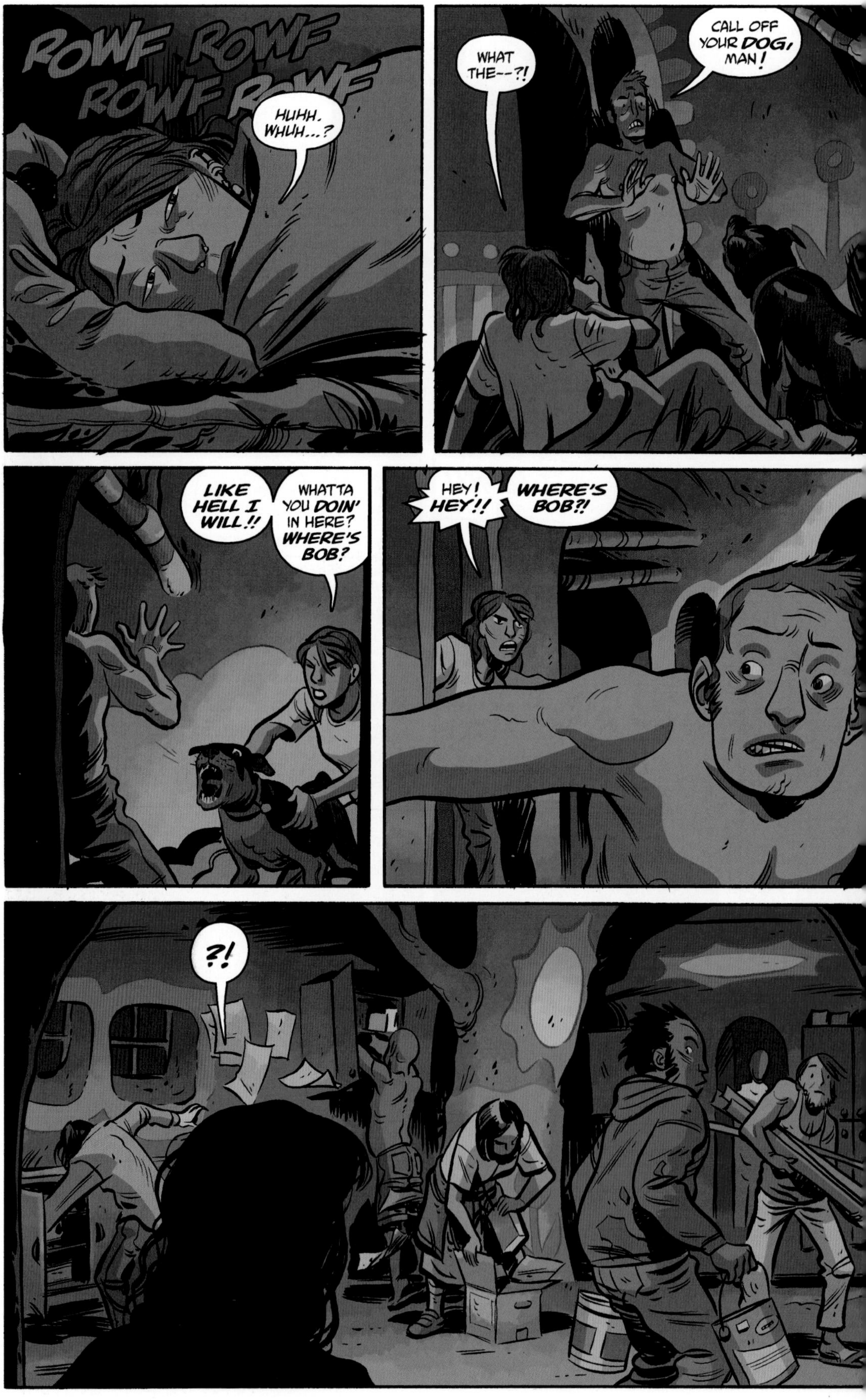
ROWF ROWF ROWF ROWF
HUHH. WHUH...?
WHAT THE--?!
CALL OFF YOUR DOG, MAN!
LIKE HELL I WILL!!
WHATTA YOU DOIN' IN HERE? WHERE'S BOB?
HEY! HEY!!
WHERE'S BOB?!
?!

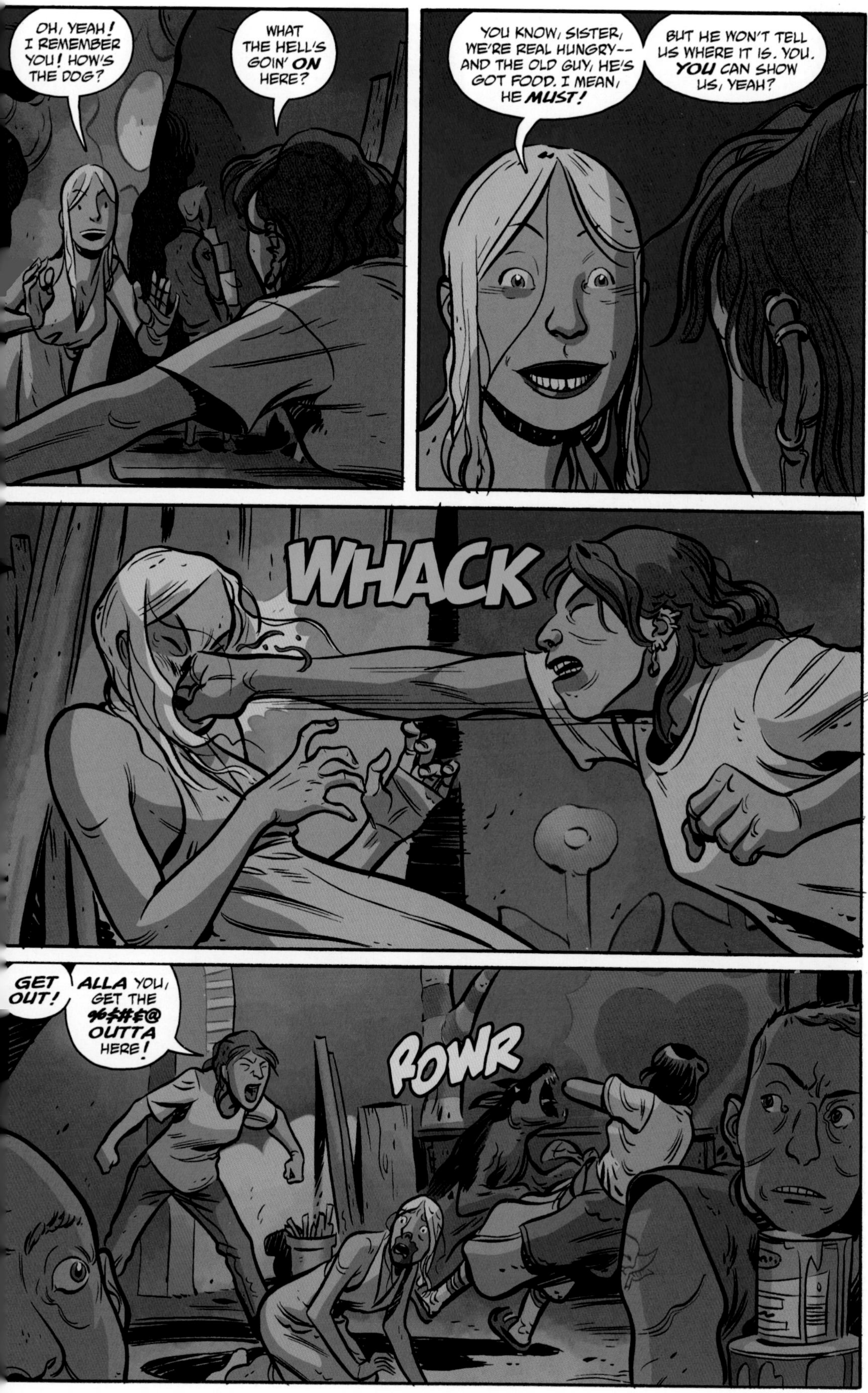

OH, YEAH! I REMEMBER YOU! HOW'S THE DOG?
WHAT THE HELL'S GOIN' ON HERE?
YOU KNOW, SISTER, WE'RE REAL HUNGRY-- AND THE OLD GUY, HE'S GOT FOOD. I MEAN, HE MUST!
BUT HE WON'T TELL US WHERE IT IS. YOU. YOU CAN SHOW US, YEAH?
WHACK
GET OUT!
ALLA YOU, GET THE %$#£@ OUTTA HERE!
ROWR

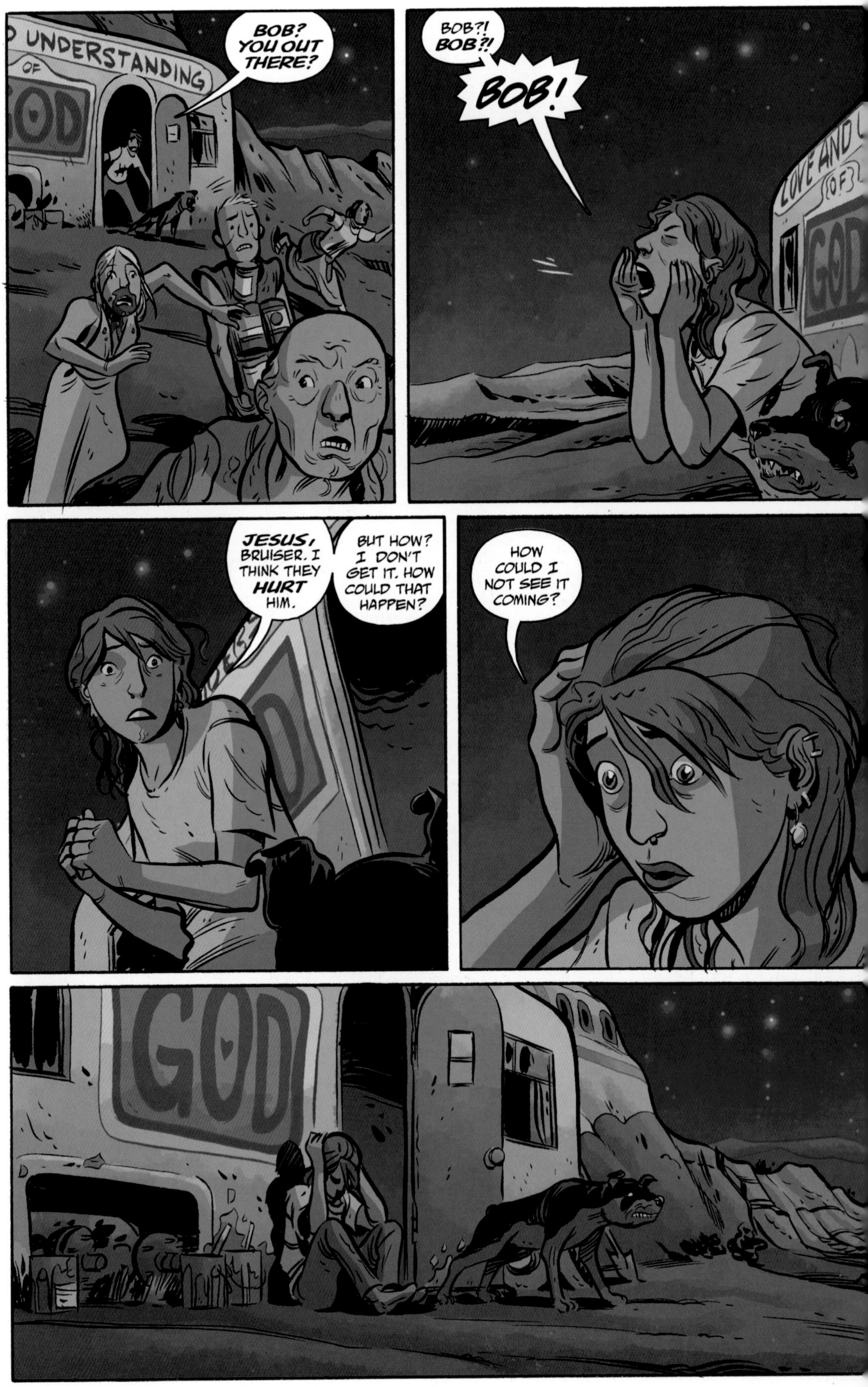
UNDERSTANDING
OF
GOD
BOB? YOU OUT THERE?
BOB?! BOB?!
BOB!
LOVE AND
OF
GOD
JESUS, BRUISER. I THINK THEY HURT HIM.
BUT HOW? I DON'T GET IT. HOW COULD THAT HAPPEN?
HOW COULD I NOT SEE IT COMING?
GOD

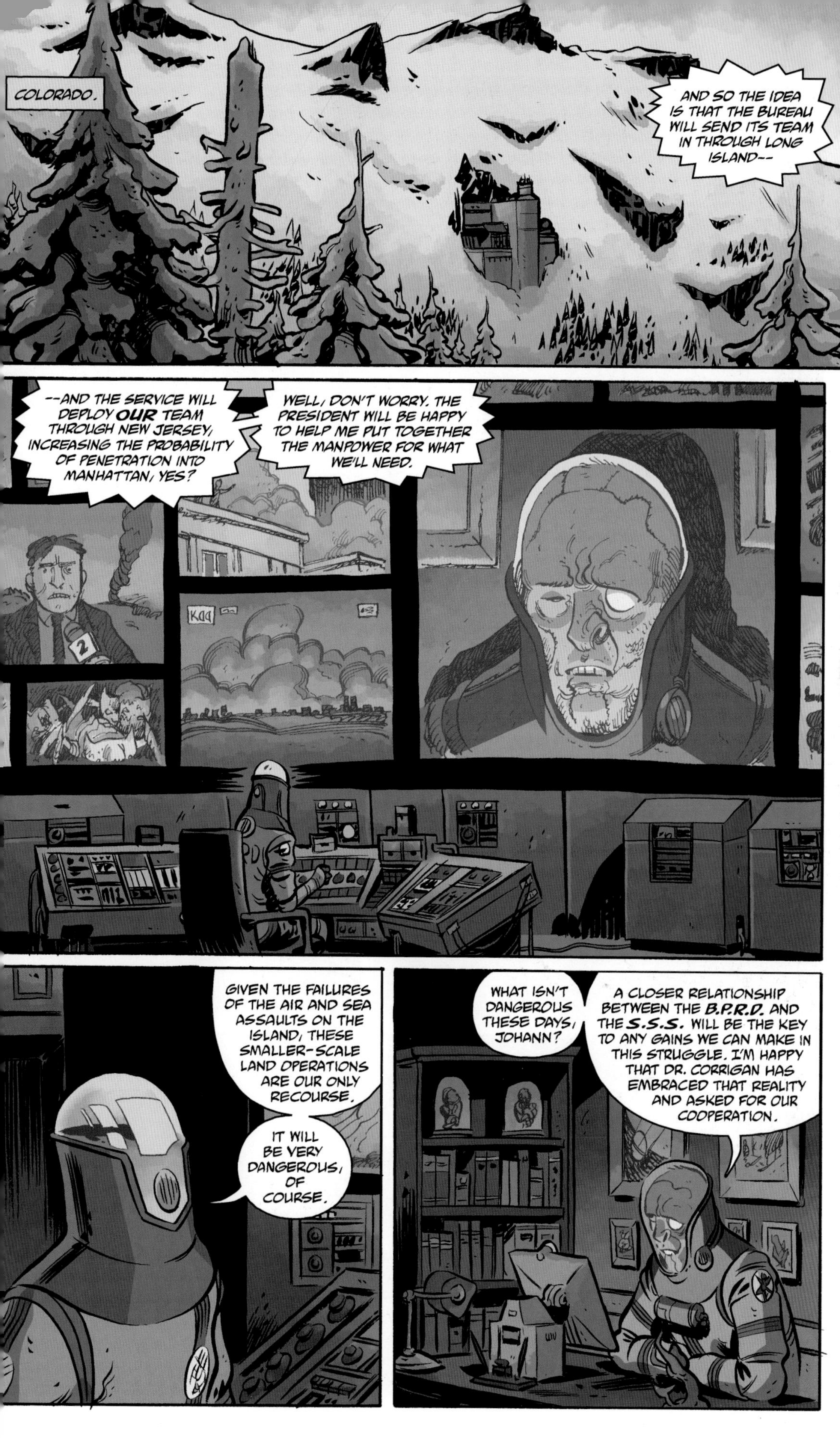
COLORADO.
AND SO THE IDEA IS THAT THE BUREAU WILL SEND ITS TEAM IN THROUGH LONG ISLAND--
--AND THE SERVICE WILL DEPLOY OUR TEAM THROUGH NEW JERSEY, INCREASING THE PROBABILITY OF PENETRATION INTO MANHATTAN, YES?
WELL, DON'T WORRY. THE PRESIDENT WILL BE HAPPY TO HELP ME PUT TOGETHER THE MANPOWER FOR WHAT WE'LL NEED.
GIVEN THE FAILURES OF THE AIR AND SEA ASSAULTS ON THE ISLAND, THESE SMALLER-SCALE LAND OPERATIONS ARE OUR ONLY RECOURSE.
IT WILL BE VERY DANGEROUS, OF COURSE.
WHAT ISN'T DANGEROUS THESE DAYS, JOHANN?
A CLOSER RELATIONSHIP BETWEEN THE B.P.R.D. AND THE S.S.S. WILL BE THE KEY TO ANY GAINS WE CAN MAKE IN THIS STRUGGLE. I'M HAPPY THAT DR. CORRIGAN HAS EMBRACED THAT REALITY AND ASKED FOR OUR COOPERATION.

I SUPPOSE THE SUCCESS OF OUR RECENT COLLABORATION IN DOYONEK MAY HAVE HAD SOME-THING TO DO WITH THAT.

ACTUALLY, WE HAVE SO MANY OPERATIONS UNDERWAY RIGHT NOW KATE WAS UNABLE TO FIND ENOUGH B.P.R.D. AGENTS FOR THIS MISSION.

HA HA HA.

WELL, WHATEVER THE CASE, I WELCOME THE PARTNERSHIP.

NOW LISTEN, JOHAN, THIS IS INTERESTING. THE ZINCO CORPORATION WAS HEADQUARTERED IN MANHATTAN. YOU REMEMBER THEM.

ZINCO...

YES, THE PEOPLE WHO WERE WORKING ON THE REHABILITATION OF THE PARTIALLY FORMED CLONE WE HAD HERE.

I HAVEN'T THOUGHT OF THEM IN SOME TIME.

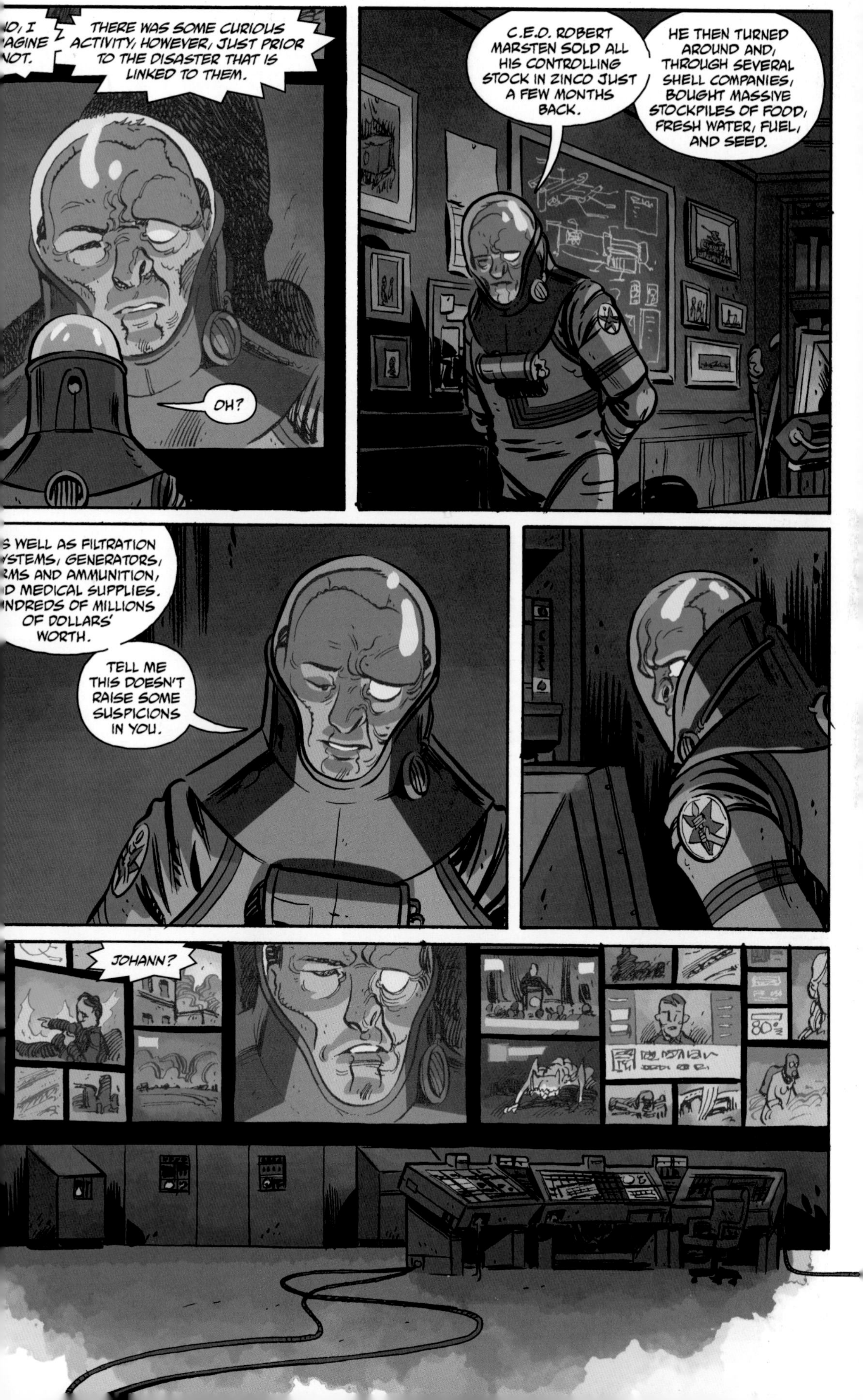
NO, I
...AGINE
NOT.
THERE WAS SOME CURIOUS ACTIVITY, HOWEVER, JUST PRIOR TO THE DISASTER THAT IS LINKED TO THEM.
OH?
C.E.O. ROBERT MARSTEN SOLD ALL HIS CONTROLLING STOCK IN ZINCO JUST A FEW MONTHS BACK.
HE THEN TURNED AROUND AND, THROUGH SEVERAL SHELL COMPANIES, BOUGHT MASSIVE STOCKPILES OF FOOD, FRESH WATER, FUEL, AND SEED.
S WELL AS FILTRATION YSTEMS, GENERATORS, RMS AND AMMUNITION, D MEDICAL SUPPLIES. NDREDS OF MILLIONS OF DOLLARS' WORTH.
TELL ME THIS DOESN'T RAISE SOME SUSPICIONS IN YOU.
JOHANN?

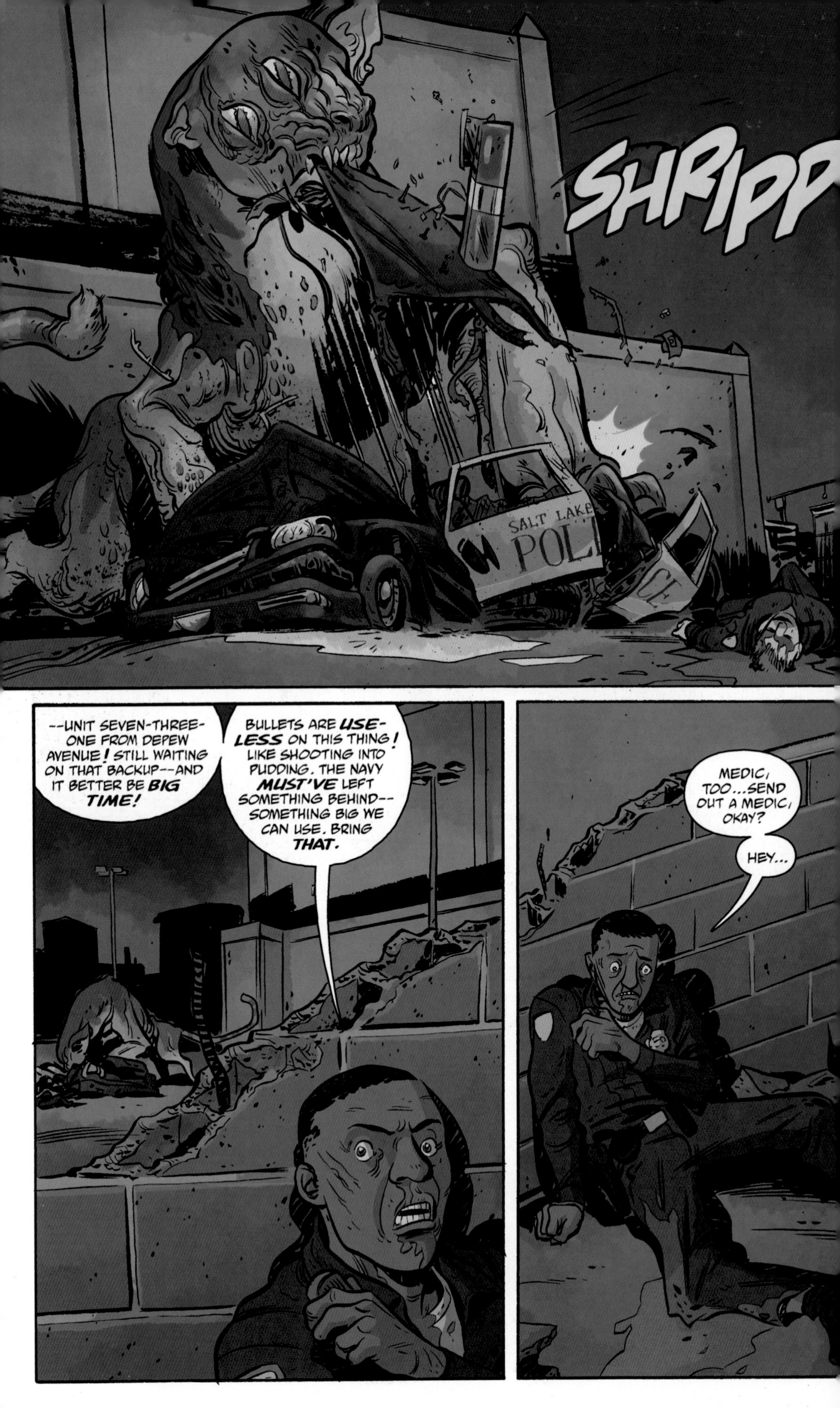
SHRIPP
SALT LAKE POLI
--UNIT SEVEN-THREE-ONE FROM DEPEW AVENUE! STILL WAITING ON THAT BACKUP--AND IT BETTER BE BIG TIME!
BULLETS ARE USELESS ON THIS THING! LIKE SHOOTING INTO PUDDING. THE NAVY MUST'VE LEFT SOMETHING BEHIND--SOMETHING BIG WE CAN USE. BRING THAT.
MEDIC, TOO...SEND OUT A MEDIC, OKAY?
HEY...

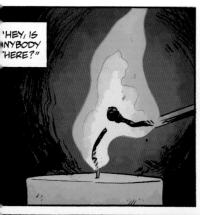

"HEY, IS
NYBODY
HERE?"

WHAT'S
WRONG
WITH ME?

AAAAAUUK

NDREA STUCK THERE
N THAT HOSPITAL WITH
LYBURN--OF COURSE
THAT'S TERRIBLE.

BUT OTHER PEOPLE LEAVE
IT TO THE COPS, THE ARMY,
WHATEVER. THEY NEVER
GET INVOLVED AND FEEL
JUST FINE ABOUT THAT.

WHY
CAN'T
I?

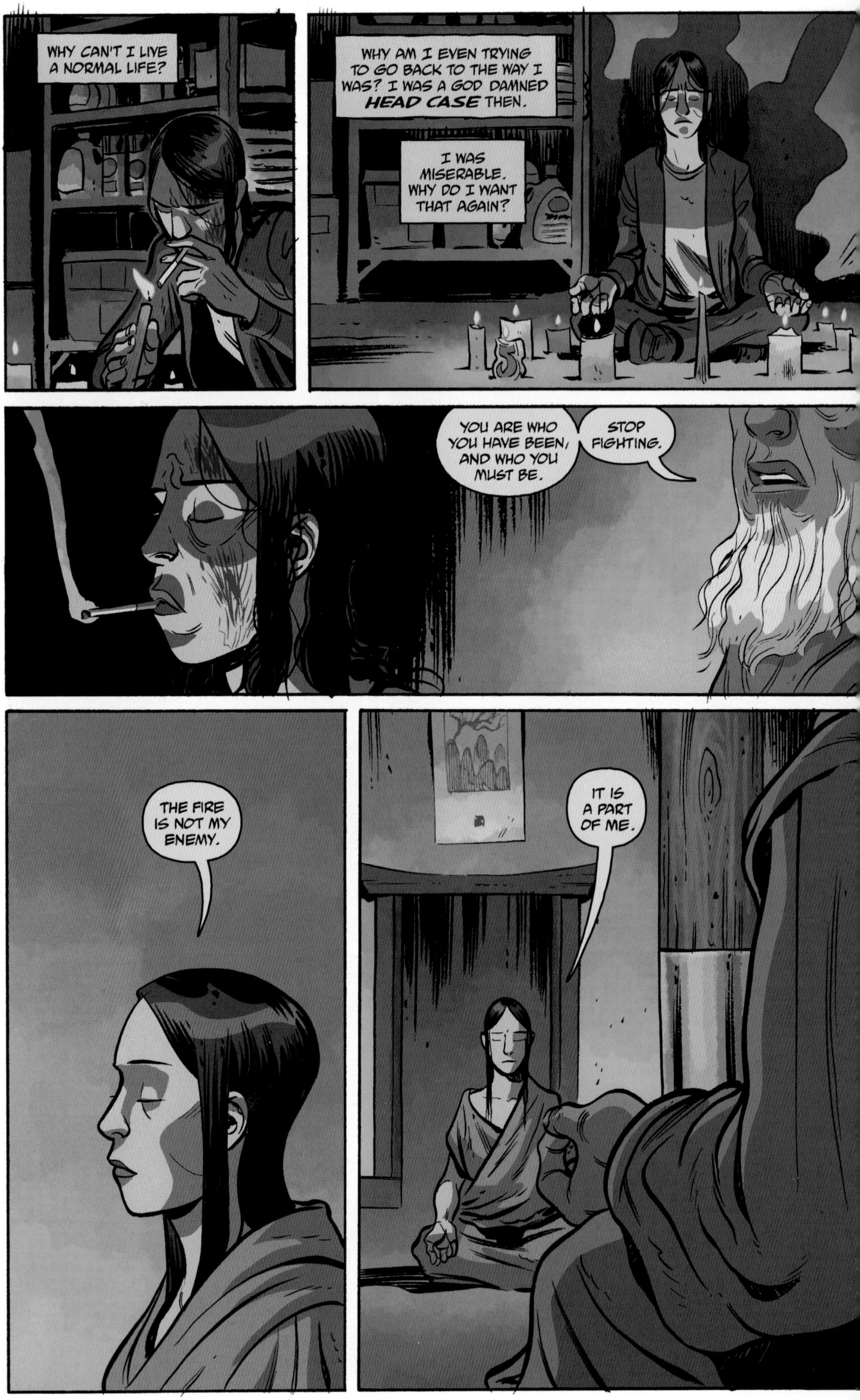
WHY CAN'T I LIVE A NORMAL LIFE?
WHY AM I EVEN TRYING TO GO BACK TO THE WAY I WAS? I WAS A GOD DAMNED HEAD CASE THEN.
I WAS MISERABLE. WHY DO I WANT THAT AGAIN?
YOU ARE WHO YOU HAVE BEEN, AND WHO YOU MUST BE.
STOP FIGHTING.
THE FIRE IS NOT MY ENEMY.
IT IS A PART OF ME.

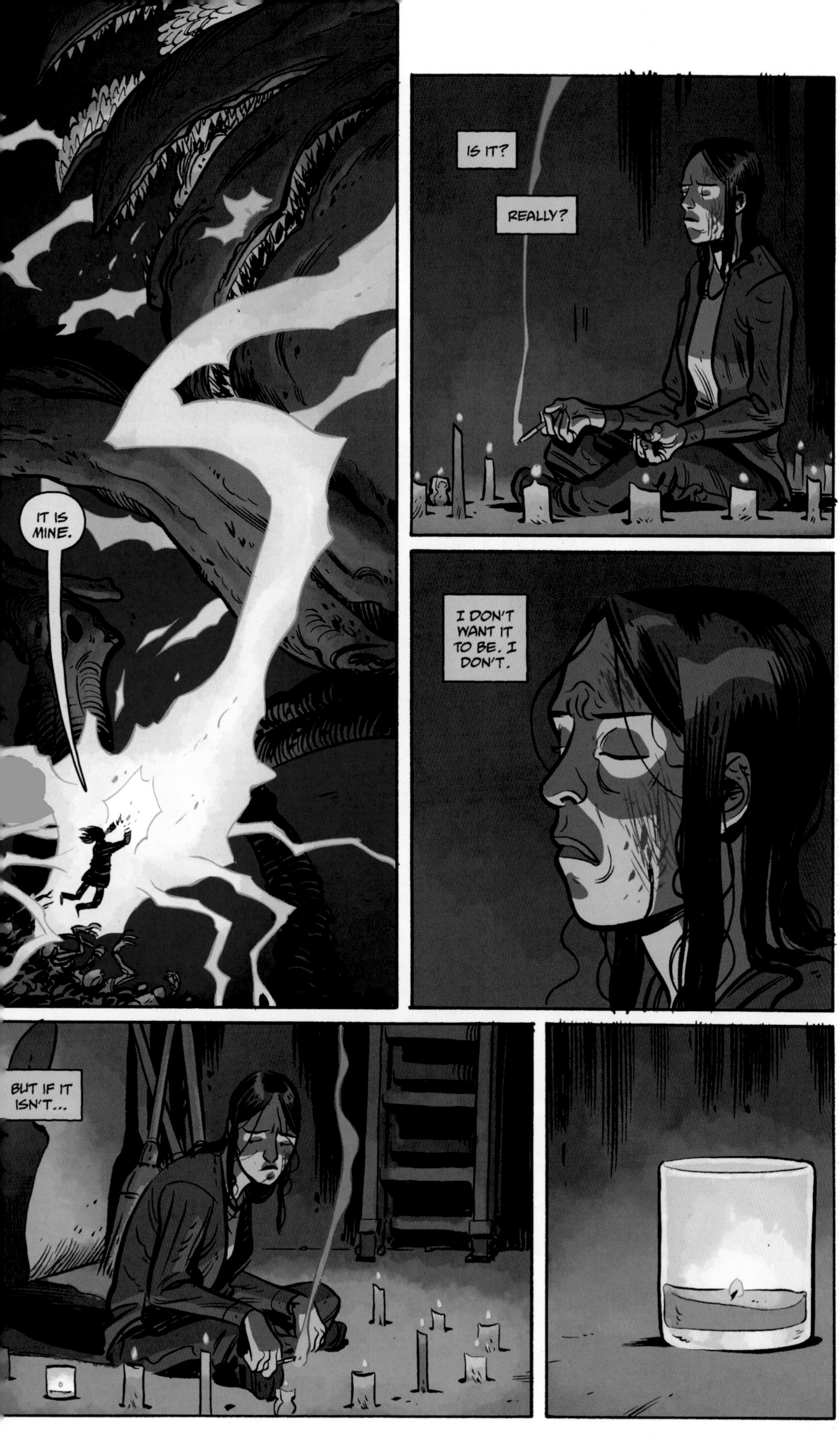
IT IS MINE.
IS IT?
REALLY?
I DON'T WANT IT TO BE. I DON'T.
BUT IF IT ISN'T...

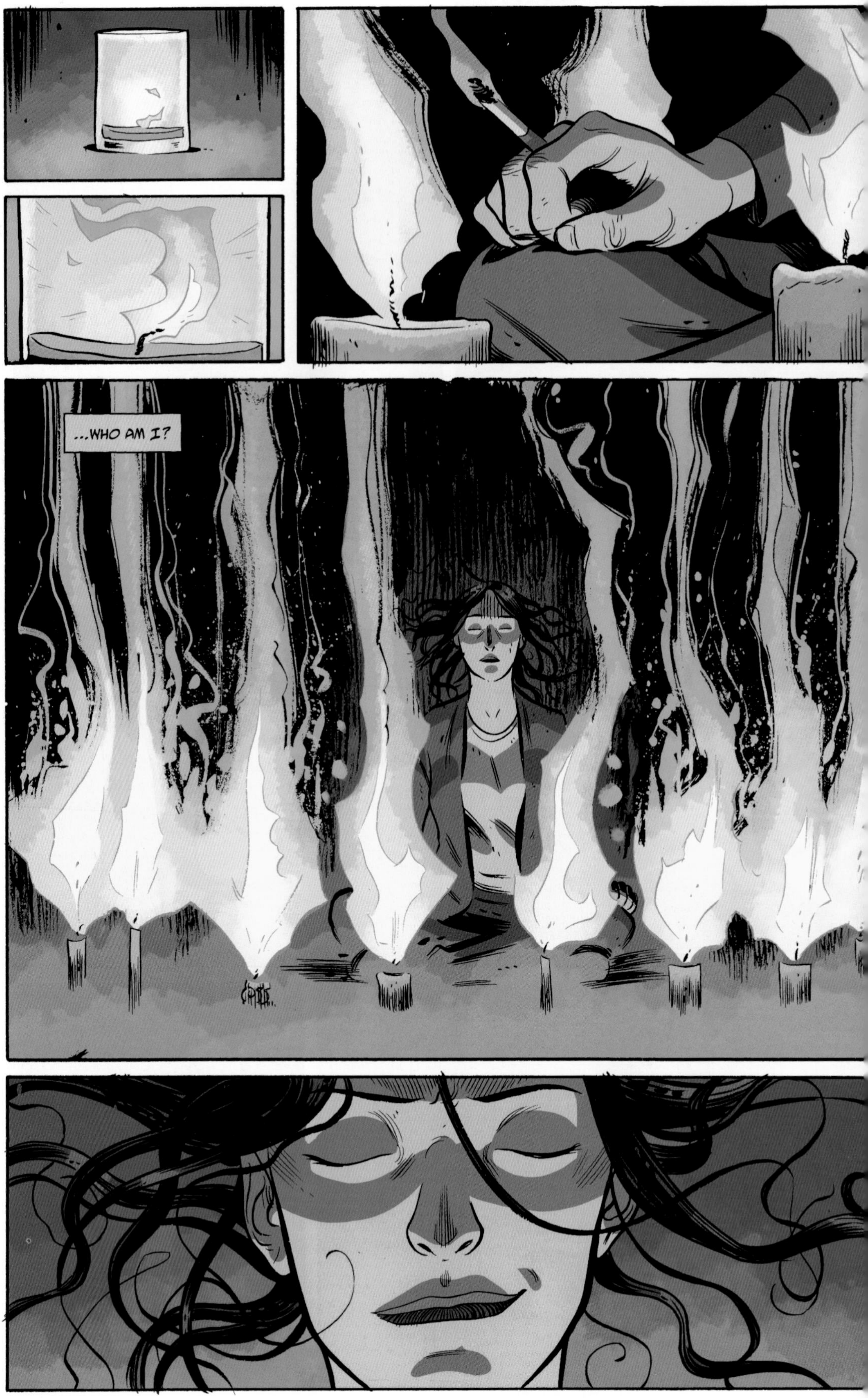
...WHO AM I?

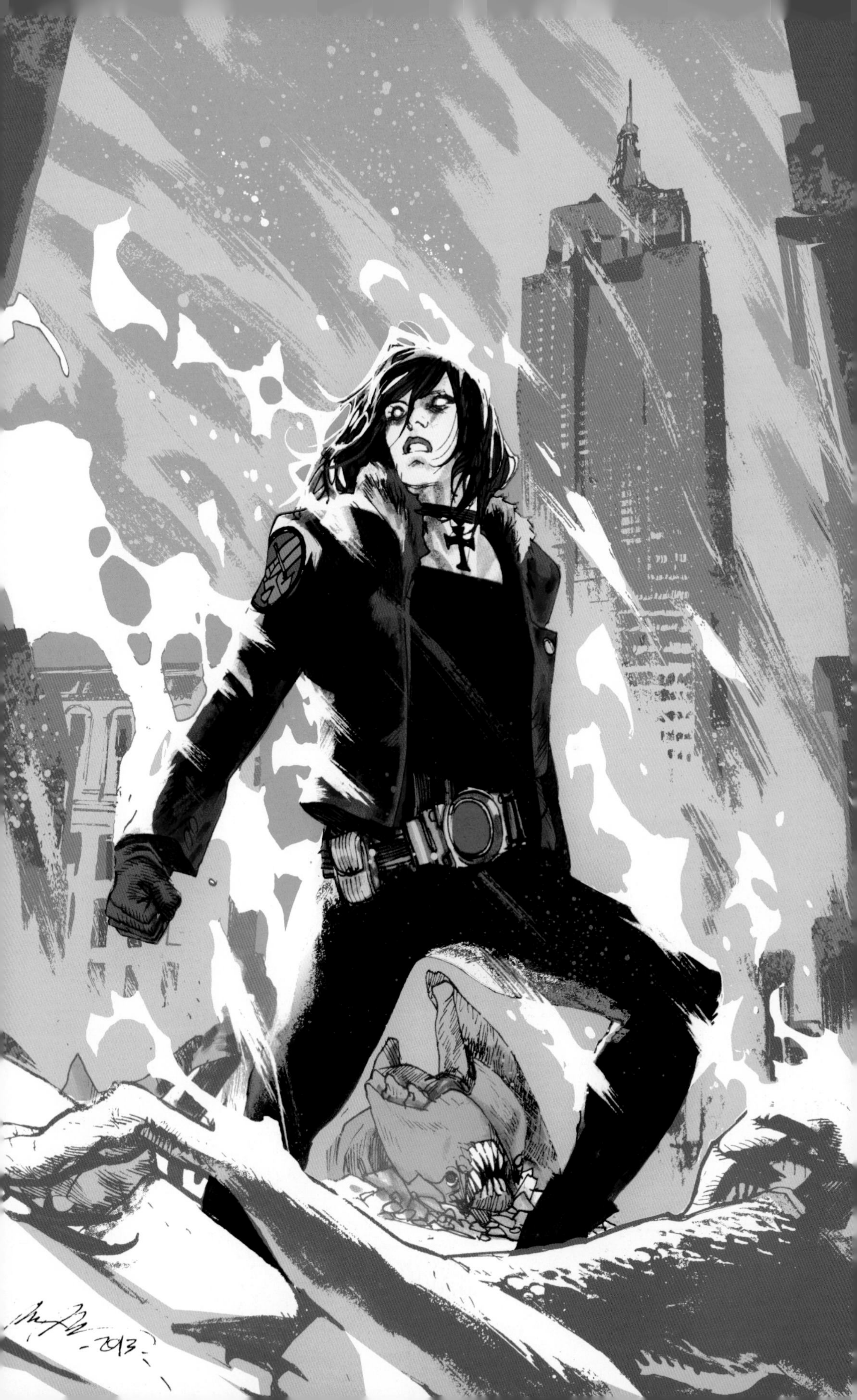

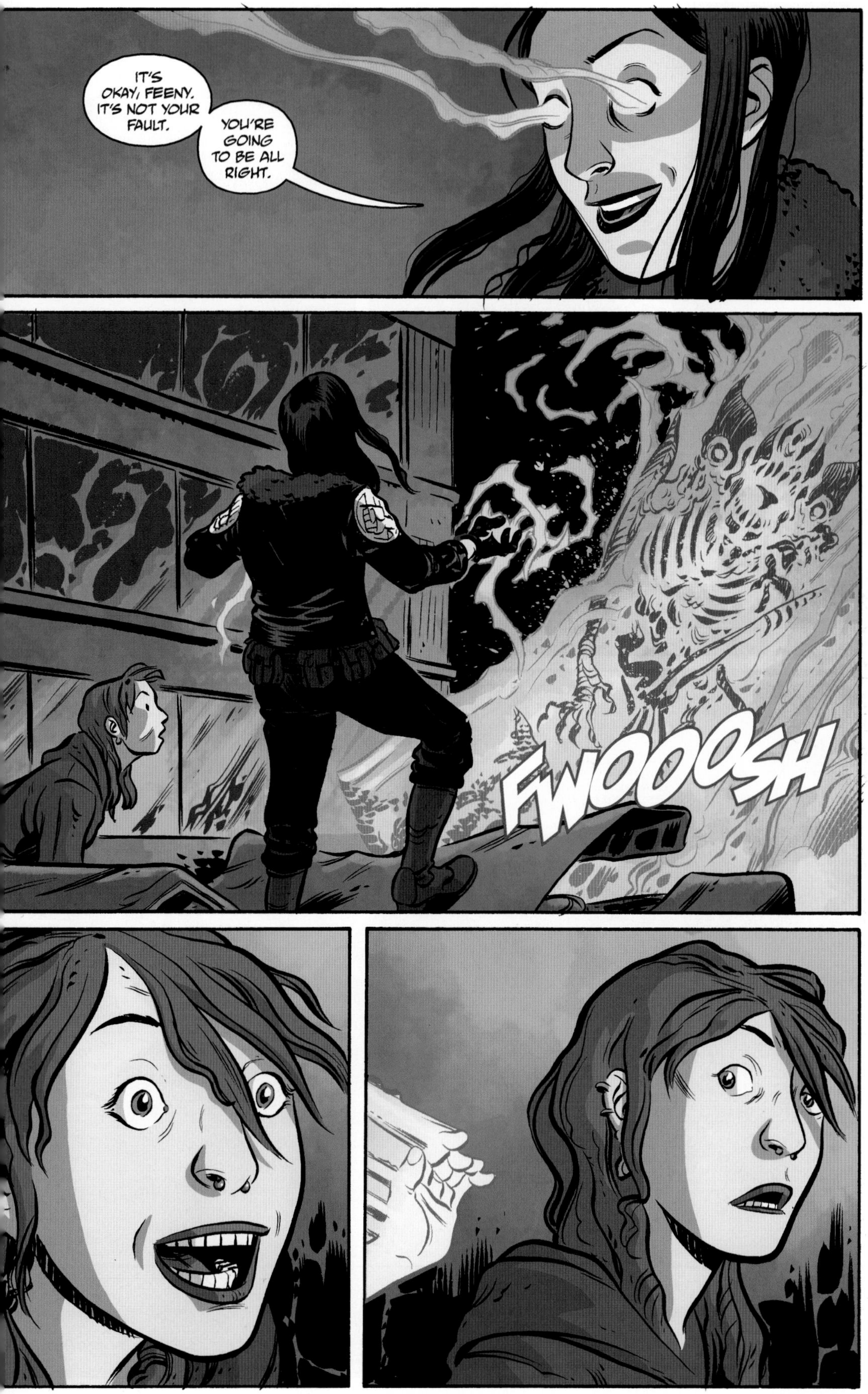
IT'S OKAY, FEENY. IT'S NOT YOUR FAULT.
YOU'RE GOING TO BE ALL RIGHT.
FWOOOSH

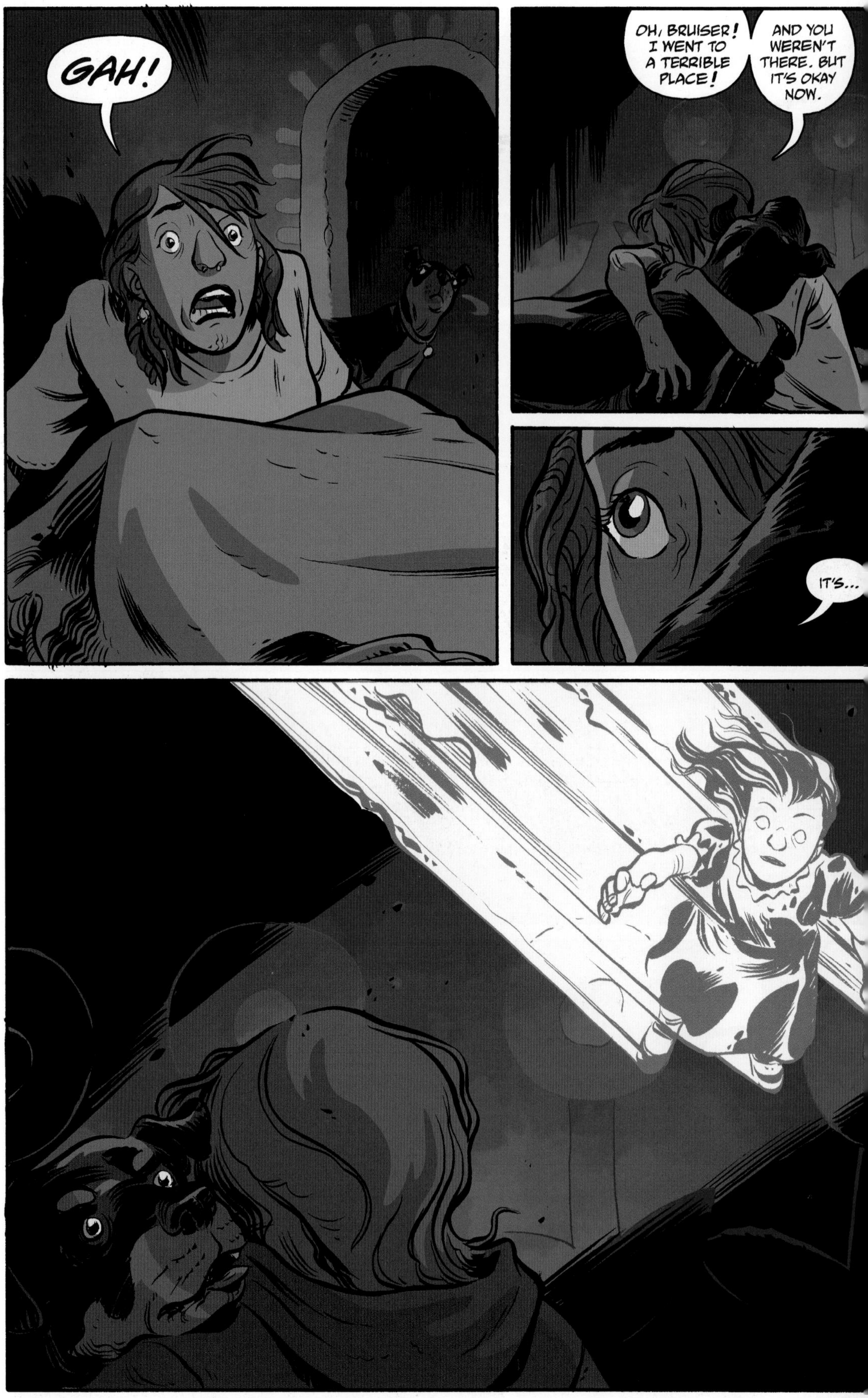
GAH!
OH, BRUISER! I WENT TO A TERRIBLE PLACE!
AND YOU WEREN'T THERE. BUT IT'S OKAY NOW.
IT'S...

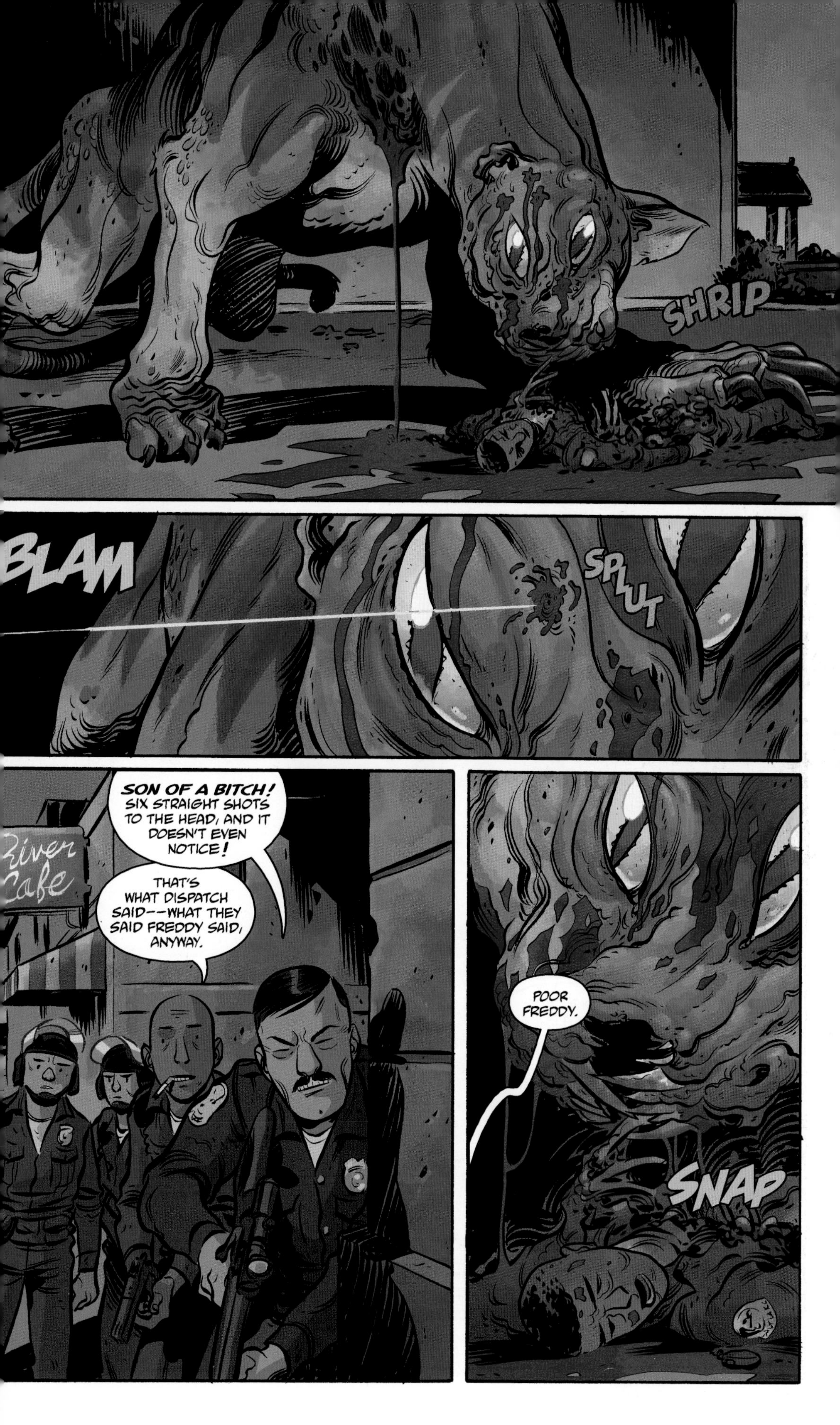
SHRIP
BLAM
SPLUT
SON OF A BITCH! SIX STRAIGHT SHOTS TO THE HEAD, AND IT DOESN'T EVEN NOTICE!
THAT'S WHAT DISPATCH SAID--WHAT THEY SAID FREDDY SAID, ANYWAY.
River Cafe
POOR FREDDY.
SNAP

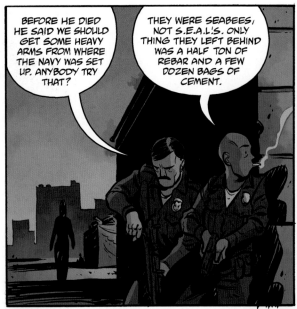

BEFORE HE DIED HE SAID WE SHOULD GET SOME HEAVY ARMS FROM WHERE THE NAVY WAS SET UP. ANYBODY TRY THAT?

THEY WERE SEABEES, NOT S.E.A.L.'S. ONLY THING THEY LEFT BEHIND WAS A HALF TON OF REBAR AND A FEW DOZEN BAGS OF CEMENT.

HEY, OFFICER. SPARE ONE OF THOSE?

WHA--? HEY, MISS, YOU CAN'T BE HERE! THIS IS A RESTRICTED AREA!

"RESTRICTED" TO WHO? *YOU* FOUR?

I'VE BEEN LISTENING TO YOU TAKE POTSHOTS AT THAT MONSTER ALL NIGHT. WHERE'S IT GETTING YOU?

HOW 'BOUT THAT CIGARETTE?

OKAY, SO WE'RE A BUNCH OF CLOWNS--BUT REALLY, YOU HAVE TO LEAVE.

LET ME ASK YOU SOME-THING.

YOU "CLOW THOUGH ABOUT US FIRE ON T THING

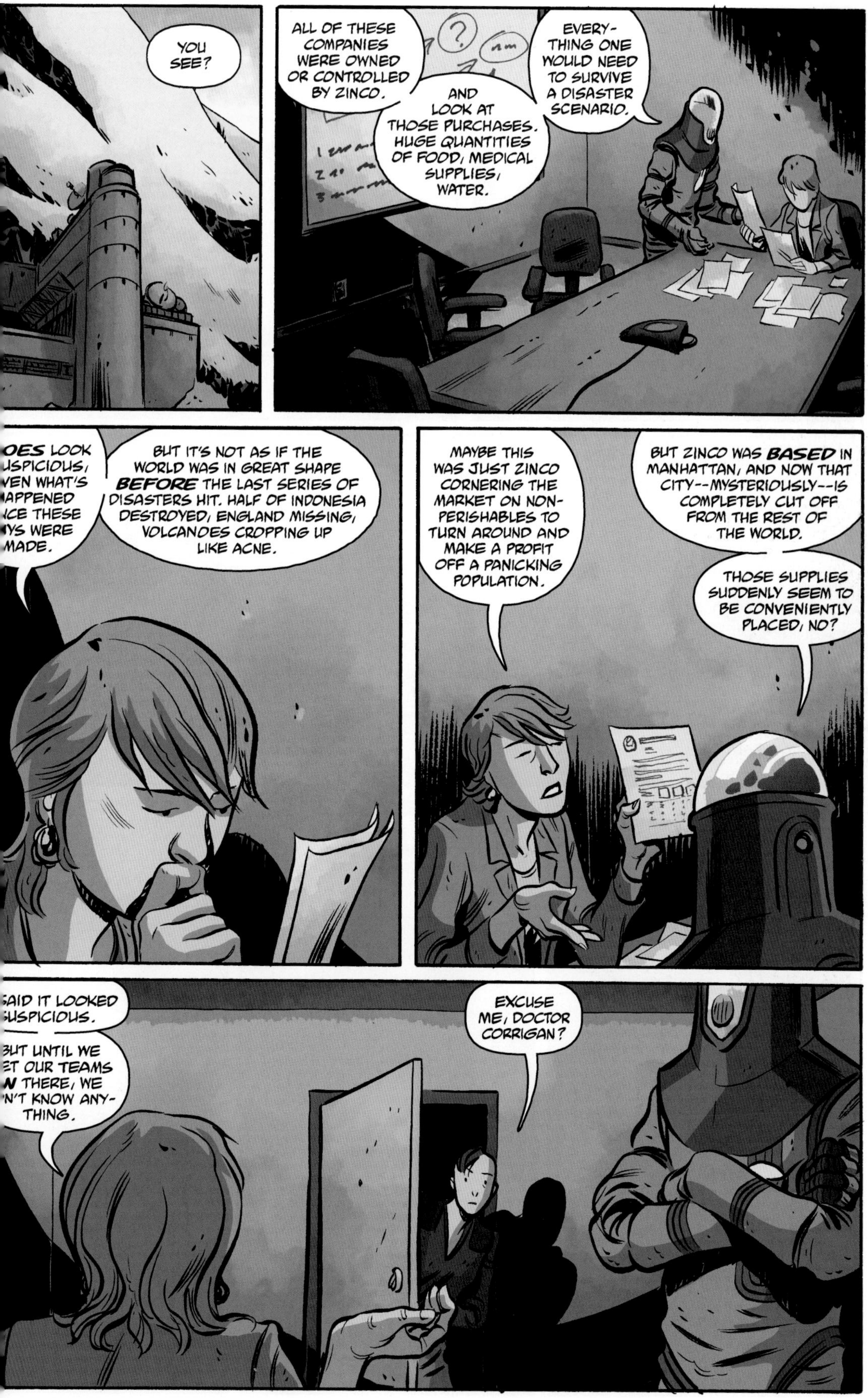
YOU SEE?
ALL OF THESE COMPANIES WERE OWNED OR CONTROLLED BY ZINCO.
AND LOOK AT THOSE PURCHASES. HUGE QUANTITIES OF FOOD, MEDICAL SUPPLIES, WATER.
EVERY-THING ONE WOULD NEED TO SURVIVE A DISASTER SCENARIO.
OES LOOK USPICIOUS, VEN WHAT'S APPENED NCE THESE YS WERE MADE.
BUT IT'S NOT AS IF THE WORLD WAS IN GREAT SHAPE BEFORE THE LAST SERIES OF DISASTERS HIT. HALF OF INDONESIA DESTROYED, ENGLAND MISSING, VOLCANOES CROPPING UP LIKE ACNE.
MAYBE THIS WAS JUST ZINCO CORNERING THE MARKET ON NON-PERISHABLES TO TURN AROUND AND MAKE A PROFIT OFF A PANICKING POPULATION.
BUT ZINCO WAS BASED IN MANHATTAN, AND NOW THAT CITY--MYSTERIOUSLY--IS COMPLETELY CUT OFF FROM THE REST OF THE WORLD.
THOSE SUPPLIES SUDDENLY SEEM TO BE CONVENIENTLY PLACED, NO?
AID IT LOOKED USPICIOUS.
BUT UNTIL WE ET OUR TEAMS N THERE, WE N'T KNOW ANY-THING.
EXCUSE ME, DOCTOR CORRIGAN?

OH, HI CARLA. WHAT'S UP?

HI.

HEY, NICHOLS TOLD ME YOU'RE MAKING UP THE ROSTERS FOR THE TWO TEAMS HEADING INTO NEW YORK NEXT MONTH.

HOLD ON. DON'T TELL ME. YOU WANT ME TO GIVE YOU HOWARDS, RIGHT?

uhhh...

TOO LATE. JOHANN ALREADY PUT IN HIS REQUEST.

DAMN.

YOUR TEAM WILL HAVE DIRECTOR NICHAYKO, AND, HE ASSURES ME, AT LEAST ONE HIGHLY SPECIALIZED AGENT. ASIDE FROM ME, MY TEAM IS HUMAN. WE NEED THE ADVANTAGE.

WHAT'S TH BIG DEAL W HOWARD ANYWAY

"HE DOESN'T LOOK LIKE MUCH TO ME."

"YOU STILL HAVEN'T READ MY REPORT ON CHICAGO, HAVE YOU, KATE?"

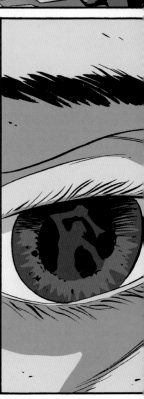

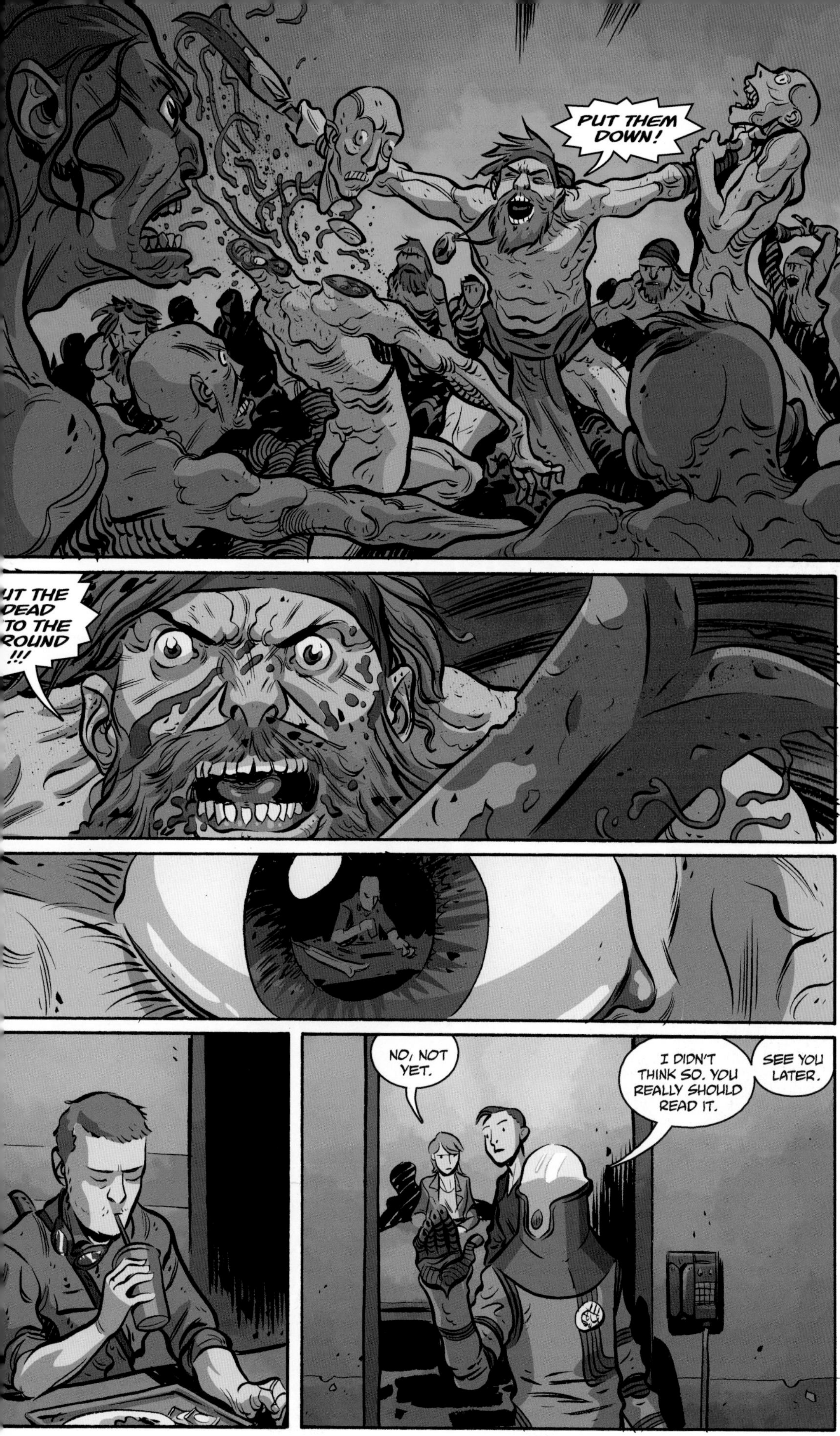
PUT THEM DOWN!
UT THE DEAD TO THE ROUND !!!
NO, NOT YET.
I DIDN'T THINK SO. YOU REALLY SHOULD READ IT.
SEE YOU LATER.

IT'S REALLY HAPPENING, ISN'T IT, GENE? SHE'S COMING TODAY.

SHE IS, YES. SHE'S MOVIN[G] IN THERE SPEAKING[...]

"I CAN HEAR HER."

GOD

LOVE THY BROTHER

WORLD IS

LOVE

LOVE AND UNDERSTAND[ING]

GOD

WE SHOULDN'T BE DOWN HERE. THIS IS BOB'S PLACE.

I FEEL LIKE HE WOULDN'T WANT US SNOOPIN' THIS WAY.

WHERE IS HE...?

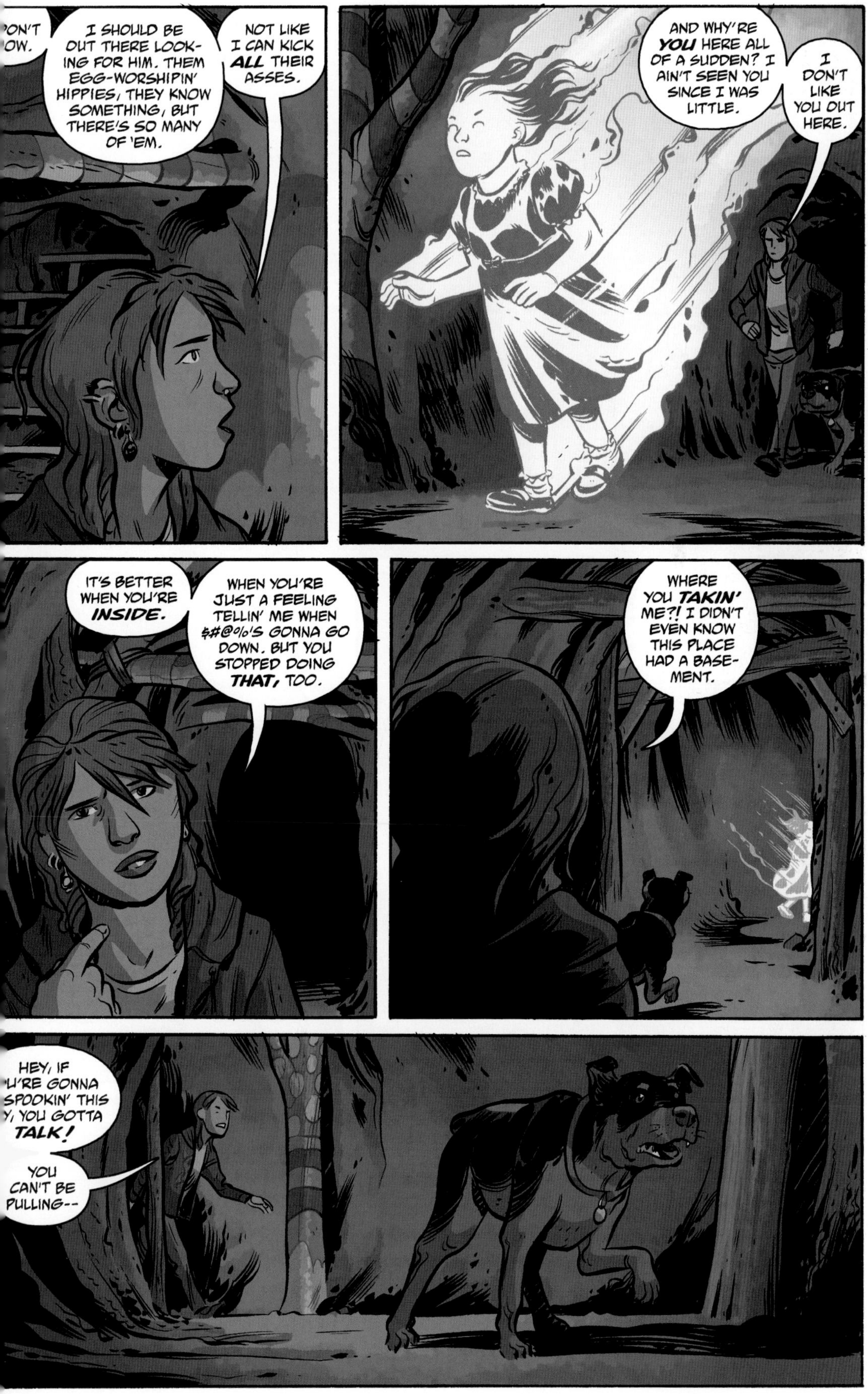

'ON'T
'OW.
I SHOULD BE OUT THERE LOOKING FOR HIM. THEM EGG-WORSHIPIN' HIPPIES, THEY KNOW SOMETHING, BUT THERE'S SO MANY OF 'EM.
NOT LIKE I CAN KICK ALL THEIR ASSES.
AND WHY'RE YOU HERE ALL OF A SUDDEN? I AIN'T SEEN YOU SINCE I WAS LITTLE.
I DON'T LIKE YOU OUT HERE.
IT'S BETTER WHEN YOU'RE INSIDE.
WHEN YOU'RE JUST A FEELING TELLIN' ME WHEN $#@%'S GONNA GO DOWN. BUT YOU STOPPED DOING THAT, TOO.
WHERE YOU TAKIN' ME?! I DIDN'T EVEN KNOW THIS PLACE HAD A BASEMENT.
HEY, IF 'U'RE GONNA SPOOKIN' THIS Y, YOU GOTTA TALK!
YOU CAN'T BE PULLING--

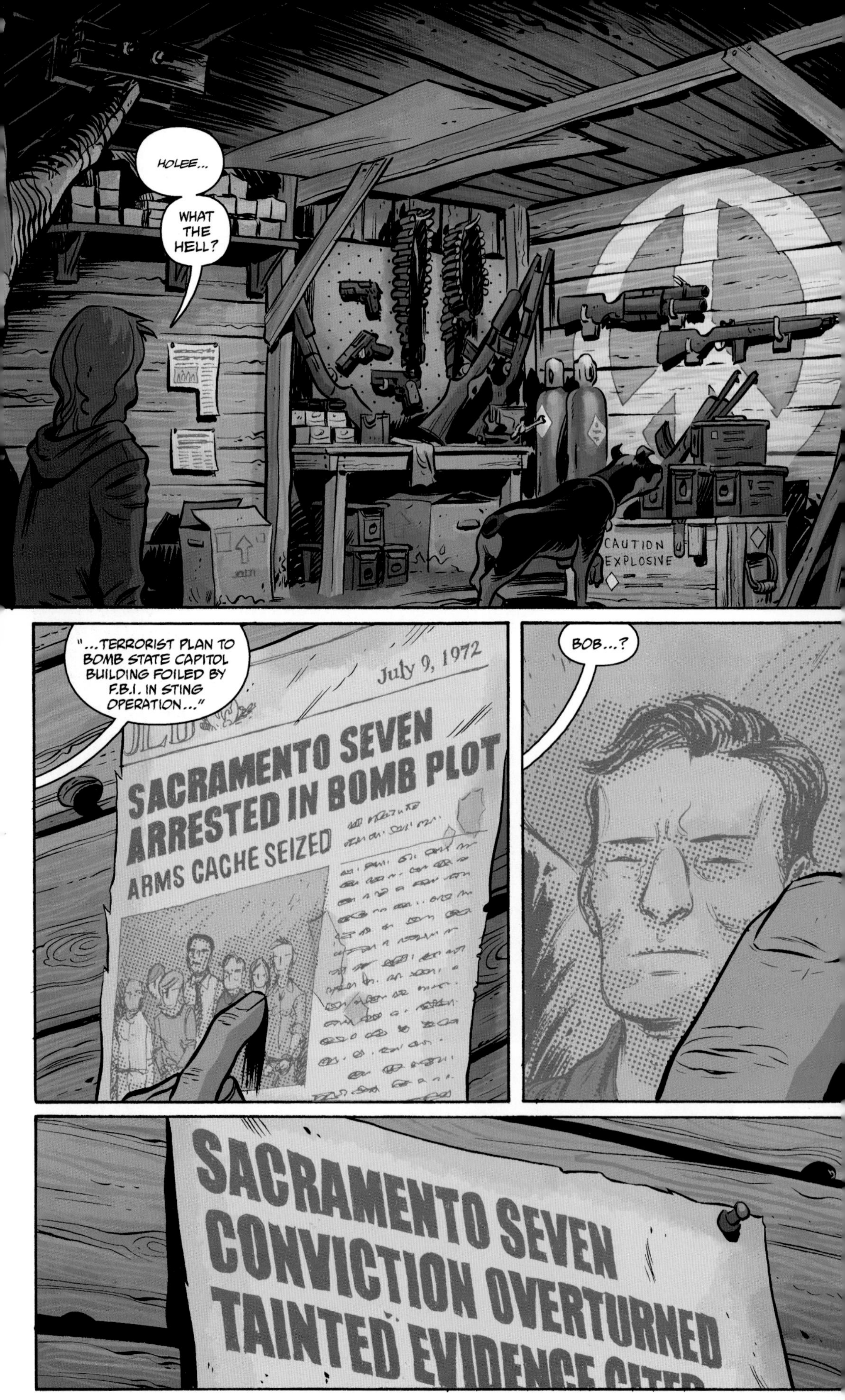
HOLEE...
WHAT THE HELL?
CAUTION EXPLOSIVE
"...TERRORIST PLAN TO BOMB STATE CAPITOL BUILDING FOILED BY F.B.I. IN STING OPERATION..."
July 9, 1972
SACRAMENTO SEVEN ARRESTED IN BOMB PLOT
ARMS CACHE SEIZED
BOB...?
SACRAMENTO SEVEN CONVICTION OVERTURNED TAINTED EVIDENCE CITED

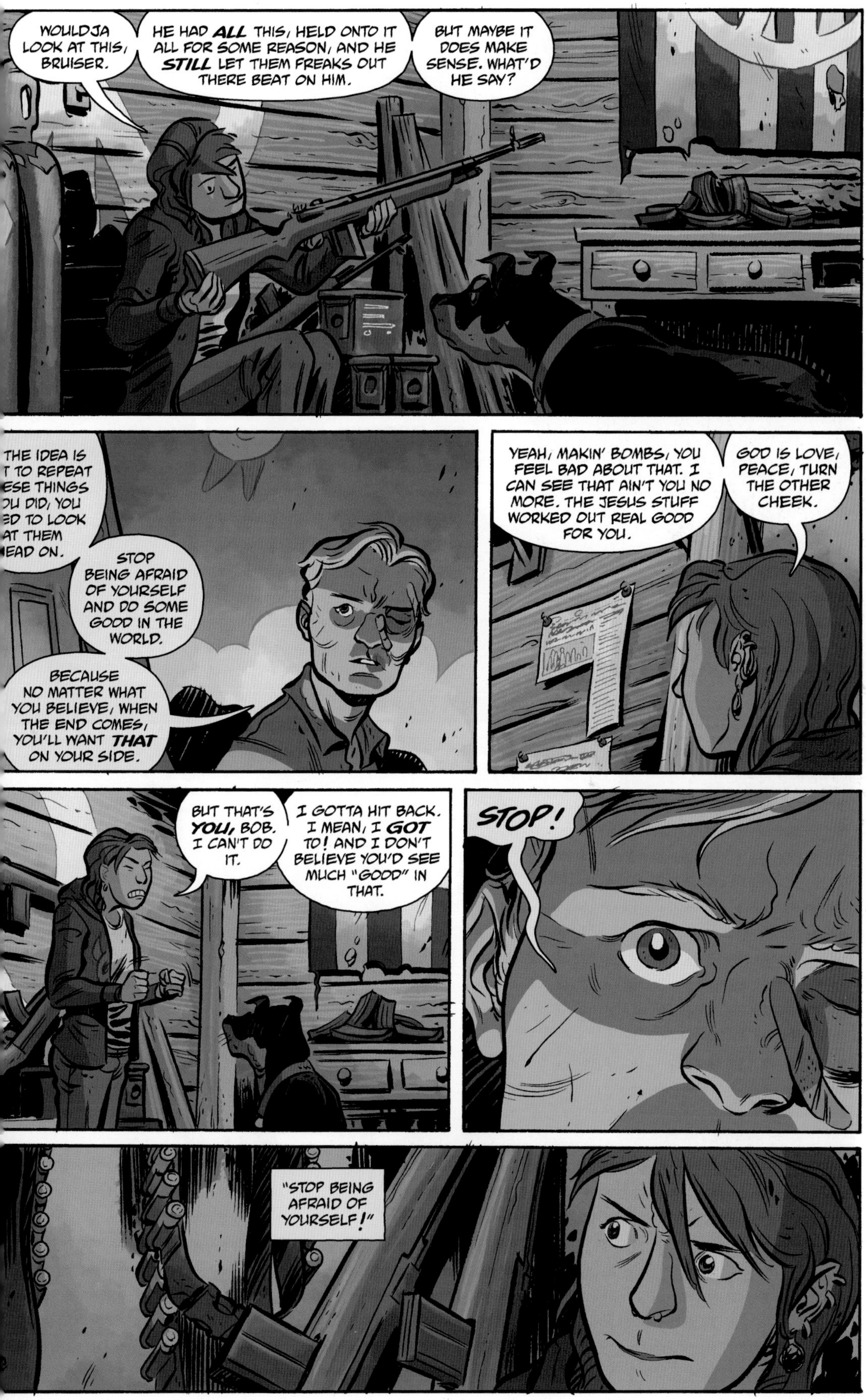
WOULDJA LOOK AT THIS, BRUISER.
HE HAD **ALL** THIS, HELD ONTO IT ALL FOR SOME REASON, AND HE **STILL** LET THEM FREAKS OUT THERE BEAT ON HIM.
BUT MAYBE IT DOES MAKE SENSE. WHAT'D HE SAY?
THE IDEA IS T TO REPEAT ESE THINGS OU DID, YOU ED TO LOOK AT THEM EAD ON.
STOP BEING AFRAID OF YOURSELF AND DO SOME GOOD IN THE WORLD.
BECAUSE NO MATTER WHAT YOU BELIEVE, WHEN THE END COMES, YOU'LL WANT **THAT** ON YOUR SIDE.
YEAH, MAKIN' BOMBS, YOU FEEL BAD ABOUT THAT. I CAN SEE THAT AIN'T YOU NO MORE. THE JESUS STUFF WORKED OUT REAL GOOD FOR YOU.
GOD IS LOVE, PEACE, TURN THE OTHER CHEEK.
BUT THAT'S **YOU,** BOB. I CAN'T DO IT.
I GOTTA HIT BACK. I MEAN, I **GOT** TO! AND I DON'T BELIEVE YOU'D SEE MUCH "GOOD" IN THAT.
STOP!
"STOP BEING AFRAID OF YOURSELF!"

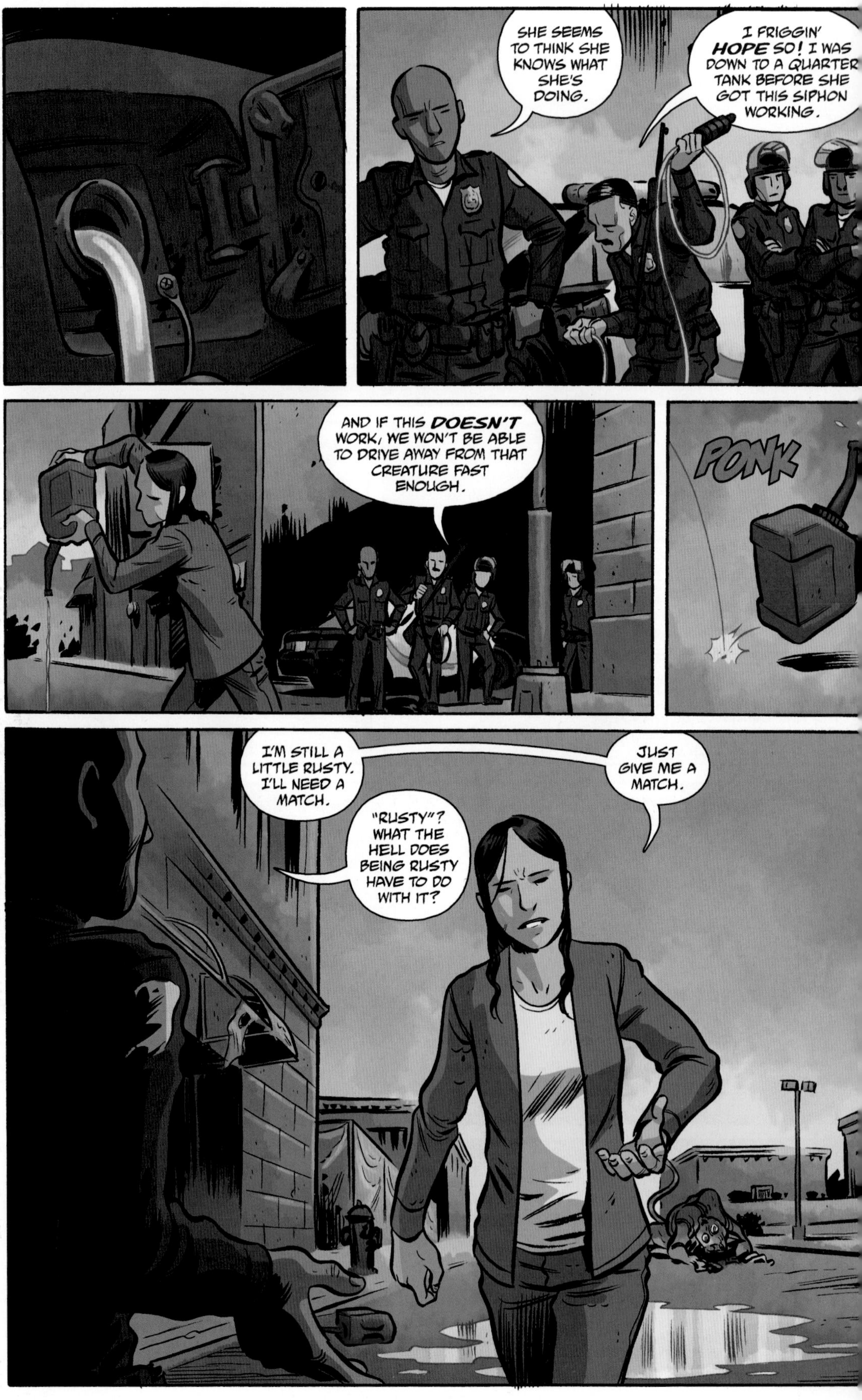
SHE SEEMS TO THINK SHE KNOWS WHAT SHE'S DOING.
I FRIGGIN' HOPE SO! I WAS DOWN TO A QUARTER TANK BEFORE SHE GOT THIS SIPHON WORKING.
AND IF THIS DOESN'T WORK, WE WON'T BE ABLE TO DRIVE AWAY FROM THAT CREATURE FAST ENOUGH.
PONK
I'M STILL A LITTLE RUSTY. I'LL NEED A MATCH.
"RUSTY"? WHAT THE HELL DOES BEING RUSTY HAVE TO DO WITH IT?
JUST GIVE ME A MATCH.

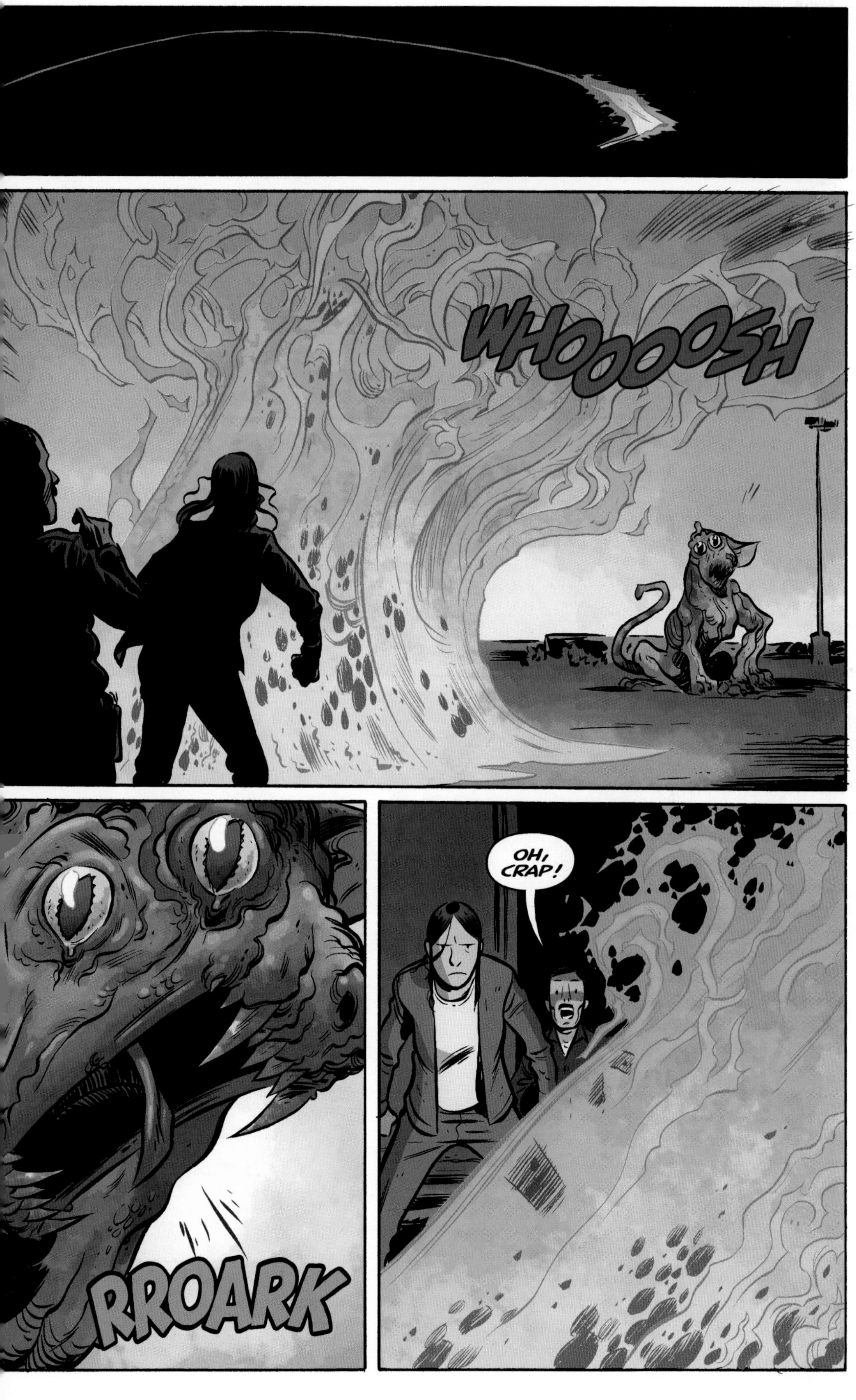
WHOOOOOSH
RROARK
OH, CRAP!

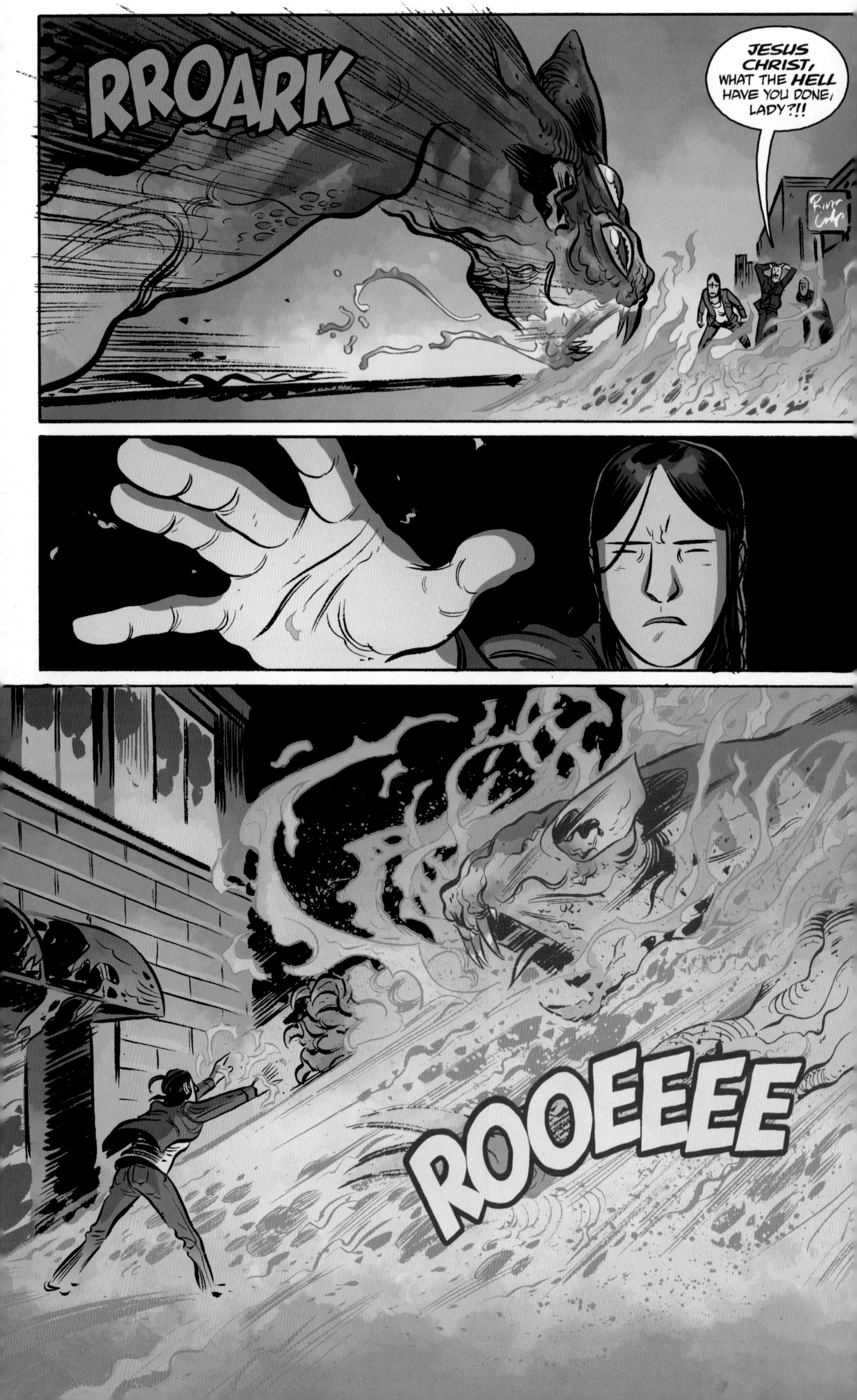
RROARK
JESUS CHRIST, WHAT THE HELL HAVE YOU DONE, LADY?!!
ROOEEEE

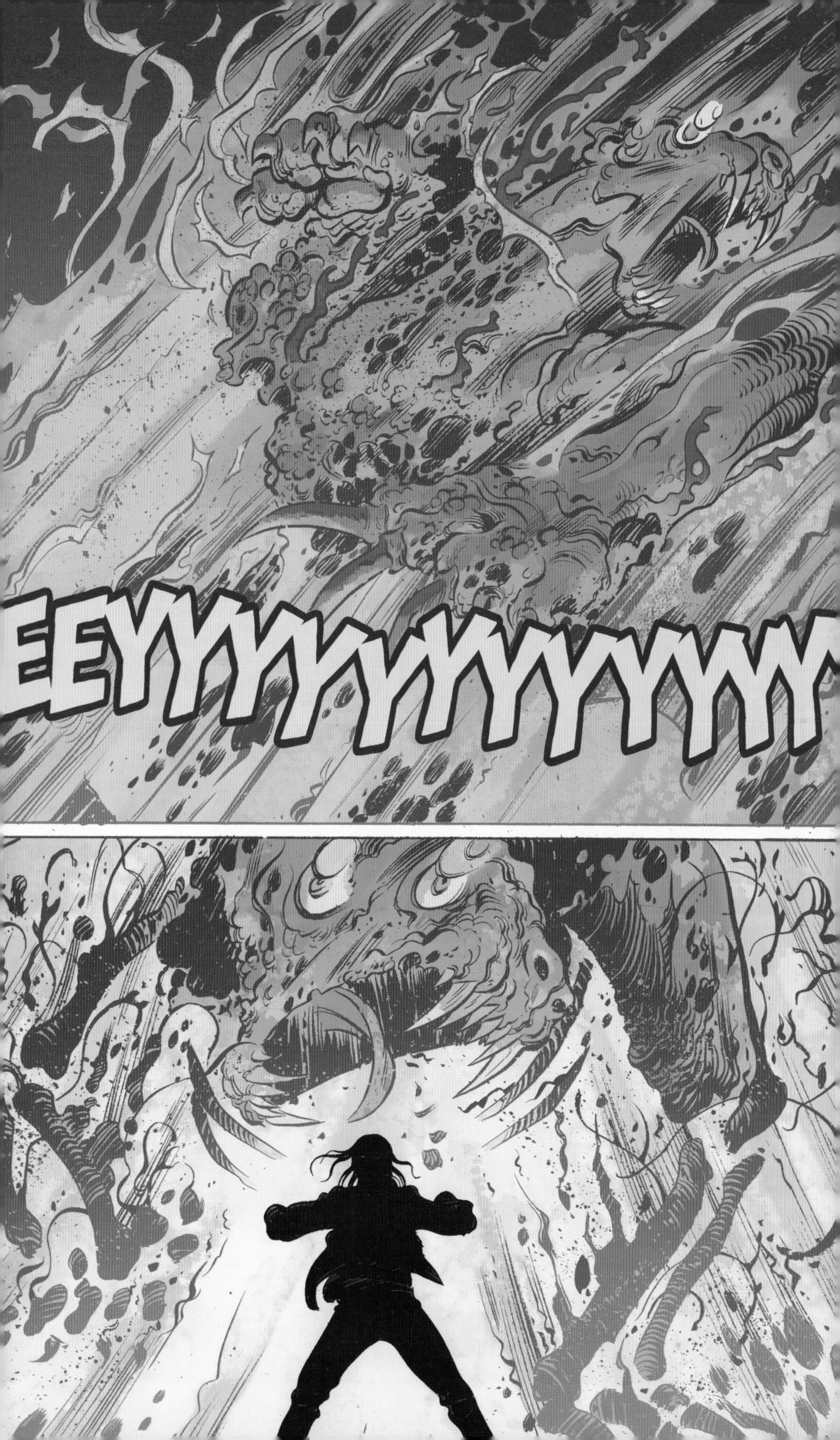
EEYYYYYYYYYYYY

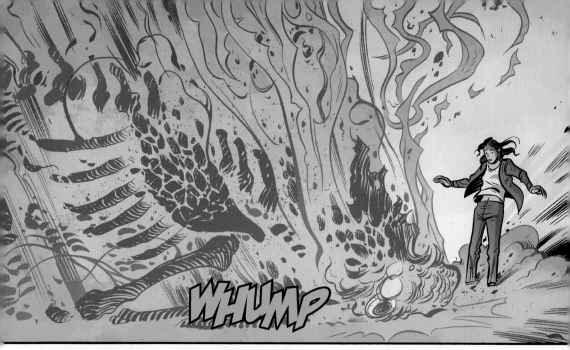

WHUMP

HOW... HOW THE HELL...?

...THE...THE HOSPITAL?

DON'T WET YOURSELF JUST YET. WE STILL NEED TO TAKE OVER THE HOSPITAL, AND FIRE'S NO GOOD IN THERE.

HOW MUCH AMMO YOU BOYS HAVE LEFT?

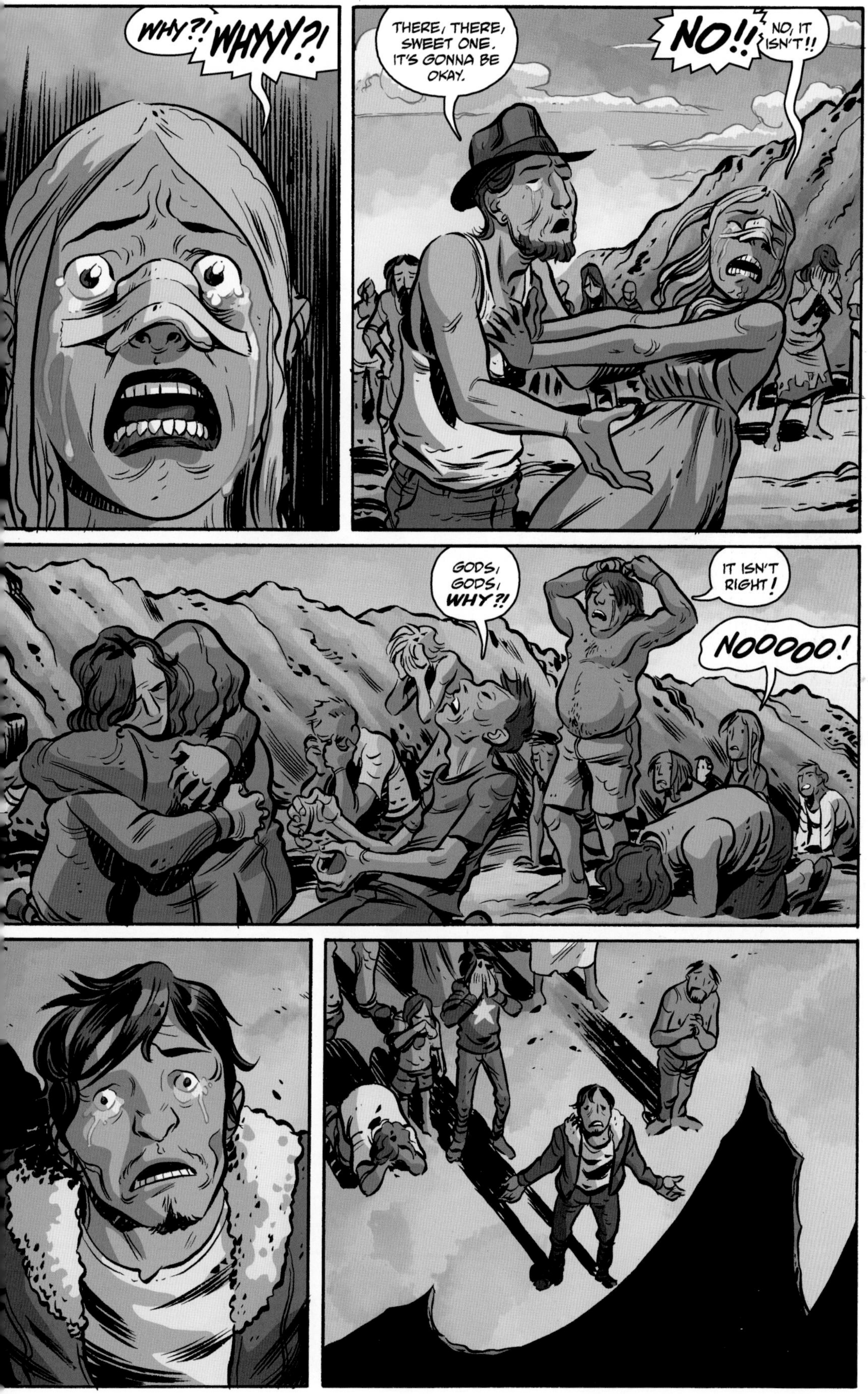
WHY?! WHYYY?!
THERE, THERE, SWEET ONE. IT'S GONNA BE OKAY.
NO!!
NO, IT ISN'T!!
GODS, GODS, WHY?!
IT ISN'T RIGHT!
NOOOOO!

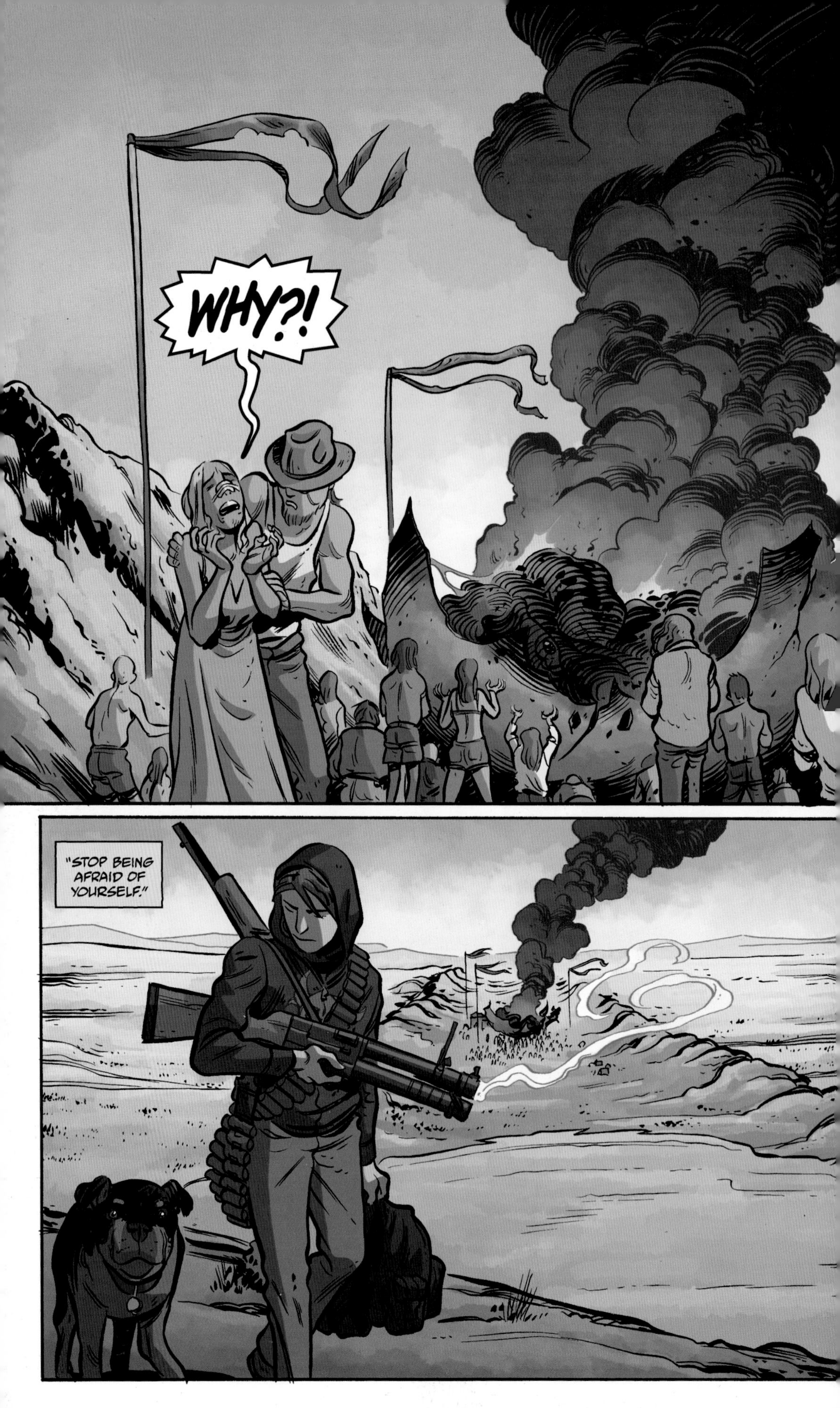
WHY?!
"STOP BEING AFRAID OF YOURSELF."

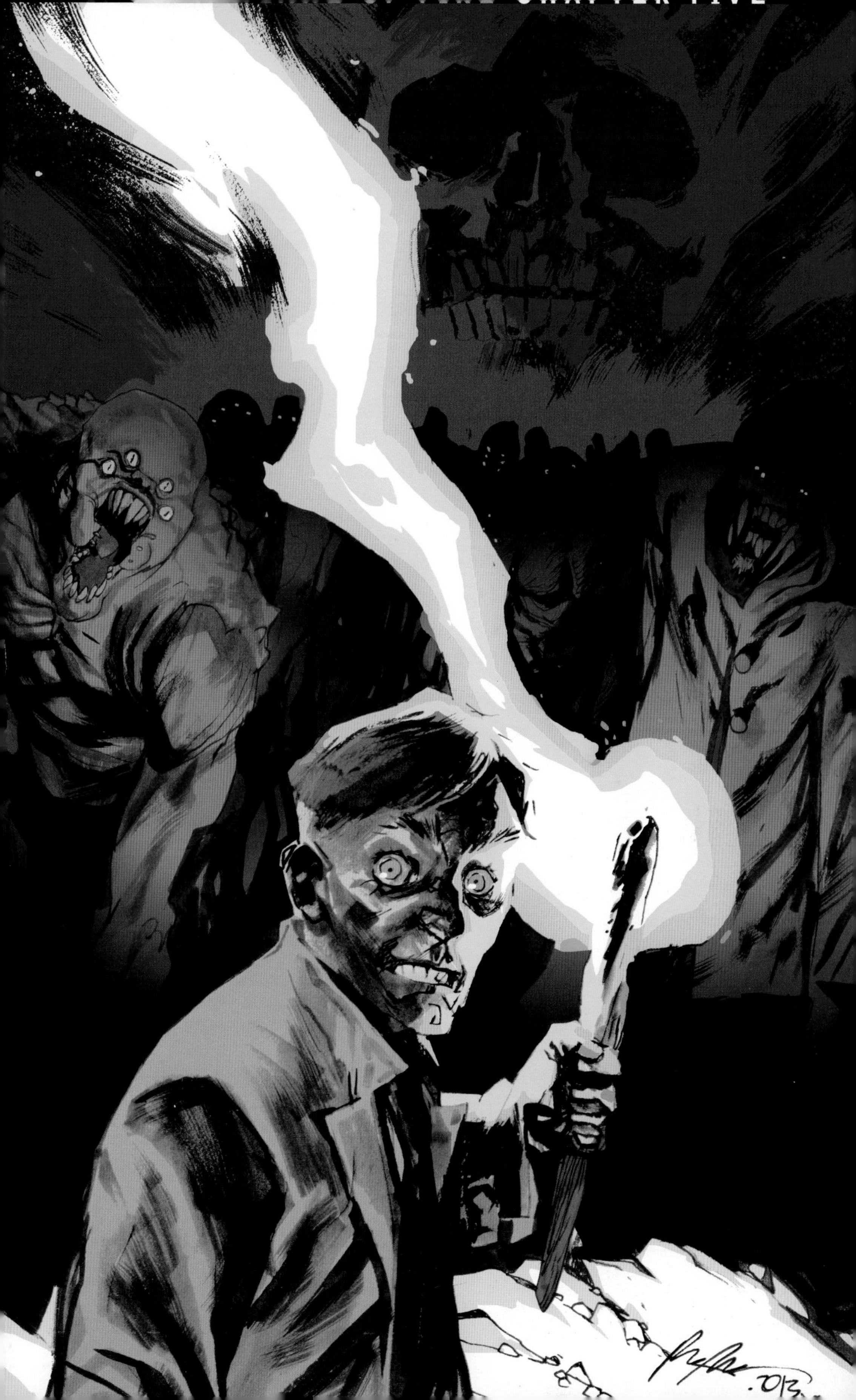

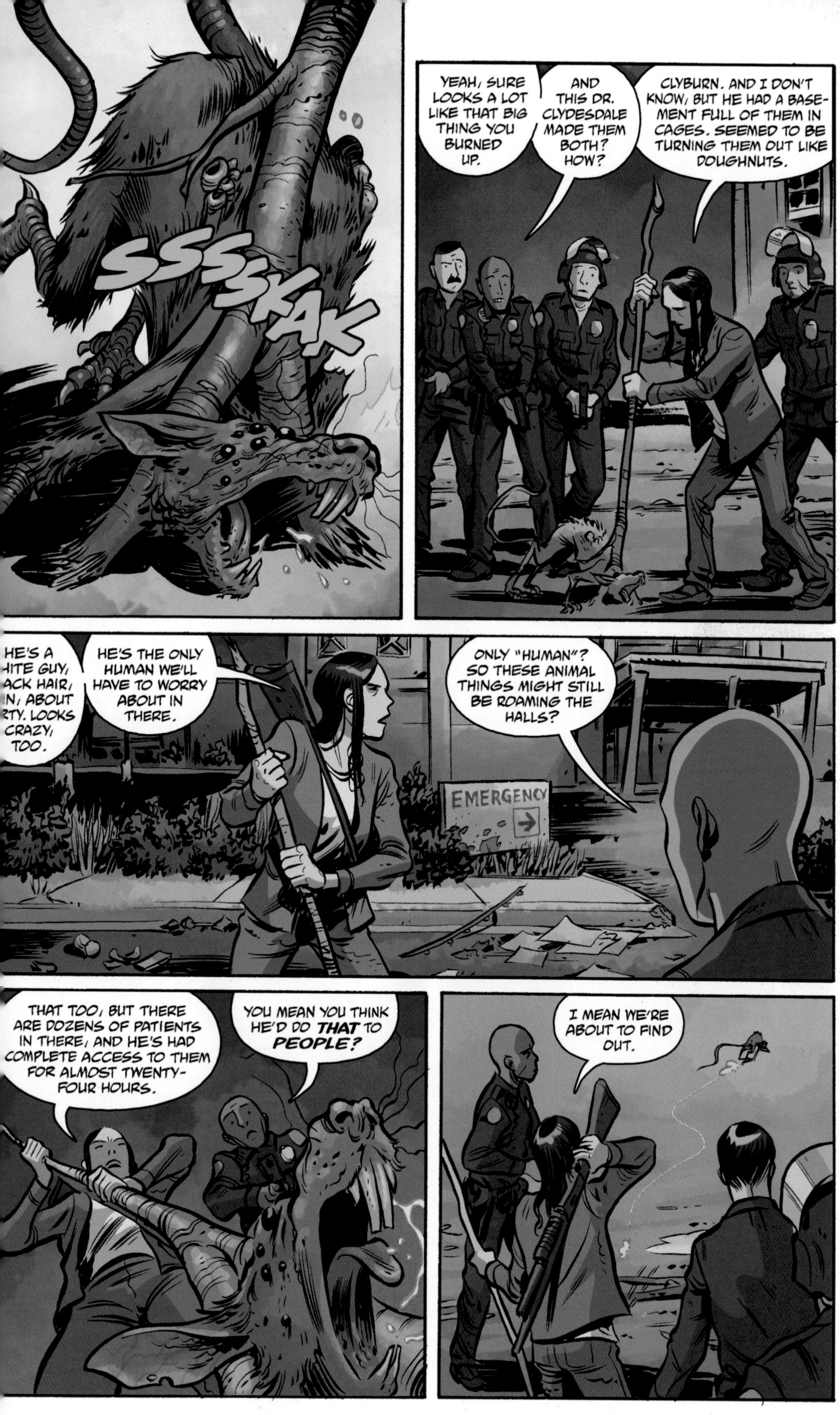
SSSSKAK
YEAH, SURE LOOKS A LOT LIKE THAT BIG THING YOU BURNED UP.
AND THIS DR. CLYDESDALE MADE THEM BOTH? HOW?
CLYBURN. AND I DON'T KNOW, BUT HE HAD A BASEMENT FULL OF THEM IN CAGES. SEEMED TO BE TURNING THEM OUT LIKE DOUGHNUTS.
HE'S A HITE GUY, ACK HAIR, IN, ABOUT RTY. LOOKS CRAZY, TOO.
HE'S THE ONLY HUMAN WE'LL HAVE TO WORRY ABOUT IN THERE.
EMERGENCY
ONLY "HUMAN"? SO THESE ANIMAL THINGS MIGHT STILL BE ROAMING THE HALLS?
THAT TOO, BUT THERE ARE DOZENS OF PATIENTS IN THERE, AND HE'S HAD COMPLETE ACCESS TO THEM FOR ALMOST TWENTY-FOUR HOURS.
YOU MEAN YOU THINK HE'D DO **THAT** TO **PEOPLE?**
I MEAN WE'RE ABOUT TO FIND OUT.

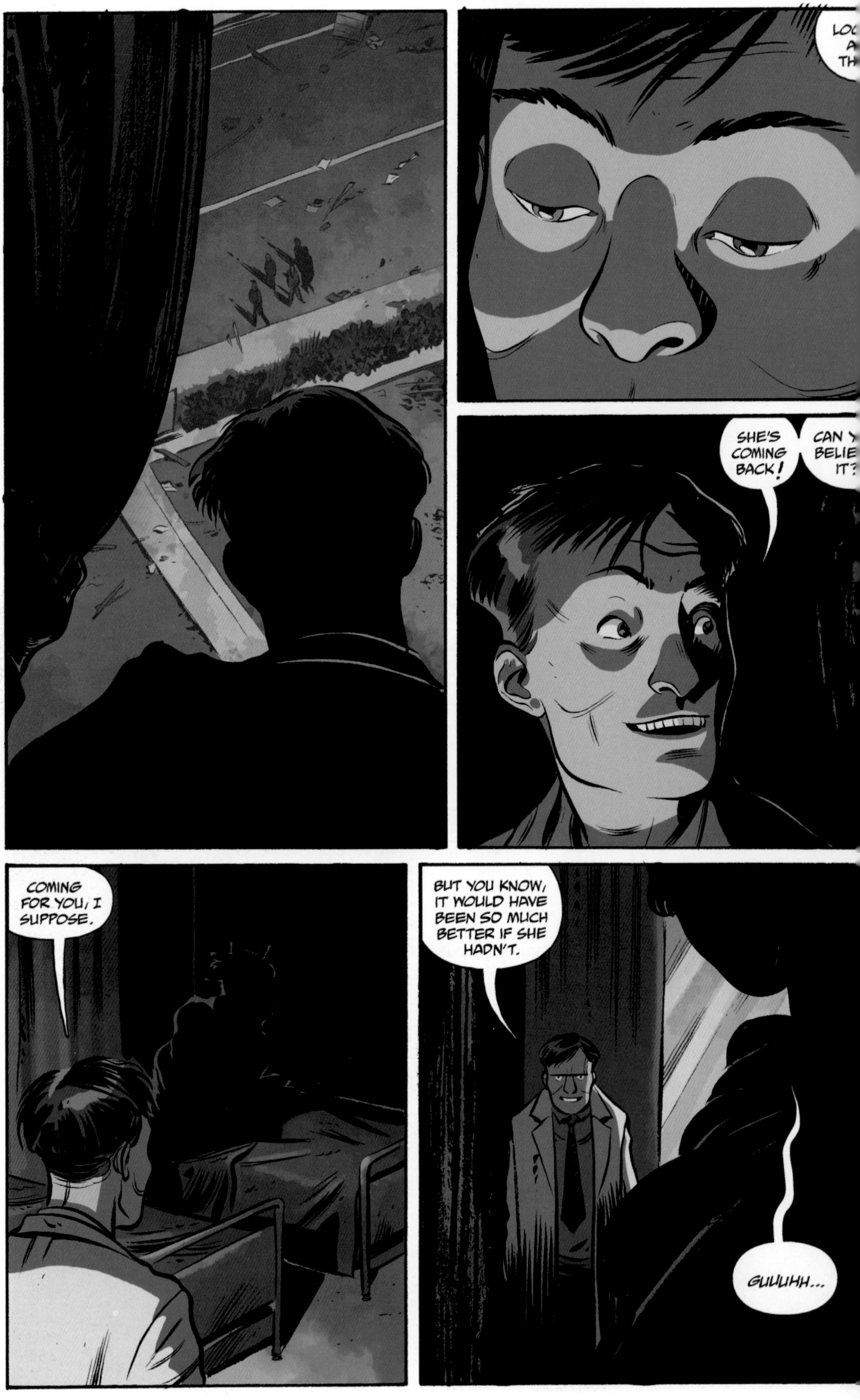
SHE'S COMING BACK!
COMING FOR YOU, I SUPPOSE.
BUT YOU KNOW, IT WOULD HAVE BEEN SO MUCH BETTER IF SHE HADN'T.
GUUUHH...

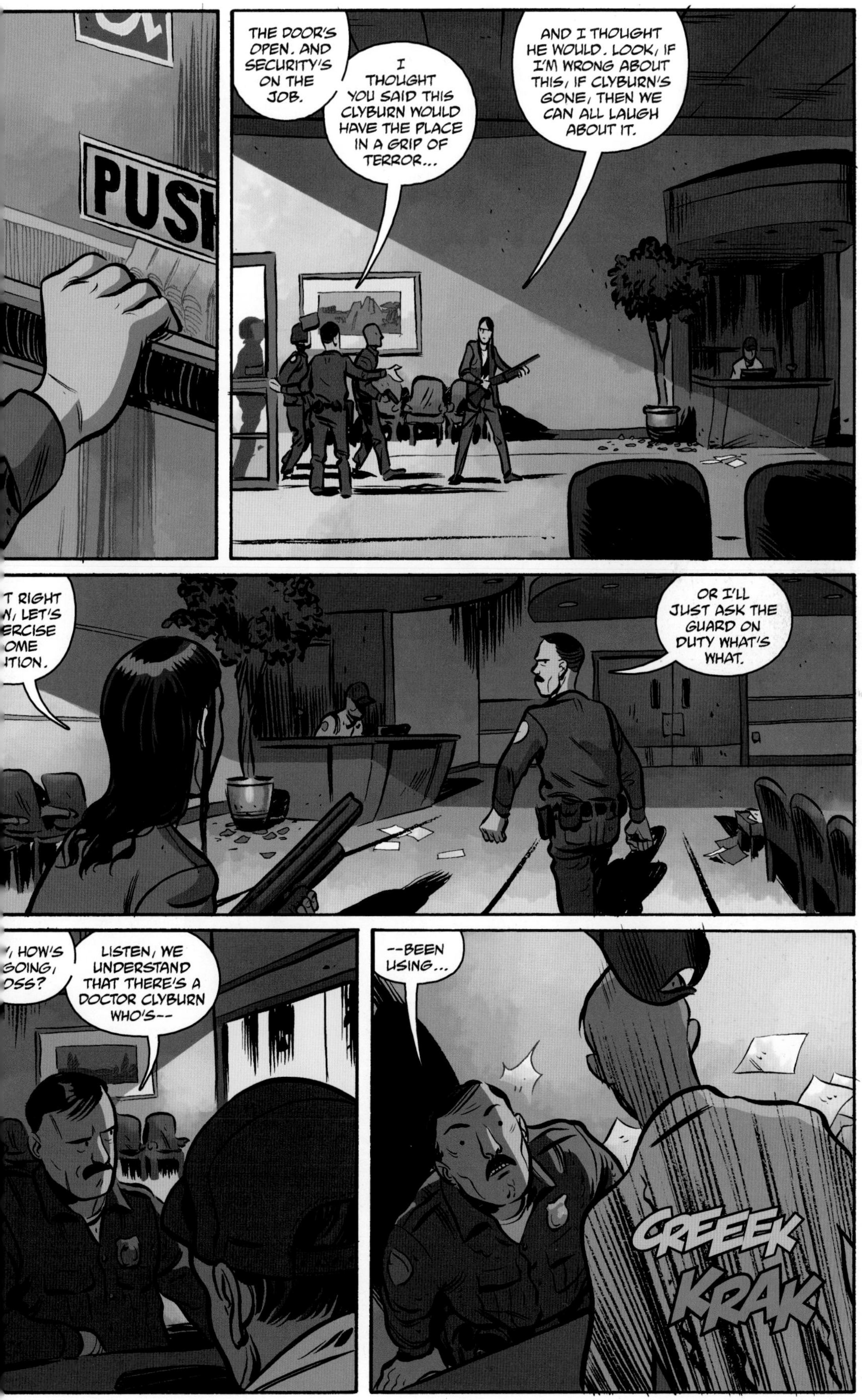
PUSH
THE DOOR'S OPEN. AND SECURITY'S ON THE JOB.
I THOUGHT YOU SAID THIS CLYBURN WOULD HAVE THE PLACE IN A GRIP OF TERROR...
AND I THOUGHT HE WOULD. LOOK, IF I'M WRONG ABOUT THIS, IF CLYBURN'S GONE, THEN WE CAN ALL LAUGH ABOUT IT.
T RIGHT W, LET'S ERCISE OME ITION.
OR I'LL JUST ASK THE GUARD ON DUTY WHAT'S WHAT.
, HOW'S GOING, OSS?
LISTEN, WE UNDERSTAND THAT THERE'S A DOCTOR CLYBURN WHO'S--
--BEEN USING...
CREEEK
KRAK

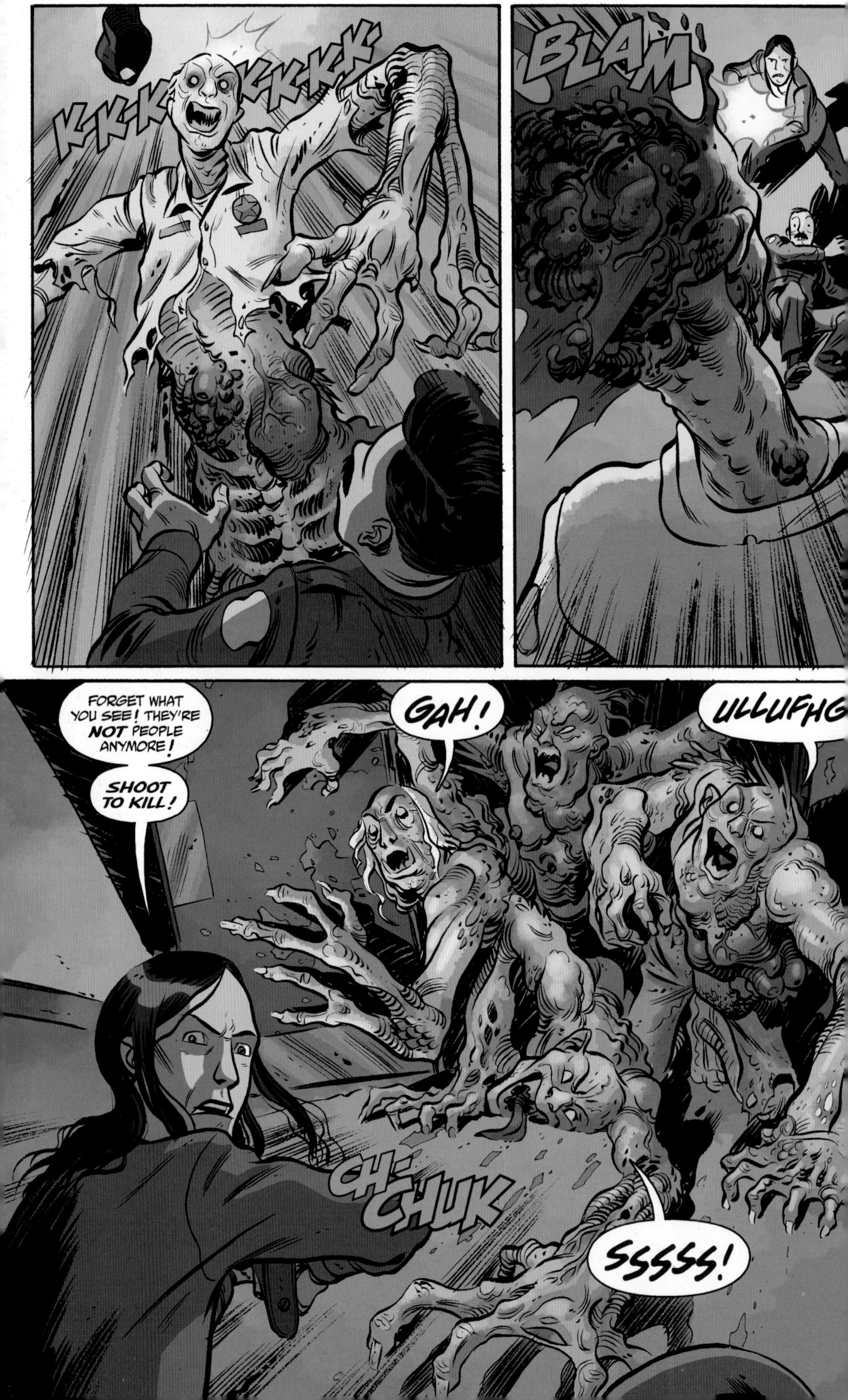
K-K-K-K-K-K-K
BLAM
FORGET WHAT YOU SEE! THEY'RE NOT PEOPLE ANYMORE!
SHOOT TO KILL!
GAH!
ULLUFHG
CH-CHUK
SSSSS!

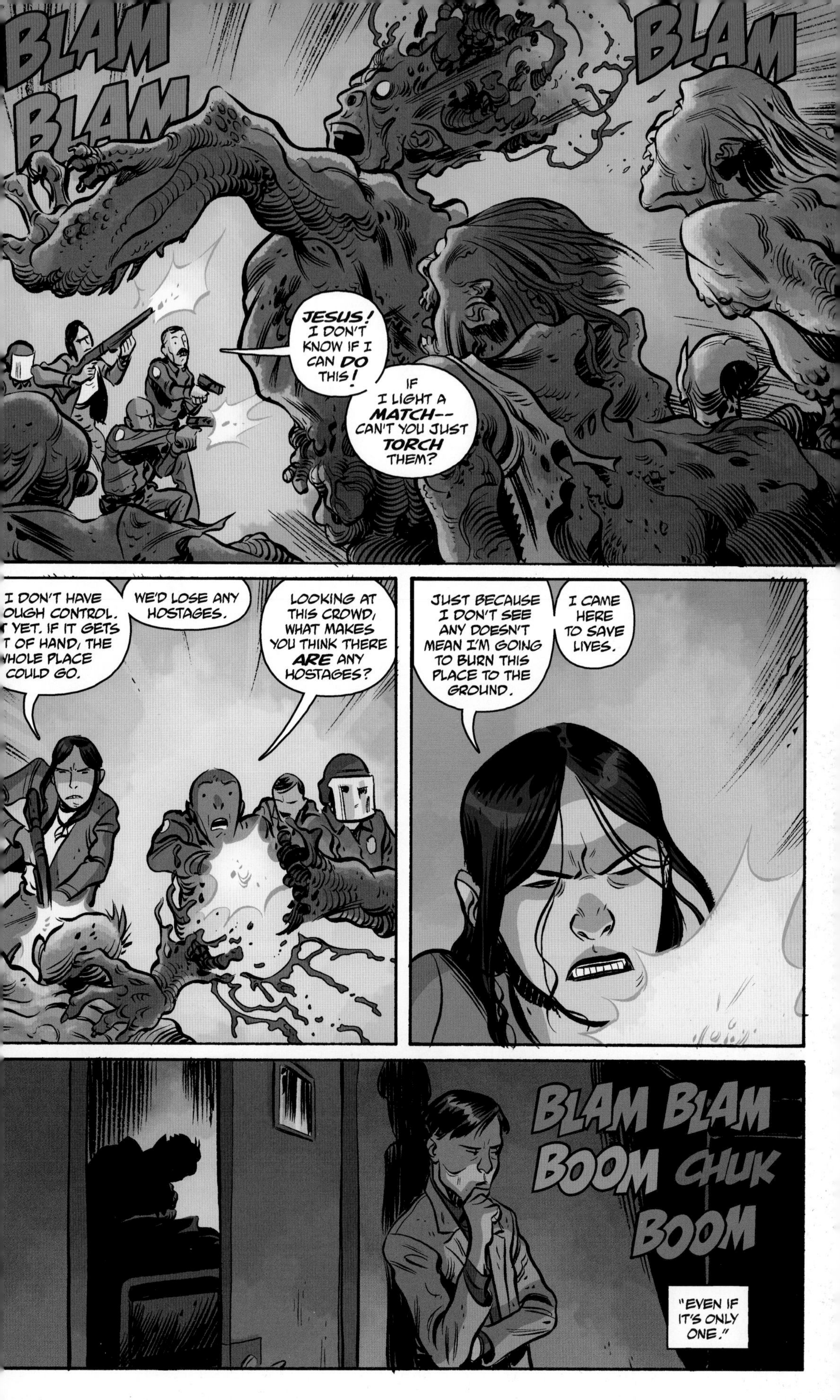
BLAM BLAM
BLAM
JESUS! I DON'T KNOW IF I CAN DO THIS!
IF I LIGHT A MATCH-- CAN'T YOU JUST TORCH THEM?
I DON'T HAVE OUGH CONTROL. T YET. IF IT GETS T OF HAND, THE HOLE PLACE COULD GO.
WE'D LOSE ANY HOSTAGES.
LOOKING AT THIS CROWD, WHAT MAKES YOU THINK THERE ARE ANY HOSTAGES?
JUST BECAUSE I DON'T SEE ANY DOESN'T MEAN I'M GOING TO BURN THIS PLACE TO THE GROUND.
I CAME HERE TO SAVE LIVES.
BLAM BLAM BOOM CHUK BOOM
"EVEN IF IT'S ONLY ONE."

--HAVE SEEN SEVERAL NEW RELIGIONS EMERGING FROM THIS CRISIS.

WHILE IT MAY JUST BE A SIGN OF PEOPLE AROUND THE WORLD TRYING TO ADAPT TO AN INCREASINGLY UNPREDICTABLE FUTURE--

--OTHERS ARE INTERPRETING THIS PROLIFERATION AS A FAILURE OF MORE CONVENTIONAL RELIGIONS TO MAKE ANY SENSE OF THE CHAOS.

JOINING ME TODAY TO DISCUSS THESE QUESTIONS ARE REVEREND WILLIAM TRABOR OF THE C.C.B. NETWORK.

AND REVEREND PAUL NEDIN OF THE FIRST CHURCH OF THE LIVING EARTH.

THANK YOU FOR HAVING ME, MARTHA.

YES, THANK YOU.

HOWEVER, LET'S STOP USING THE WORD "RELIGIONS" WHEN REFERRING TO THESE CULTS!

AND HERE WE GO.

MR. KRAUS, IS THIS REALLY THE BEST USE OF OUR MONITORING EQUIPMENT?

AN APPRECIATE R SKEPTICISM, T THIS IS OUR LY RELIABLE WSFEED.

AND MONDAY, ONE OF THE GUESTS ON THIS SAME SHOW SAID SOMETHING THAT LED US TO A LARVAL BEHEMOTH IN MISSISSIPPI.

WE DESTROYED IT BEFORE IT BECAME A THREAT.

MMMM.

BY THE WAY, I READ YOUR ABSTRACT ABOUT ZINCO'S STOCKPILING BEFORE THE DISASTER.

AH. KATE THINKS I'M OVERREACTING. PERHAPS I AM.

PERHAPS. *EVERY-BODY* WAS STOCKPILING, AFTER ALL.

BUT BILLS OF PING I FOUND CATE ALL THE APONS ZINCO UGHT WERE HIPPED TO ANHATTAN.

I THINK THAT'S WORTH TAKING NOTE OF, CONSIDERING THAT NEW YORK CITY IS OUR NEXT OBJECTIVE.

JA...

N, SO NOW 'M THE TICHRIST," THAT IT?

THIS COMING FROM A MAN WHO USED TO FIND A NEW CANDIDATE FOR "THE BEAST" WITH EVERY ELECTION CYCLE.

LOOK AROUND YOU, NEDIN!

IF THESE ARE *NOT* THE END TIMES, THEN TELL ME WHAT THEY ARE.

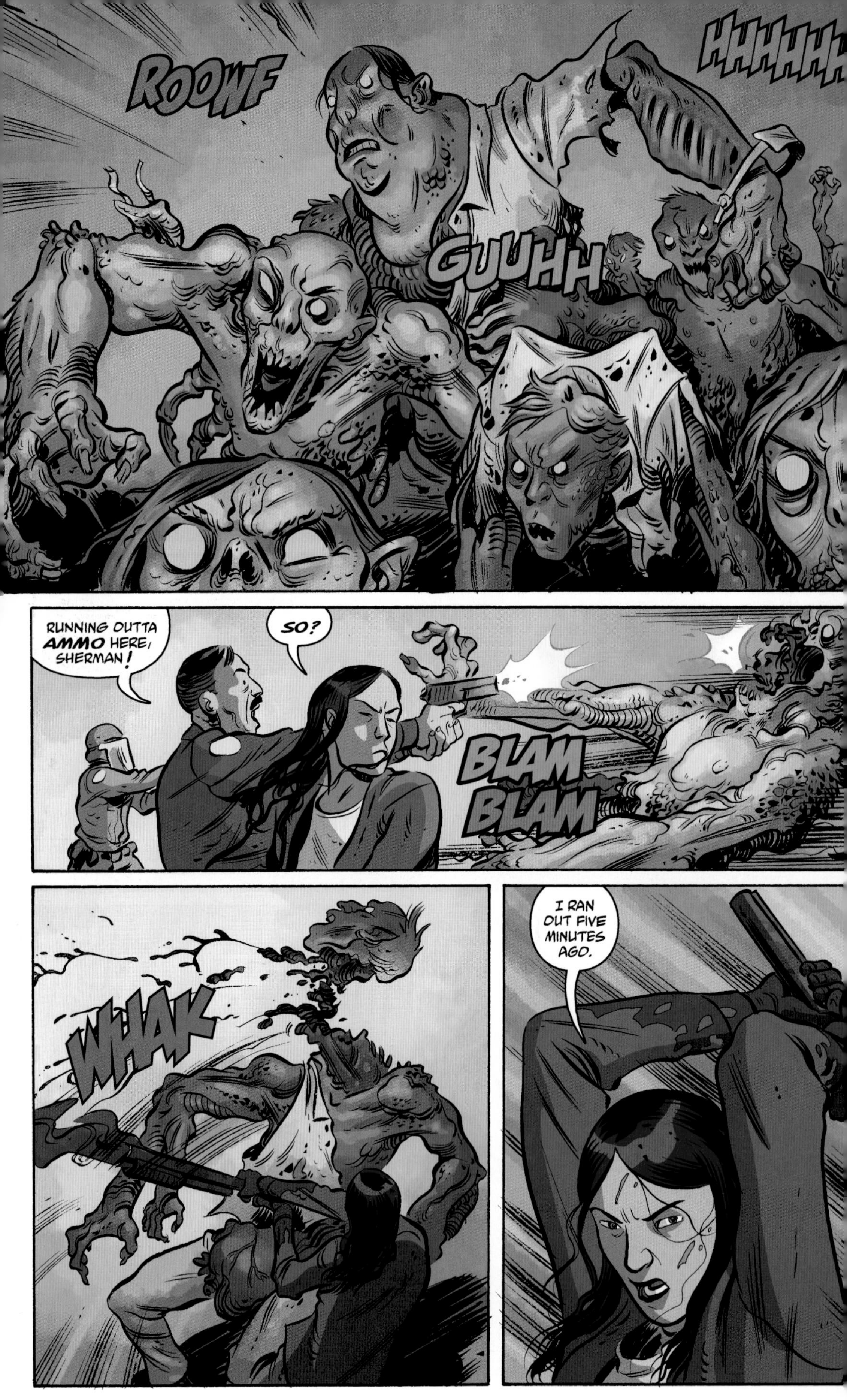

ROOWF
HHHHH
GUUHH
RUNNING OUTTA AMMO HERE, SHERMAN!
SO?
BLAM BLAM
WHAK
I RAN OUT FIVE MINUTES AGO.

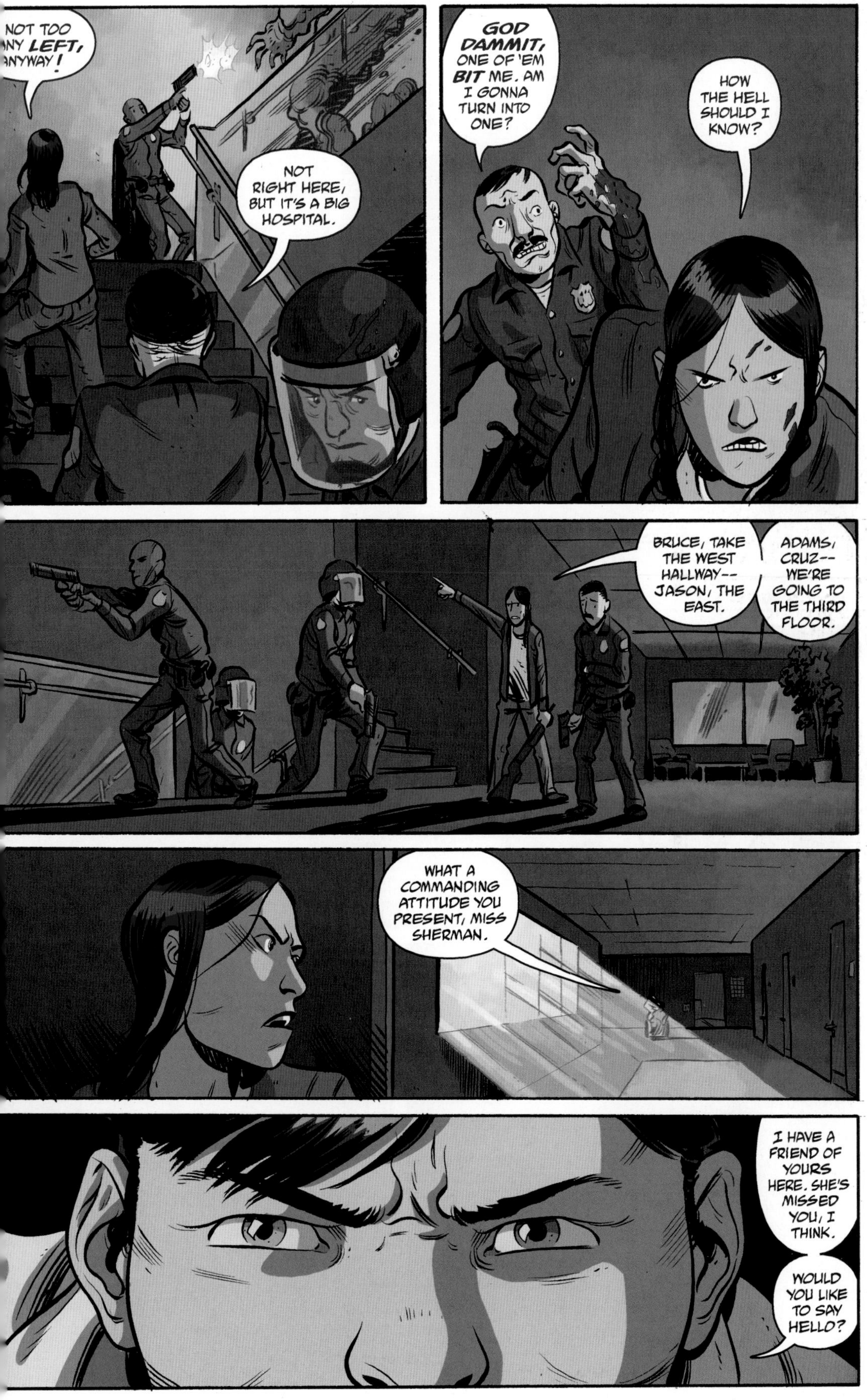
NOT TOO
NY LEFT,
NYWAY!
NOT RIGHT HERE, BUT IT'S A BIG HOSPITAL.
GOD DAMMIT, ONE OF 'EM BIT ME. AM I GONNA TURN INTO ONE?
HOW THE HELL SHOULD I KNOW?
BRUCE, TAKE THE WEST HALLWAY-- JASON, THE EAST.
ADAMS, CRUZ-- WE'RE GOING TO THE THIRD FLOOR.
WHAT A COMMANDING ATTITUDE YOU PRESENT, MISS SHERMAN.
I HAVE A FRIEND OF YOURS HERE. SHE'S MISSED YOU, I THINK.
WOULD YOU LIKE TO SAY HELLO?

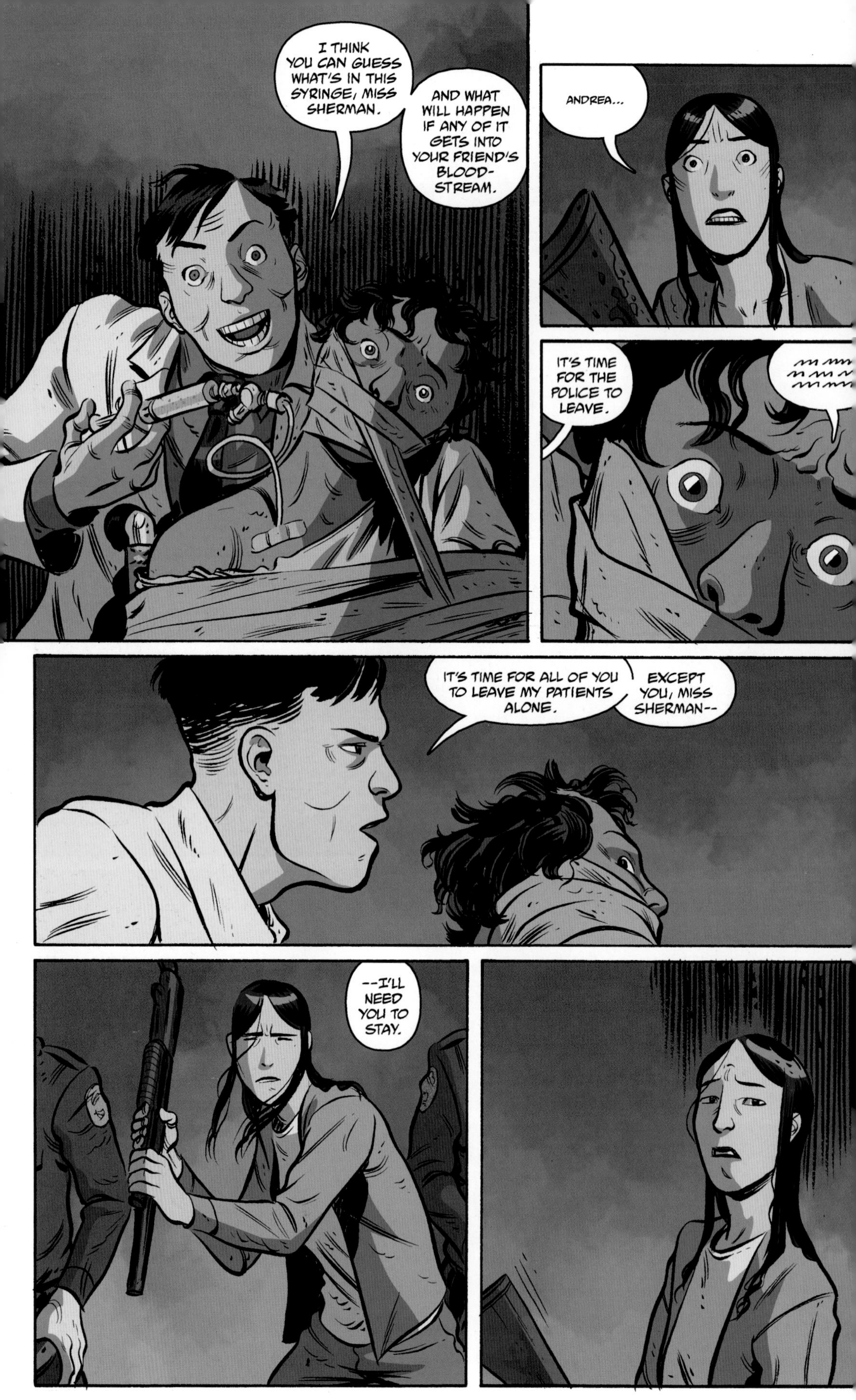
I THINK YOU CAN GUESS WHAT'S IN THIS SYRINGE, MISS SHERMAN.
AND WHAT WILL HAPPEN IF ANY OF IT GETS INTO YOUR FRIEND'S BLOOD-STREAM.
ANDREA...
IT'S TIME FOR THE POLICE TO LEAVE.
IT'S TIME FOR ALL OF YOU TO LEAVE MY PATIENTS ALONE.
EXCEPT YOU, MISS SHERMAN--
--I'LL NEED YOU TO STAY.

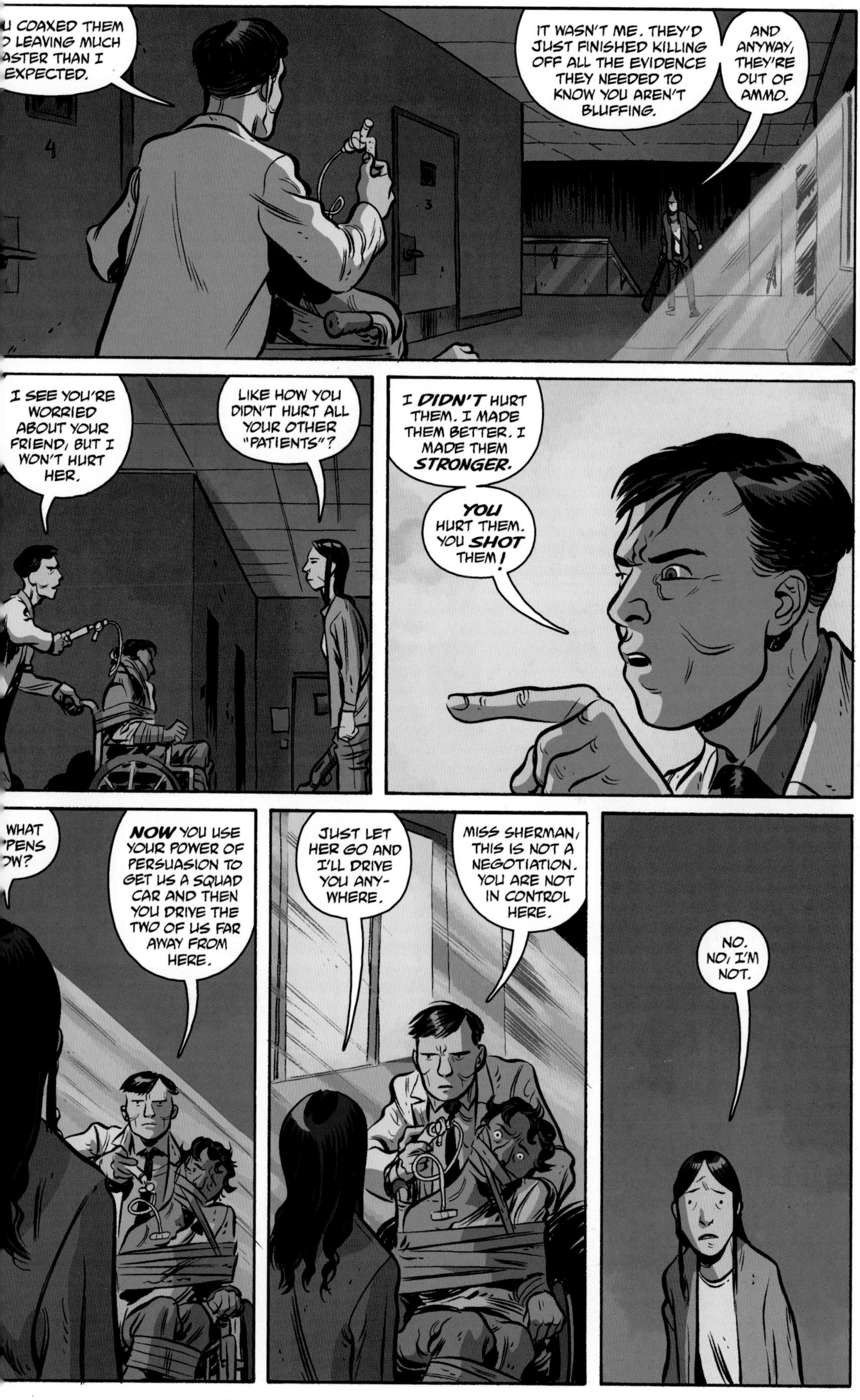
U COAXED THEM D LEAVING MUCH ASTER THAN I EXPECTED.
IT WASN'T ME. THEY'D JUST FINISHED KILLING OFF ALL THE EVIDENCE THEY NEEDED TO KNOW YOU AREN'T BLUFFING.
AND ANYWAY, THEY'RE OUT OF AMMO.
I SEE YOU'RE WORRIED ABOUT YOUR FRIEND, BUT I WON'T HURT HER.
LIKE HOW YOU DIDN'T HURT ALL YOUR OTHER "PATIENTS"?
I **DIDN'T** HURT THEM. I MADE THEM BETTER. I MADE THEM **STRONGER.**
YOU HURT THEM. YOU **SHOT** THEM!
WHAT 'PENS OW?
NOW YOU USE YOUR POWER OF PERSUASION TO GET US A SQUAD CAR AND THEN YOU DRIVE THE TWO OF US FAR AWAY FROM HERE.
JUST LET HER GO AND I'LL DRIVE YOU ANY-WHERE.
MISS SHERMAN, THIS IS NOT A NEGOTIATION. YOU ARE NOT IN CONTROL HERE.
NO. NO, I'M NOT.

"RIGHT. NOW LET'S GET HER DOWN THESE STAIRS."

OKAY--≥PUFF≤--WE'LL TAKE--≥GASP≤--TAKE A BREATHER HERE FOR A--ONLY A MOMENT.

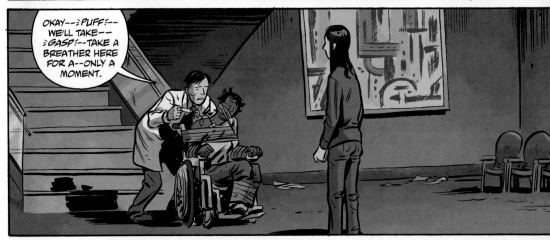

OR RATHER--≥PUFF≤--RATHER, I WILL.

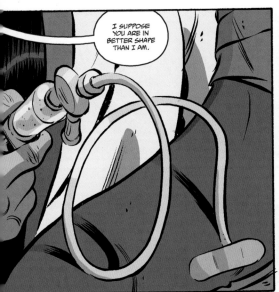

I SUPPOSE YOU ARE IN BETTER SHAPE THAN I AM.

YOU **ARE** IN CONTROL.

JUST ANOTHER MOMENT--

--ANOTHER MOMENT AND WE'LL BE--

FWSH

WHAT... I DON'T UNDER...

!

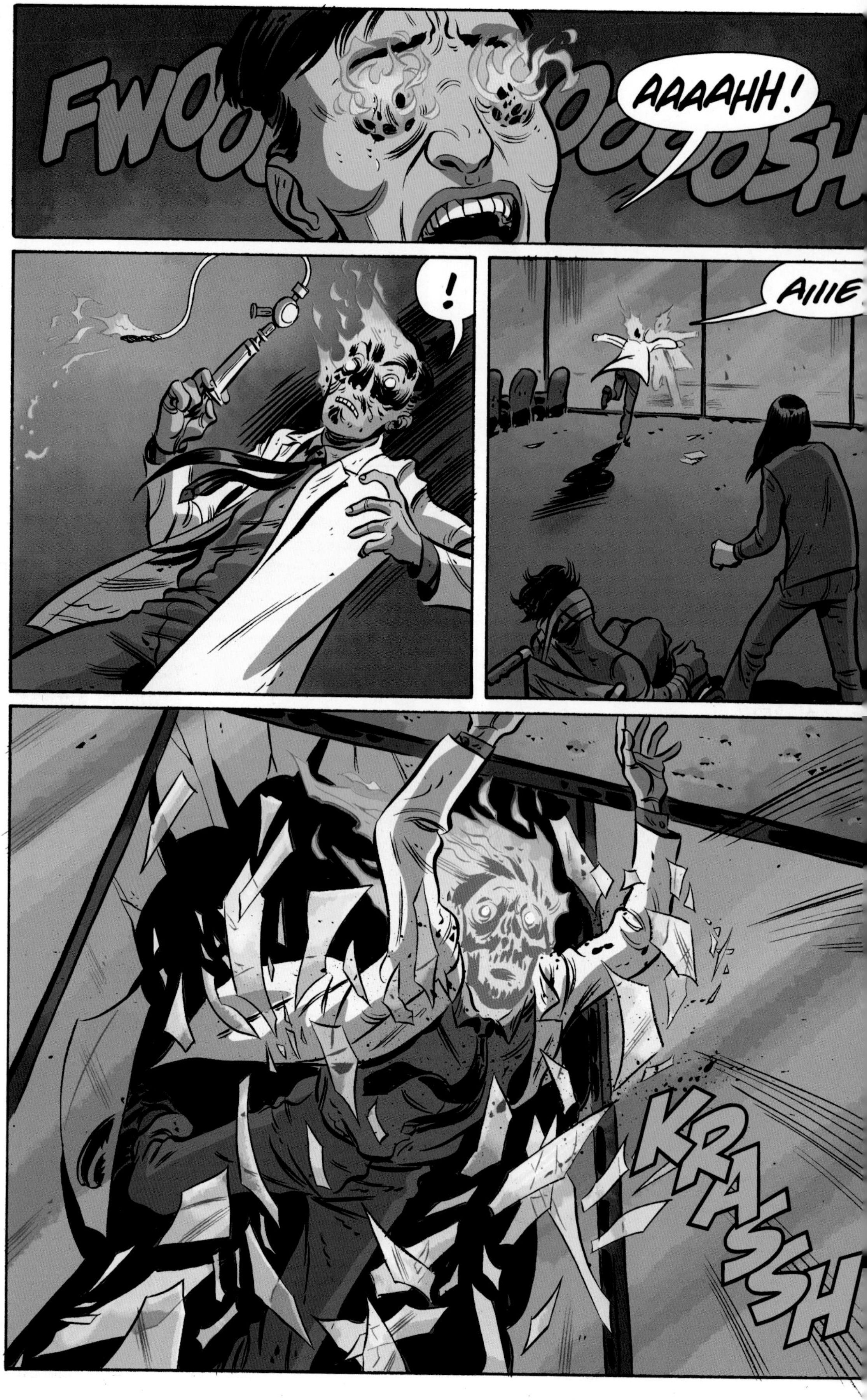
FWOOOOOOOSH
AAAAHH!
!
AIIIE
KRASSH

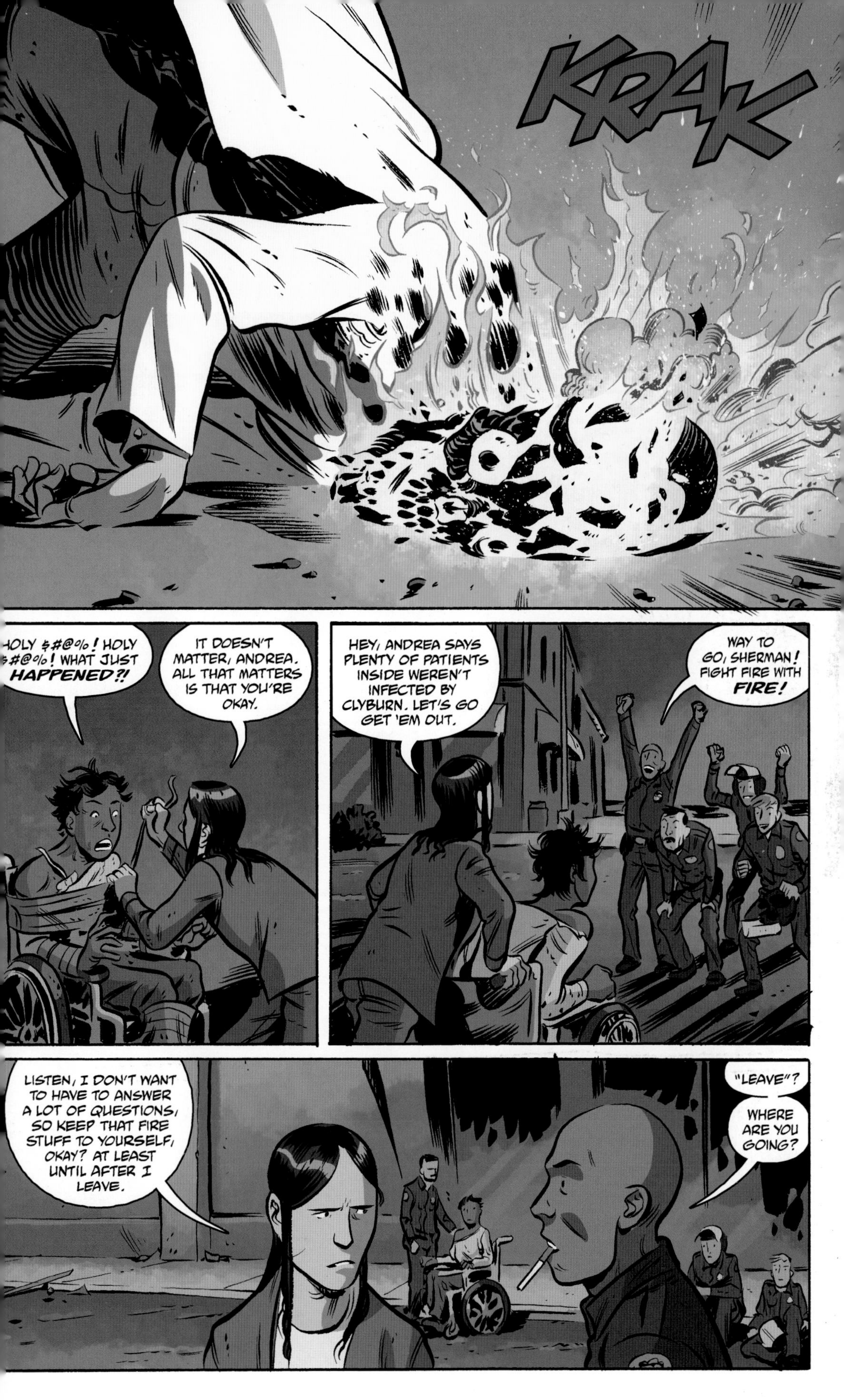
KRAK
HOLY $#@%! HOLY $#@%! WHAT JUST HAPPENED?!
IT DOESN'T MATTER, ANDREA. ALL THAT MATTERS IS THAT YOU'RE OKAY.
HEY, ANDREA SAYS PLENTY OF PATIENTS INSIDE WEREN'T INFECTED BY CLYBURN. LET'S GO GET 'EM OUT.
WAY TO GO, SHERMAN! FIGHT FIRE WITH FIRE!
LISTEN, I DON'T WANT TO HAVE TO ANSWER A LOT OF QUESTIONS, SO KEEP THAT FIRE STUFF TO YOURSELF, OKAY? AT LEAST UNTIL AFTER I LEAVE.
"LEAVE"?
WHERE ARE YOU GOING?

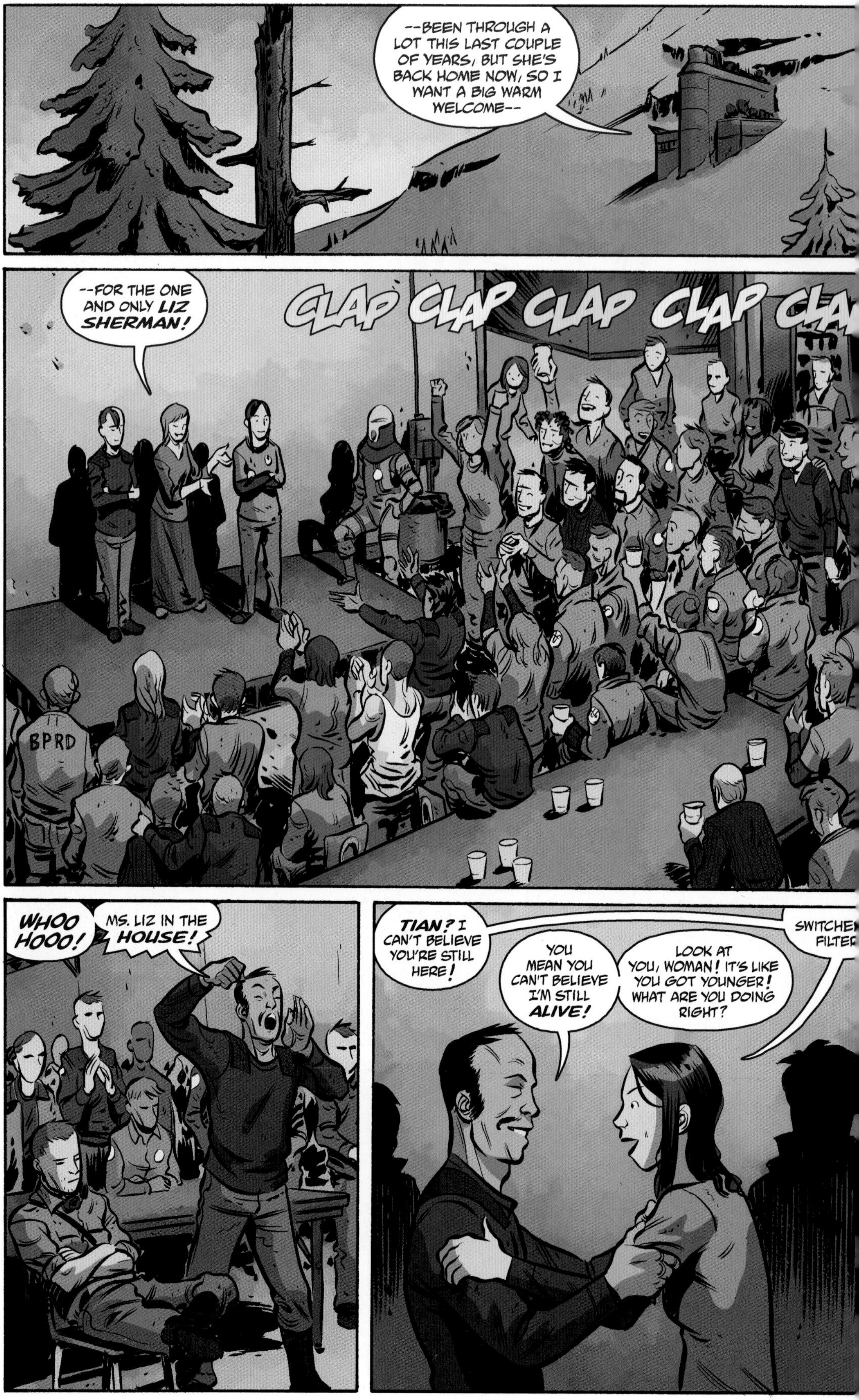
--BEEN THROUGH A LOT THIS LAST COUPLE OF YEARS, BUT SHE'S BACK HOME NOW, SO I WANT A BIG WARM WELCOME--
--FOR THE ONE AND ONLY LIZ SHERMAN!
CLAP CLAP CLAP CLAP
BPRD
WHOO HOOO!
MS. LIZ IN THE HOUSE!
TIAN? I CAN'T BELIEVE YOU'RE STILL HERE!
YOU MEAN YOU CAN'T BELIEVE I'M STILL ALIVE!
LOOK AT YOU, WOMAN! IT'S LIKE YOU GOT YOUNGER! WHAT ARE YOU DOING RIGHT?

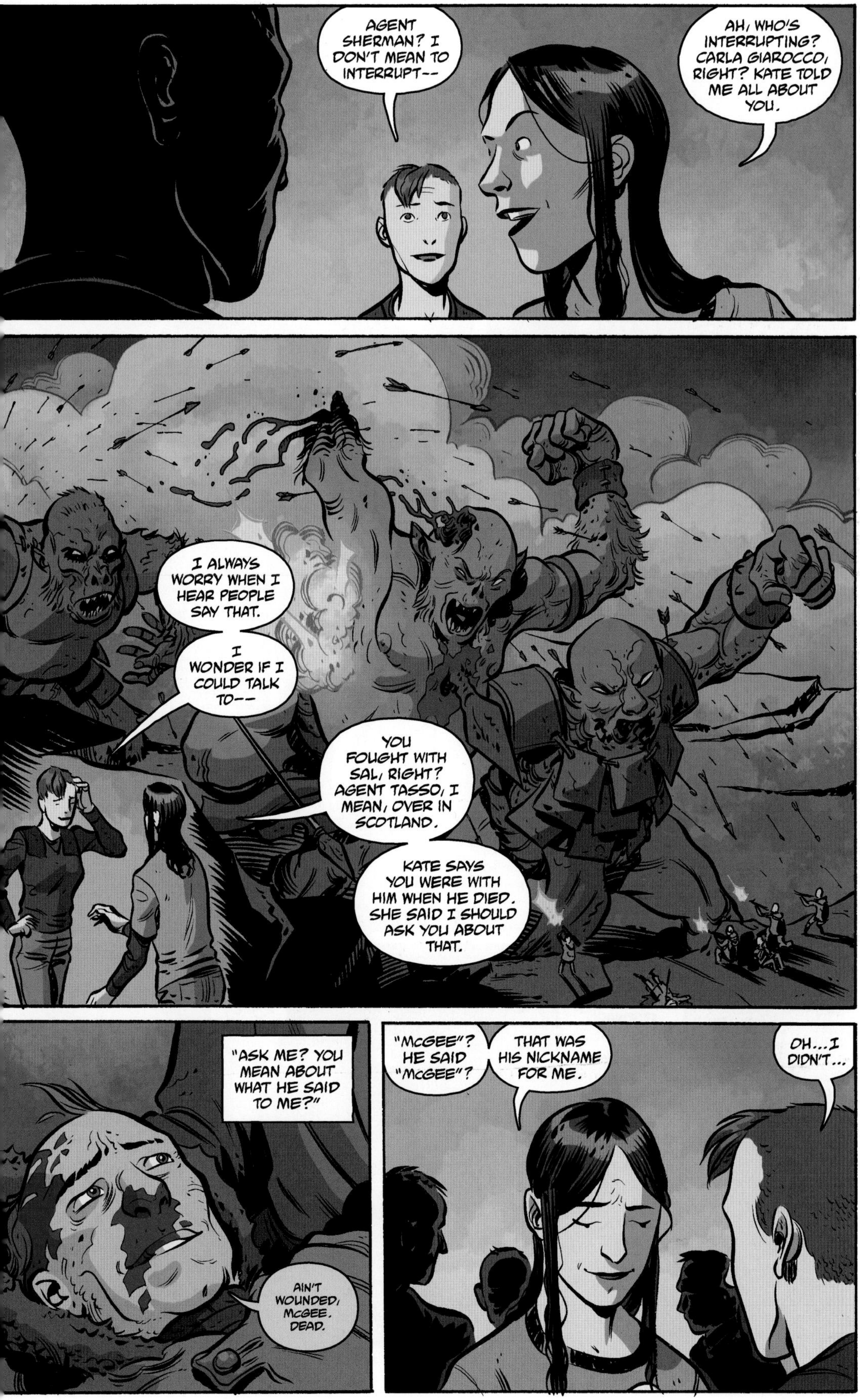
AGENT SHERMAN? I DON'T MEAN TO INTERRUPT--
AH, WHO'S INTERRUPTING? CARLA GIAROCCO, RIGHT? KATE TOLD ME ALL ABOUT YOU.
I ALWAYS WORRY WHEN I HEAR PEOPLE SAY THAT.
I WONDER IF I COULD TALK TO--
YOU FOUGHT WITH SAL, RIGHT? AGENT TASSO, I MEAN, OVER IN SCOTLAND.
KATE SAYS YOU WERE WITH HIM WHEN HE DIED. SHE SAID I SHOULD ASK YOU ABOUT THAT.
"ASK ME? YOU MEAN ABOUT WHAT HE SAID TO ME?"
AIN'T WOUNDED, McGEE. DEAD.
"McGEE"? HE SAID "McGEE"?
THAT WAS HIS NICKNAME FOR ME.
OH... I DIDN'T...

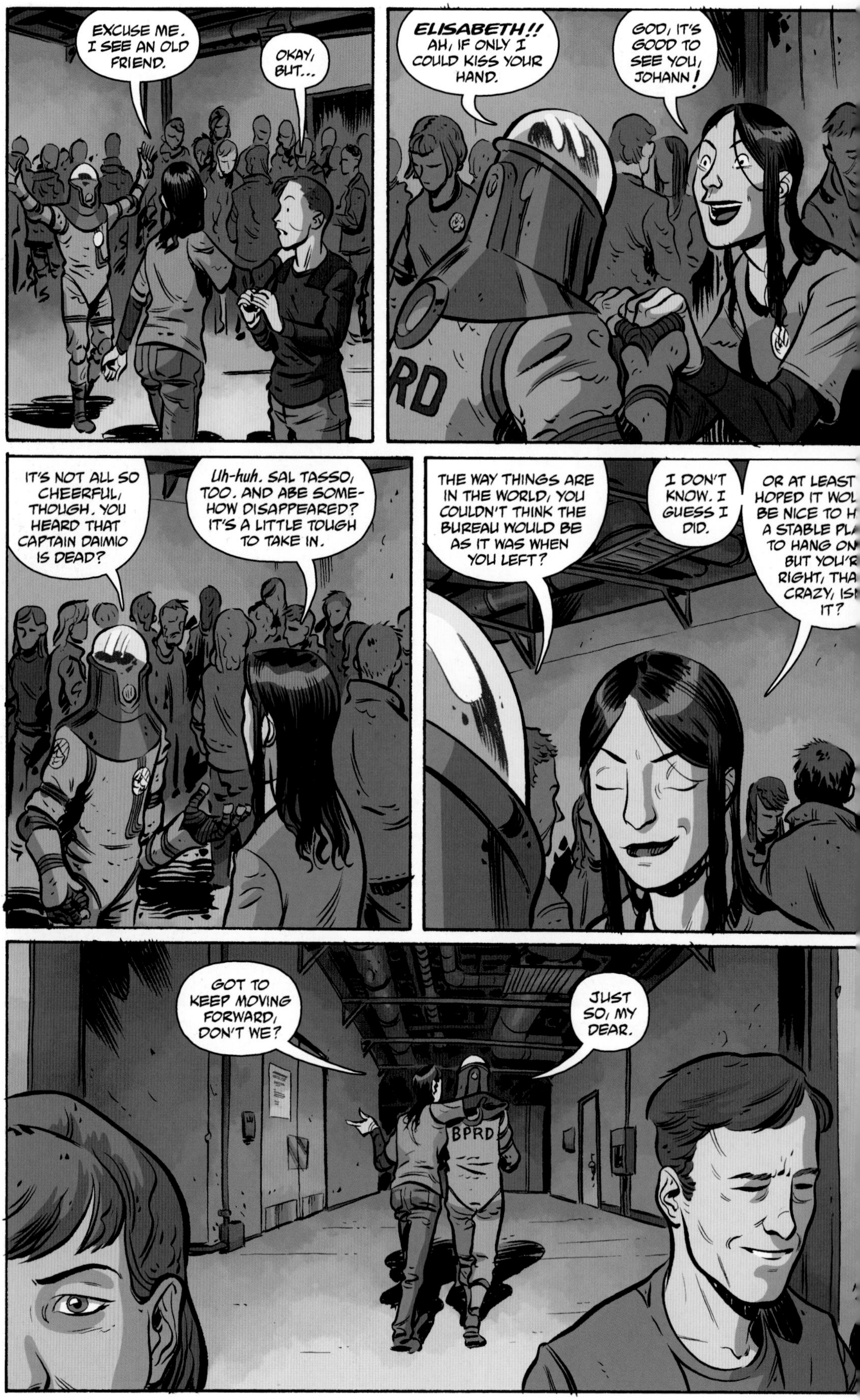
EXCUSE ME. I SEE AN OLD FRIEND.
OKAY, BUT...
ELISABETH!! AH, IF ONLY I COULD KISS YOUR HAND.
GOD, IT'S GOOD TO SEE YOU, JOHANN!
RD
IT'S NOT ALL SO CHEERFUL, THOUGH. YOU HEARD THAT CAPTAIN DAIMIO IS DEAD?
Uh-huh. SAL TASSO, TOO. AND ABE SOMEHOW DISAPPEARED? IT'S A LITTLE TOUGH TO TAKE IN.
THE WAY THINGS ARE IN THE WORLD, YOU COULDN'T THINK THE BUREAU WOULD BE AS IT WAS WHEN YOU LEFT?
I DON'T KNOW. I GUESS I DID.
OR AT LEAST HOPED IT WOU BE NICE TO H A STABLE PLA TO HANG ON BUT YOU'R RIGHT, THA CRAZY, ISN IT?
GOT TO KEEP MOVING FORWARD, DON'T WE?
JUST SO, MY DEAR.
BPRD

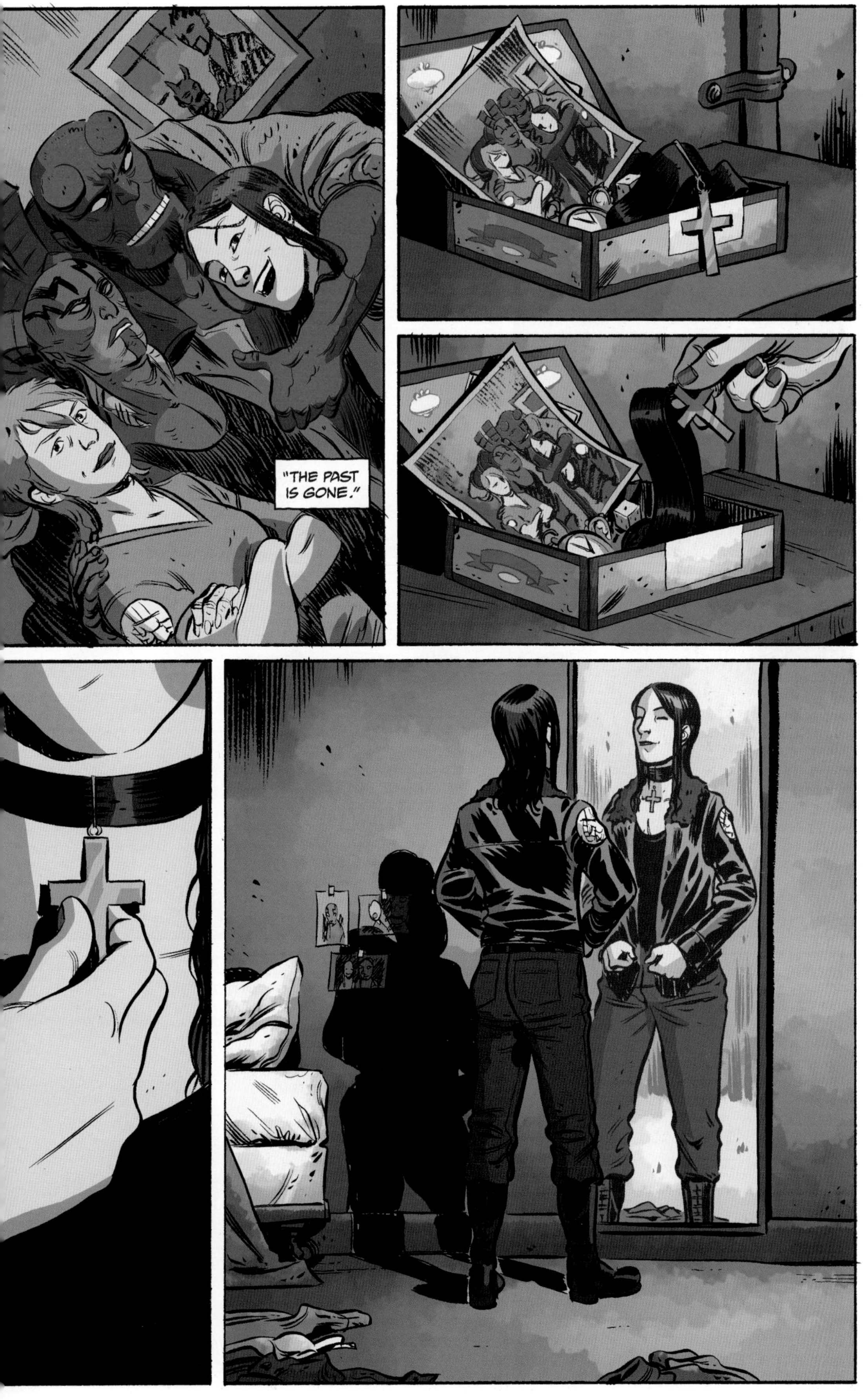
"THE PAST IS GONE."

OKAY, LET ME APOLOGIZE FOR THE GOONS.

NEW U.N. REGS. AT LEAST TWO ARMED GUARDS AT EVERY CLASSIFIED MEETING.

IT'S A GOO[D] RULE, DOCT[OR] AND IT'S MORE THAN [A] LITTLE UNF[AIR] TO CALL TH[EM] "GOONS[."]

I WANT TO GET LIZ UP TO SPEED, BUT FIRST OFF, WE HAVE A CHANGE IN TEAM ROSTERS.

LIZ WILL BE ACCOMPANYING JOHANN'S LONG ISLAND CREW.

WHAT?

I DIDN'T EV[EN] GET A CHAN[CE] TO PUT IN [MY] REQUES[T.]

CHEER UP, CARLA. YOU'LL GET HOWARDS NOW.

IT'S NICE TO BE WANTED, BUT, uhh ...WHAT FOR?

NEW YORK.

IT'S COMPLETELY CUT OFF.

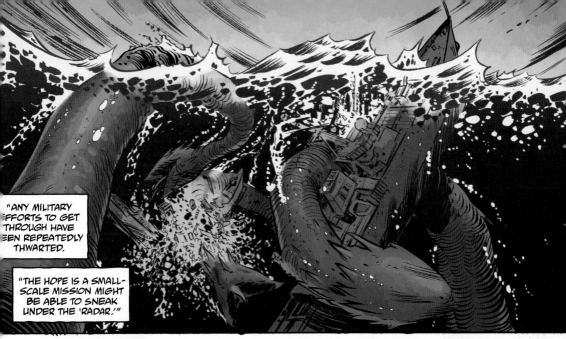

"ANY MILITARY EFFORTS TO GET THROUGH HAVE BEEN REPEATEDLY THWARTED.

"THE HOPE IS A SMALL-SCALE MISSION MIGHT BE ABLE TO SNEAK UNDER THE 'RADAR.'"

AREN'T A LOT OF CITIES CUT OFF? I MEAN, I HEARD **SEATTLE** WAS ALL BUT GONE.

YES, YOU HEARD ABOUT SEATTLE, BUT NEW YORK IS ANOTHER STORY. IT'S CUT OFF TO ALL COMMUNICATION-- EVEN TO OBSERVATION.

IT'S BEEN A YEAR NOW, ALMOST, AND WE ASSUME IT'S BAD, BUT HAVE NO IDEA **HOW** BAD--OR IN WHAT **WAYS** IT'S BAD.

PANYA'S TRIED TO MAKE A PSYCHIC LINK WITH SOMEBODY ON THE ISLAND, BUT SO FAR, NOTHING.

I CAN'T EVEN FIND A DOG OR A CAT THROUGH WHOSE EYES I CAN SEE.

AT ABOUT THE NAVY? OR THE MARINES? THEY "SMALL SCALE" BETTER THAN WE CAN.

IT'S A U.N.– MANDATED MISSION, AND THE MILITARY'S CLUELESS, TOO. NOBODY-- NOBODY AT ALL--

--KNOWS WHAT'S HAPPENING IN NEW YORK.

I DO.

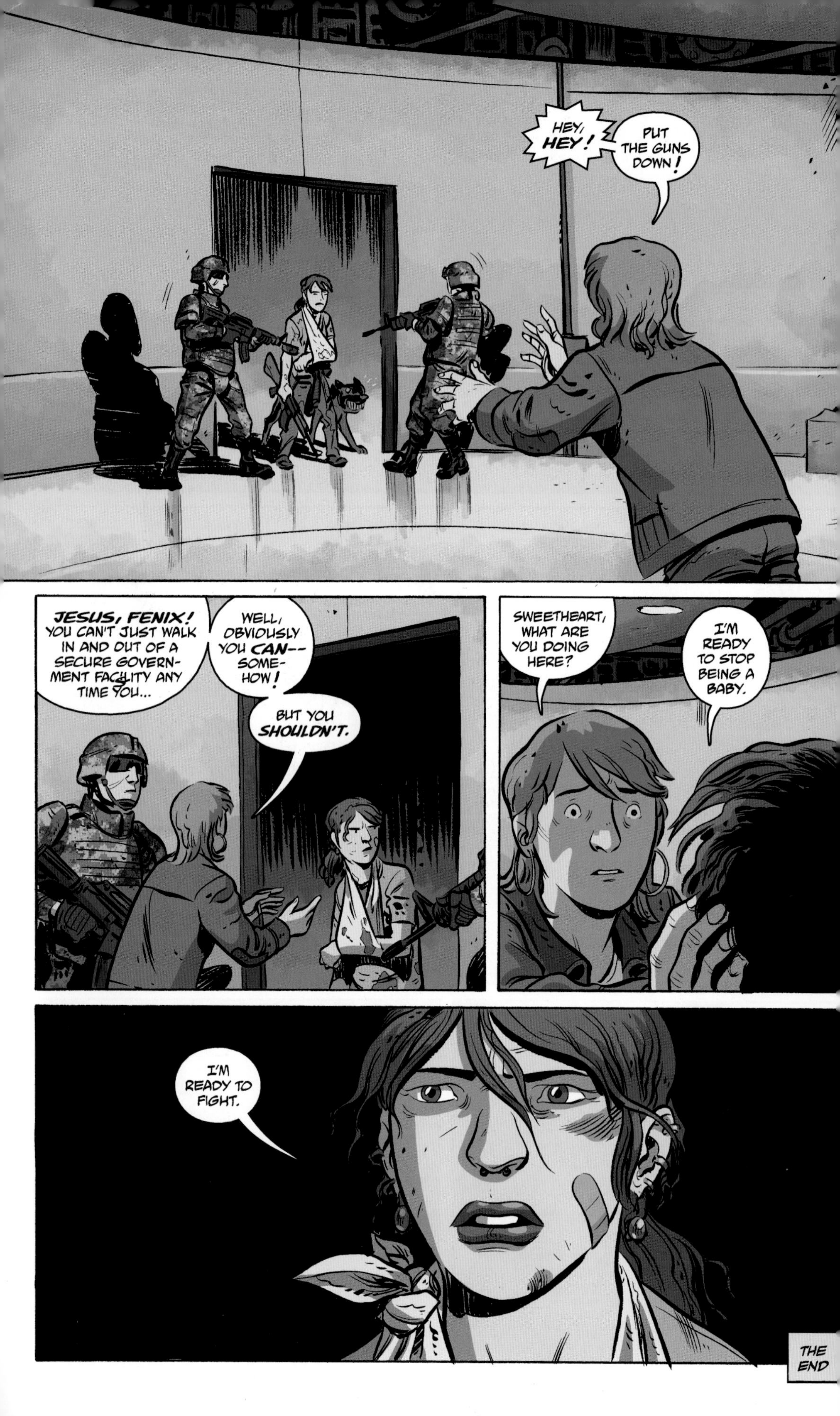
HEY, HEY!
PUT THE GUNS DOWN!
JESUS, FENIX! YOU CAN'T JUST WALK IN AND OUT OF A SECURE GOVERNMENT FACILITY ANY TIME YOU...
WELL, OBVIOUSLY YOU CAN-- SOMEHOW!
BUT YOU SHOULDN'T.
SWEETHEART, WHAT ARE YOU DOING HERE?
I'M READY TO STOP BEING A BABY.
I'M READY TO FIGHT.
THE END

B.P.R.D.™

SKETCHBOOK

Notes by Scott Allie

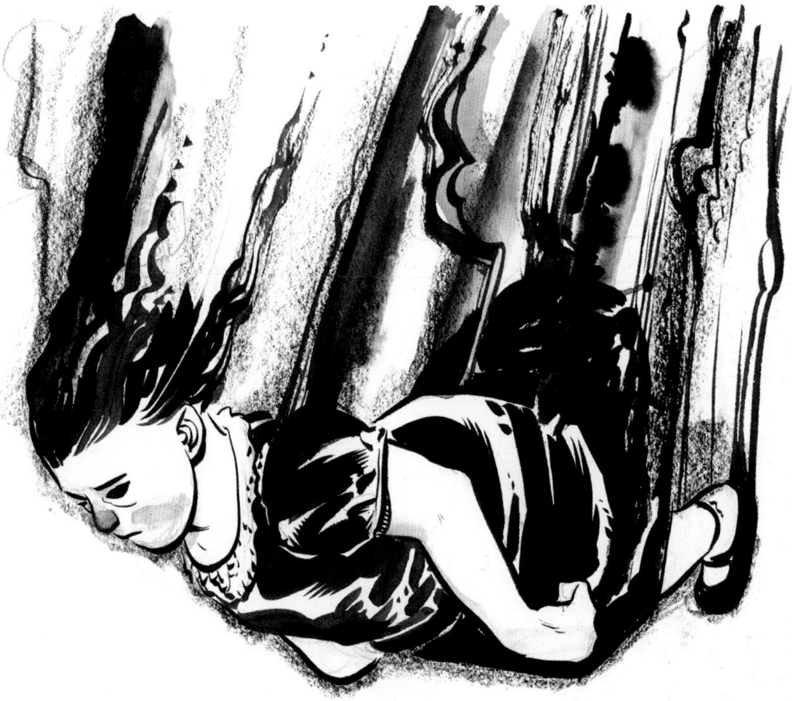

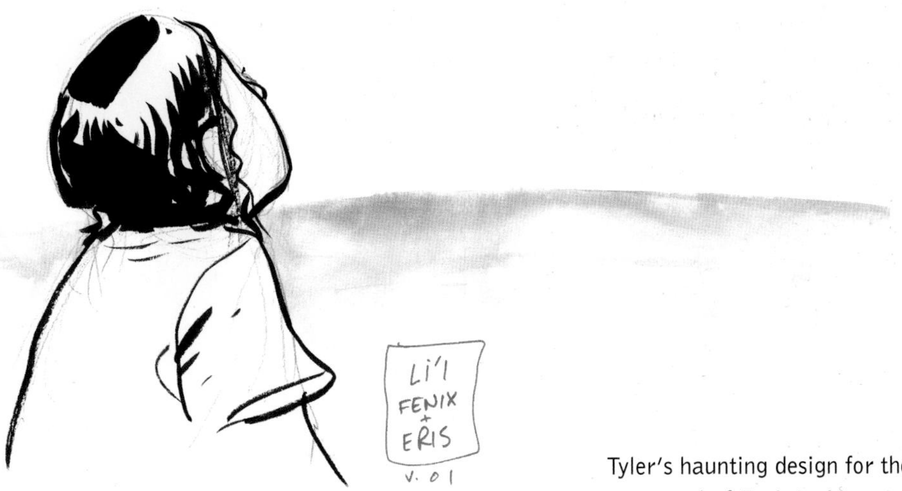
LI'L
FENIX
+
ERIS
V. 01

Tyler's haunting design for the
reveal of Fenix's sister.

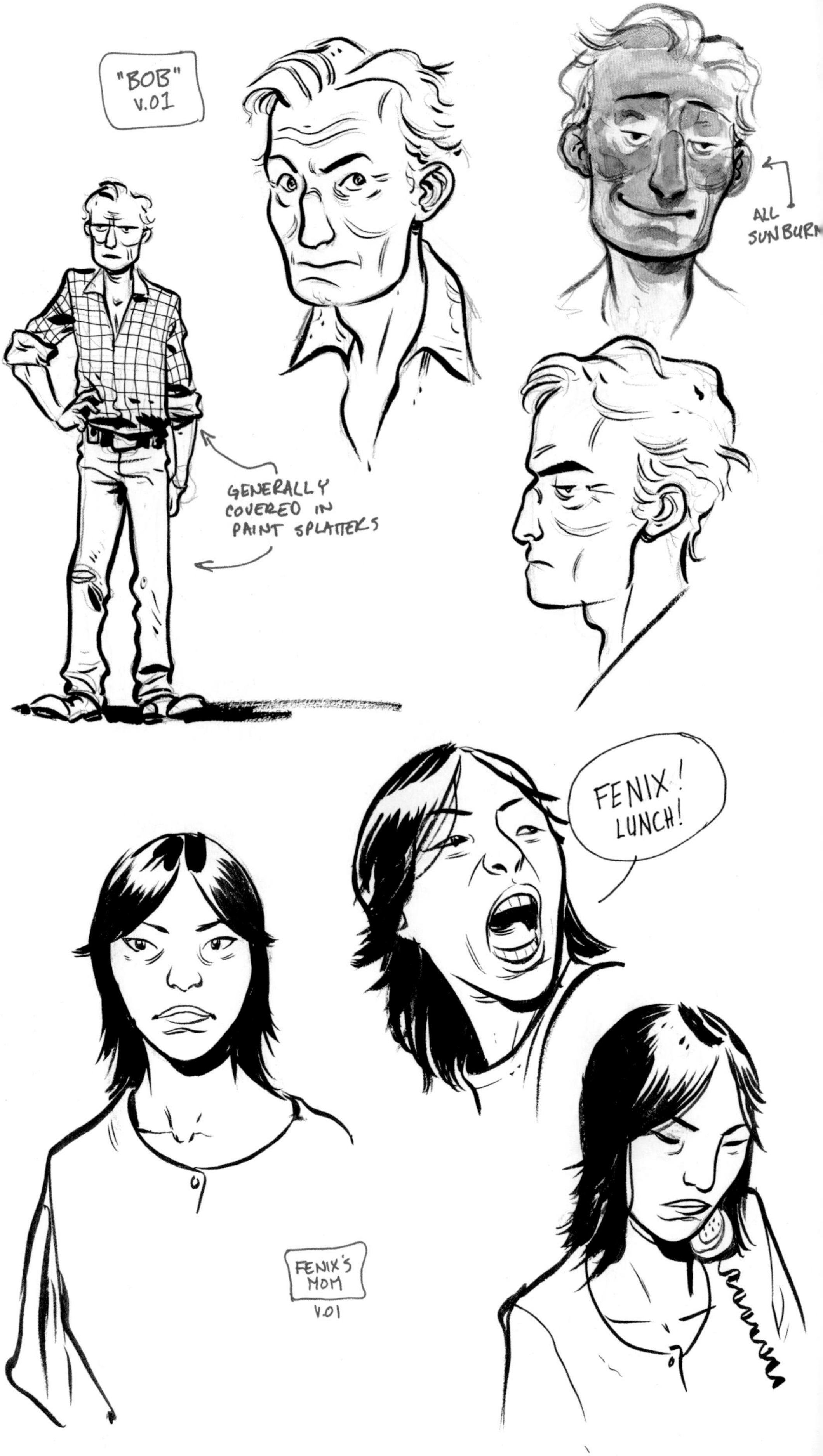
"BOB" V.01
ALL SUNBUR
GENERALLY COVERED IN PAINT SPLATTERS
FENIX! LUNCH!
FENIX'S MOM
V.01

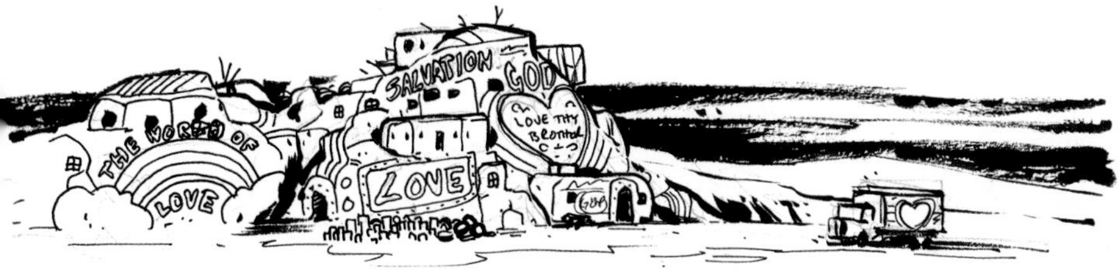
SALVATION
GOD
LOVE

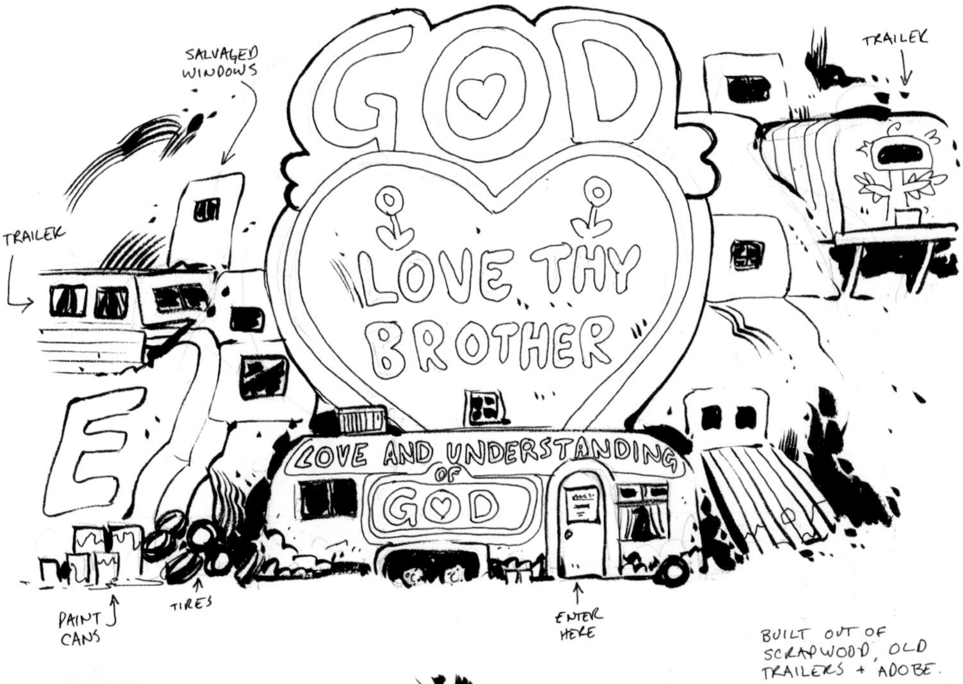
SALVAGED WINDOWS
TRAILER
TRAILER
GOD
LOVE THY BROTHER
LOVE AND UNDERSTANDING OF GOD
PAINT CANS
TIRES
ENTER HERE
BUILT OUT OF SCRAPWOOD, OLD TRAILERS + ADOBE.

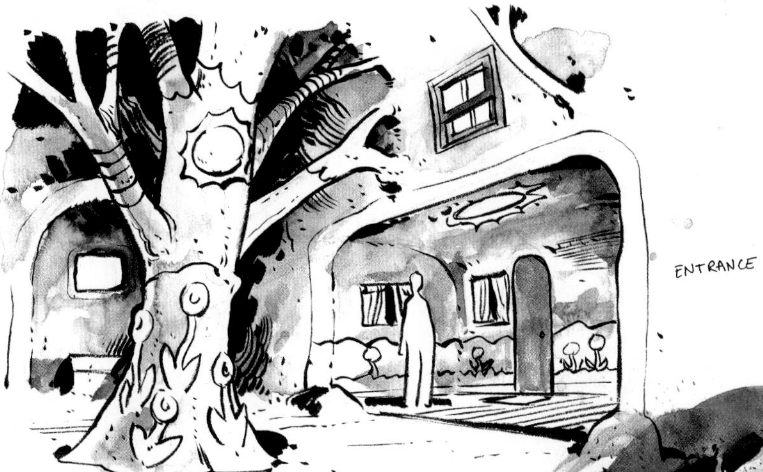
ENTRANCE

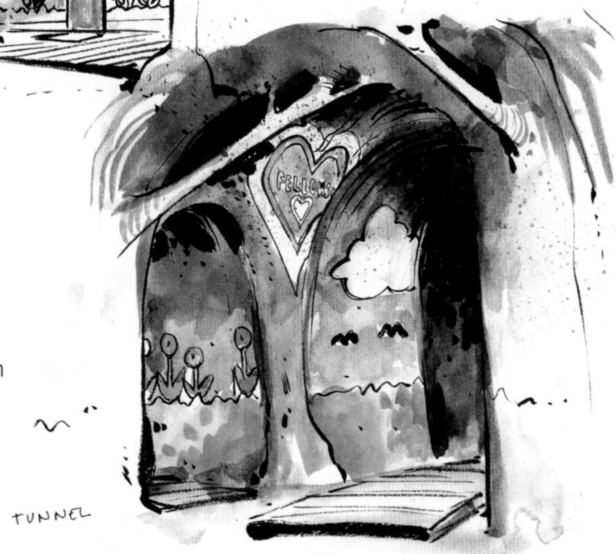
FELLOWS
TUNNEL

More designs for the Fenix section of the book. Bob's house is based on a real location in the Salton Sea. Check out the short film "The Accidental Sea" on YouTube. This house was designed early in order to facilitate a tie-in to *Abe Sapien: Dark and Terrible and the New Race of Man*, by John Arcudi and Max Fiumara.

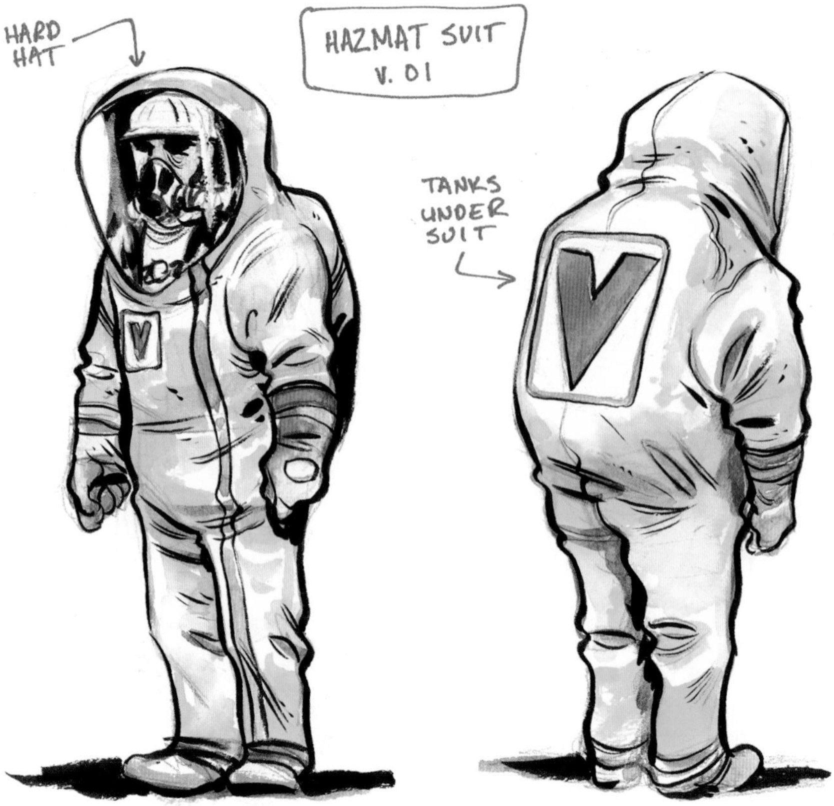
HARD HAT
HAZMAT SUIT V. 01
TANKS UNDER SUIT

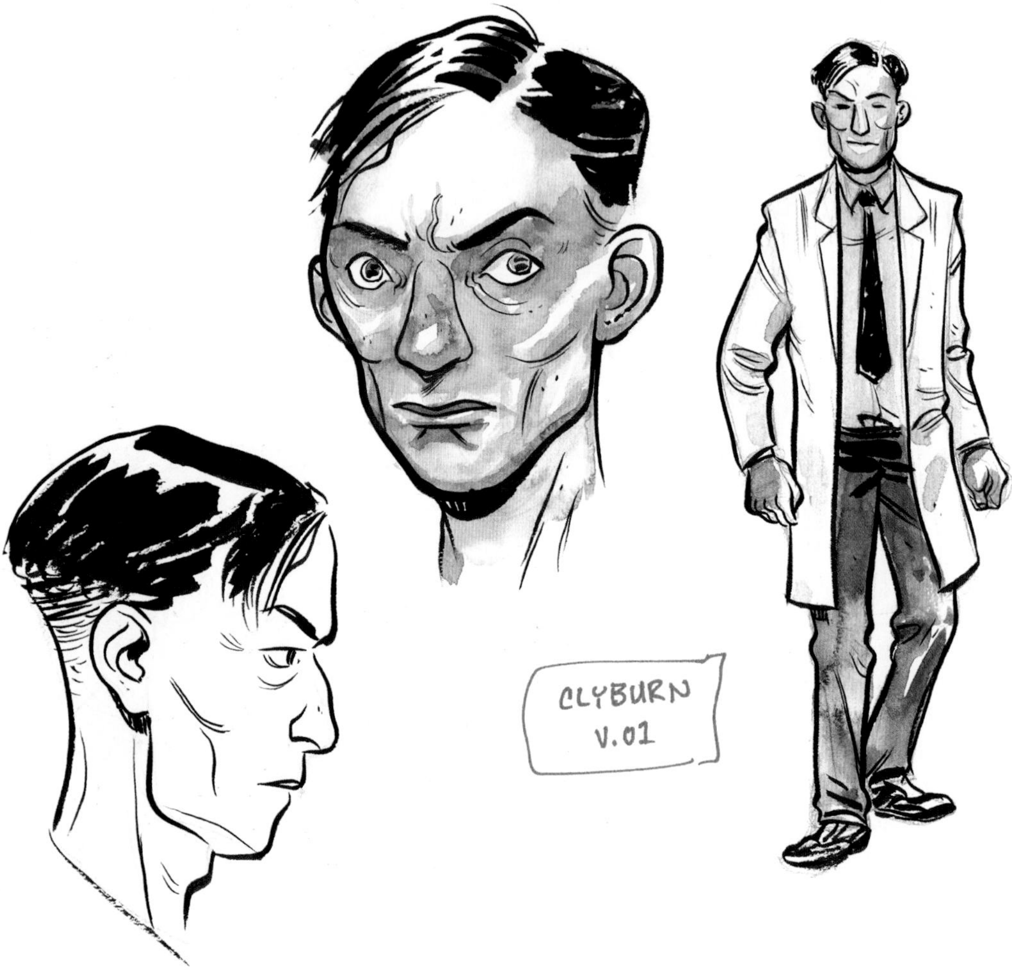
CLYBURN V.01

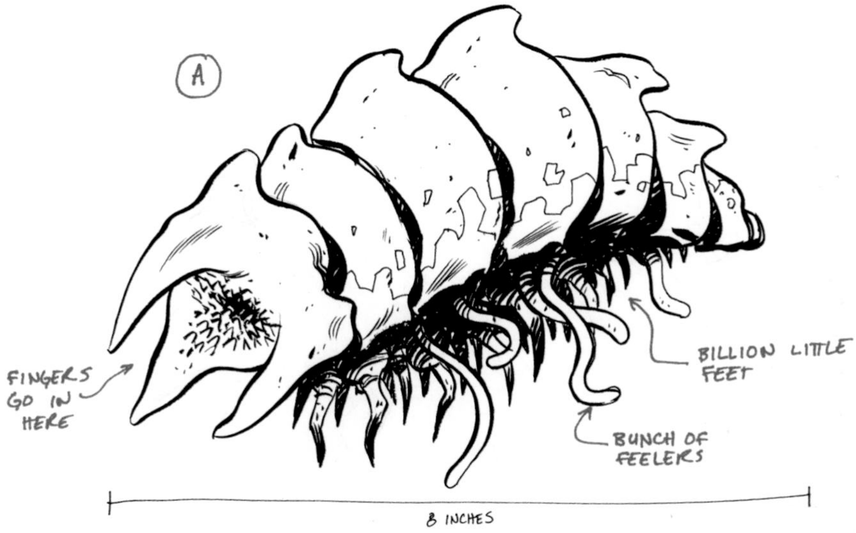
A
FINGERS GO IN HERE
BILLION LITTLE FEET
BUNCH OF FEELERS
8 INCHES

The tiny creatures that inspire Clyburn's experiments, which John described in the script as "what silverfish must look like when you're schizophrenic *and* on peyote."

Facing: The V is for volunteer.

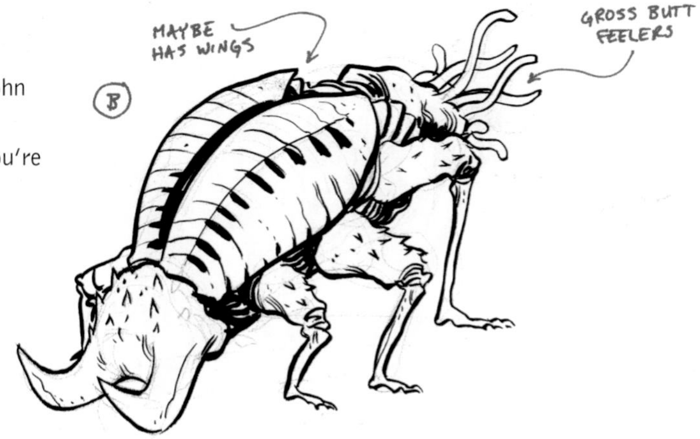
MAYBE HAS WINGS
GROSS BUTT FEELERS
B

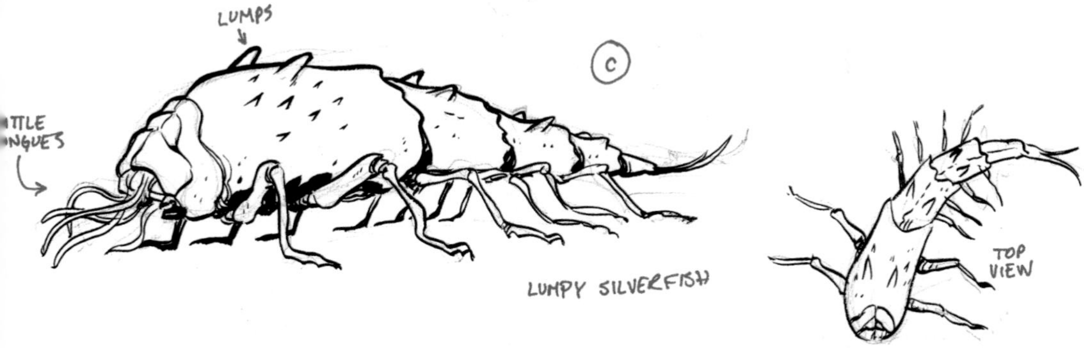
LUMPS
C
LUMPY SILVERFISH
TOP VIEW

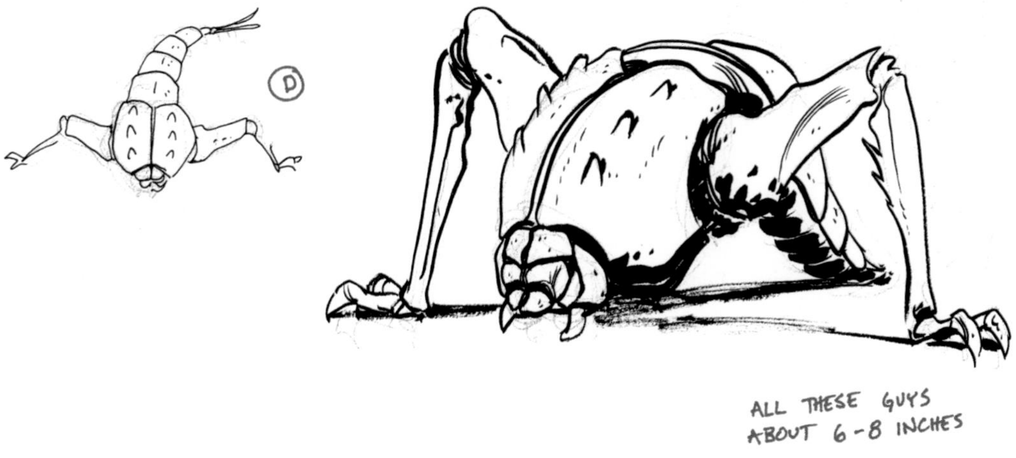
D
ALL THESE GUYS ABOUT 6-8 INCHES

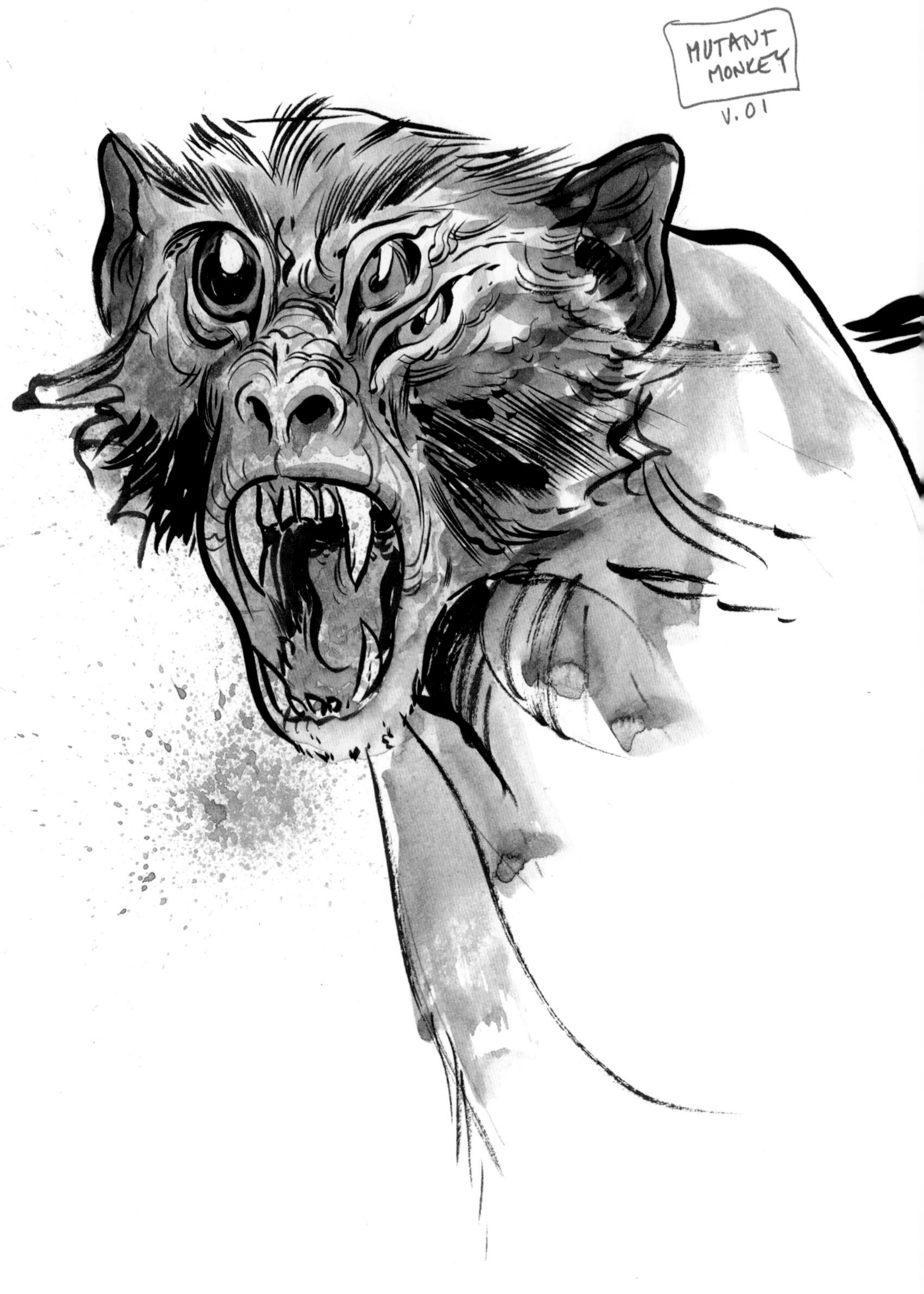
MUTANT MONKEY
V.01

We've sometimes given Tyler a hard time about his monsters being too cute. Something about Clyburn's mutant animal menagerie brought out the best in him.

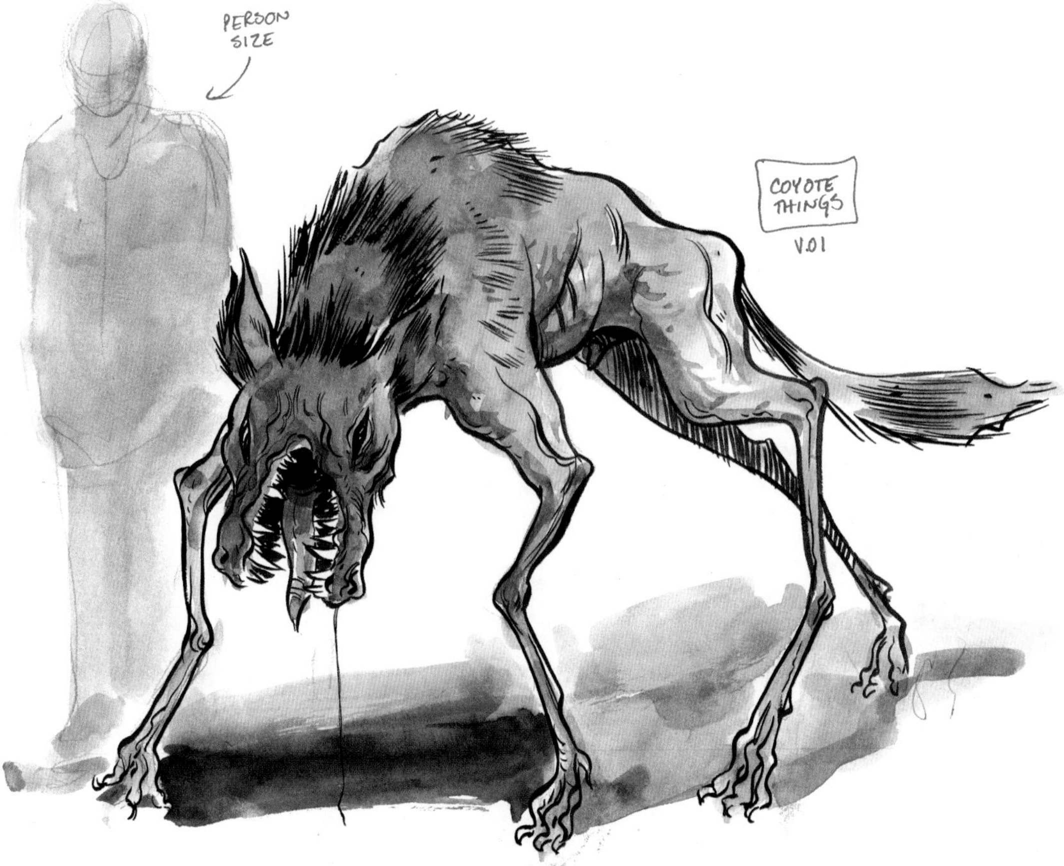
PERSON SIZE
COYOTE THINGS
V.01

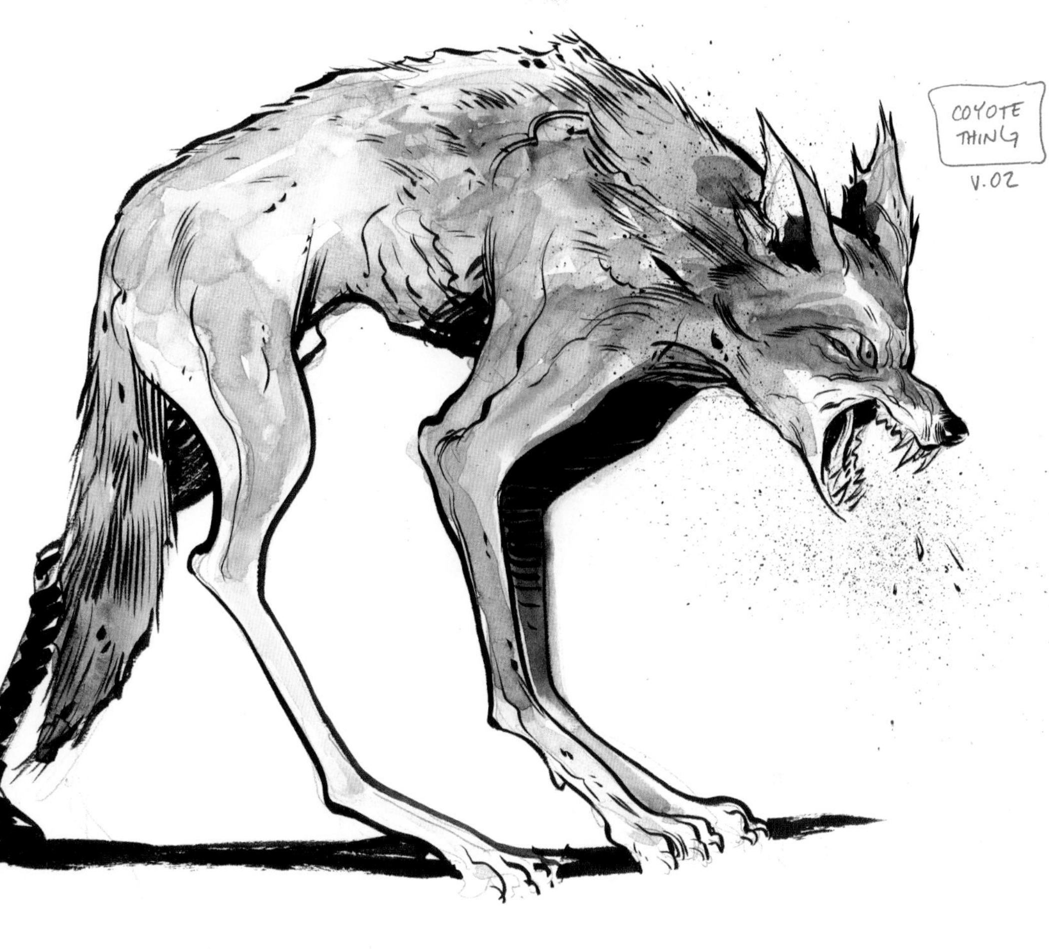
COYOTE THING
V.02

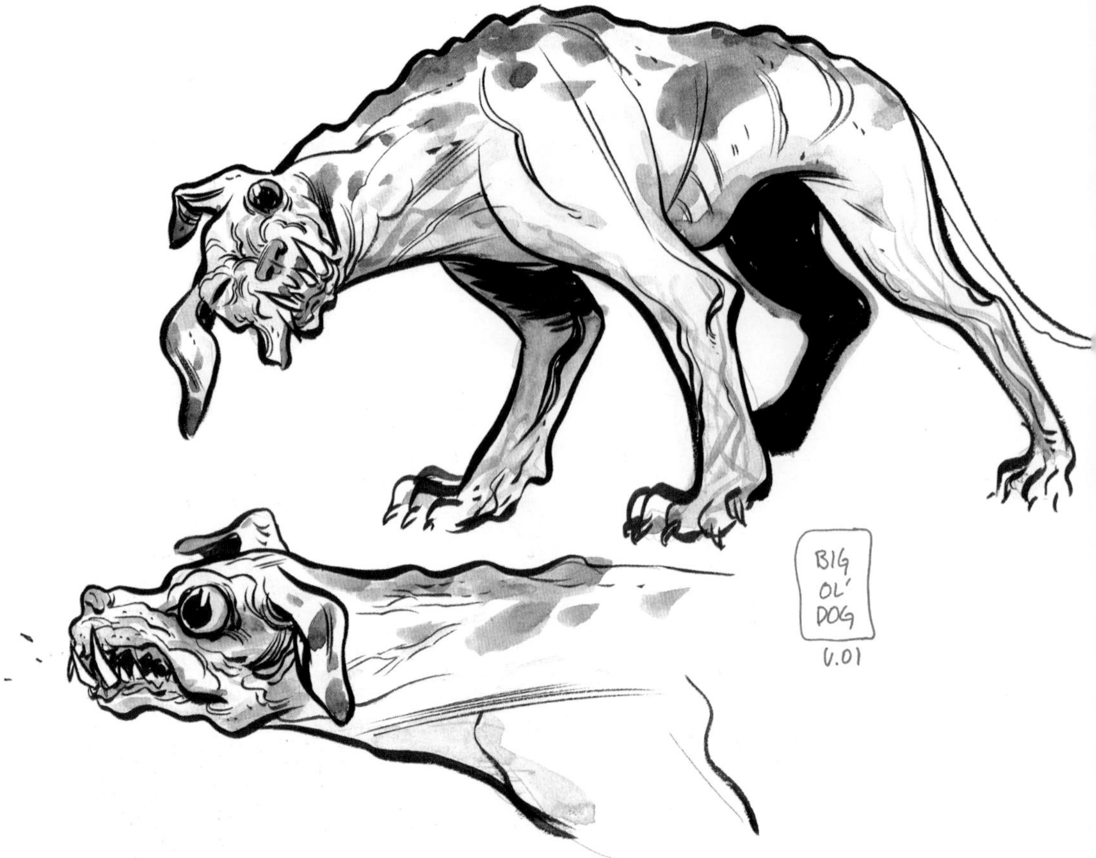
BIG OL' DOG
V.01

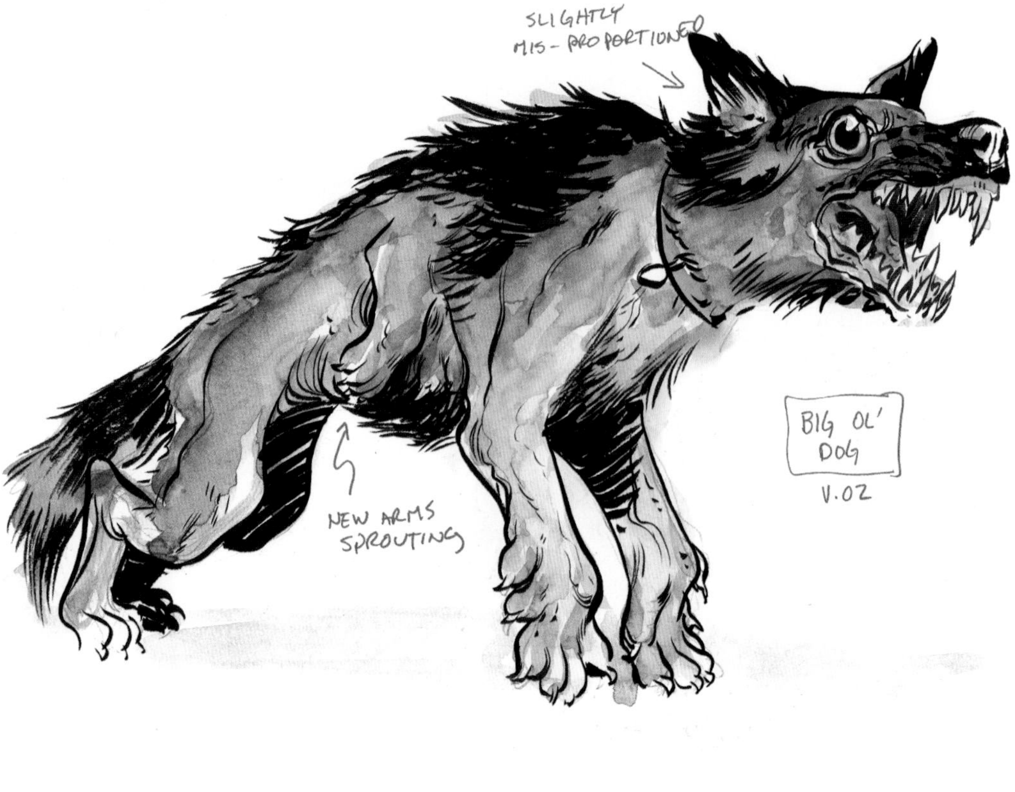
SLIGHTLY MIS-PROPORTIONED
NEW ARMS SPROUTING
BIG OL' DOG
V.02

I'm tempted to let these images go without comment, but Tyler supplied this explanation:

"I made that little maquette out of Super Sculpey and painted it with acrylic paint. I was having a hard time figuring out how to draw the monster cat's head from different angles so I thought, 'I'll take a quick break and make a little maquette.' Nine hours later I was painting it and trying to remember what I was supposed to be working on that day. It was about 4.5 inches from nose to neck. I sent it to Arcudi as a present."

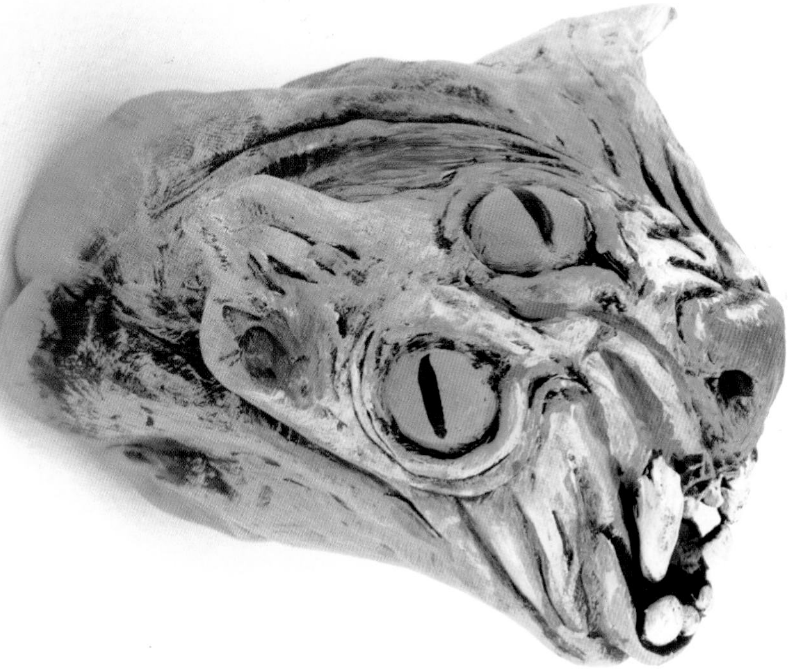

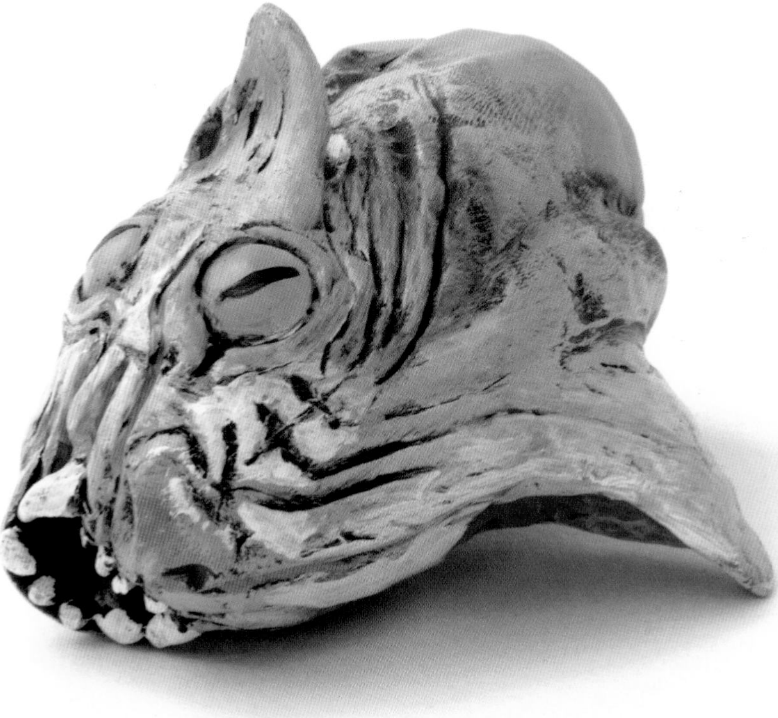

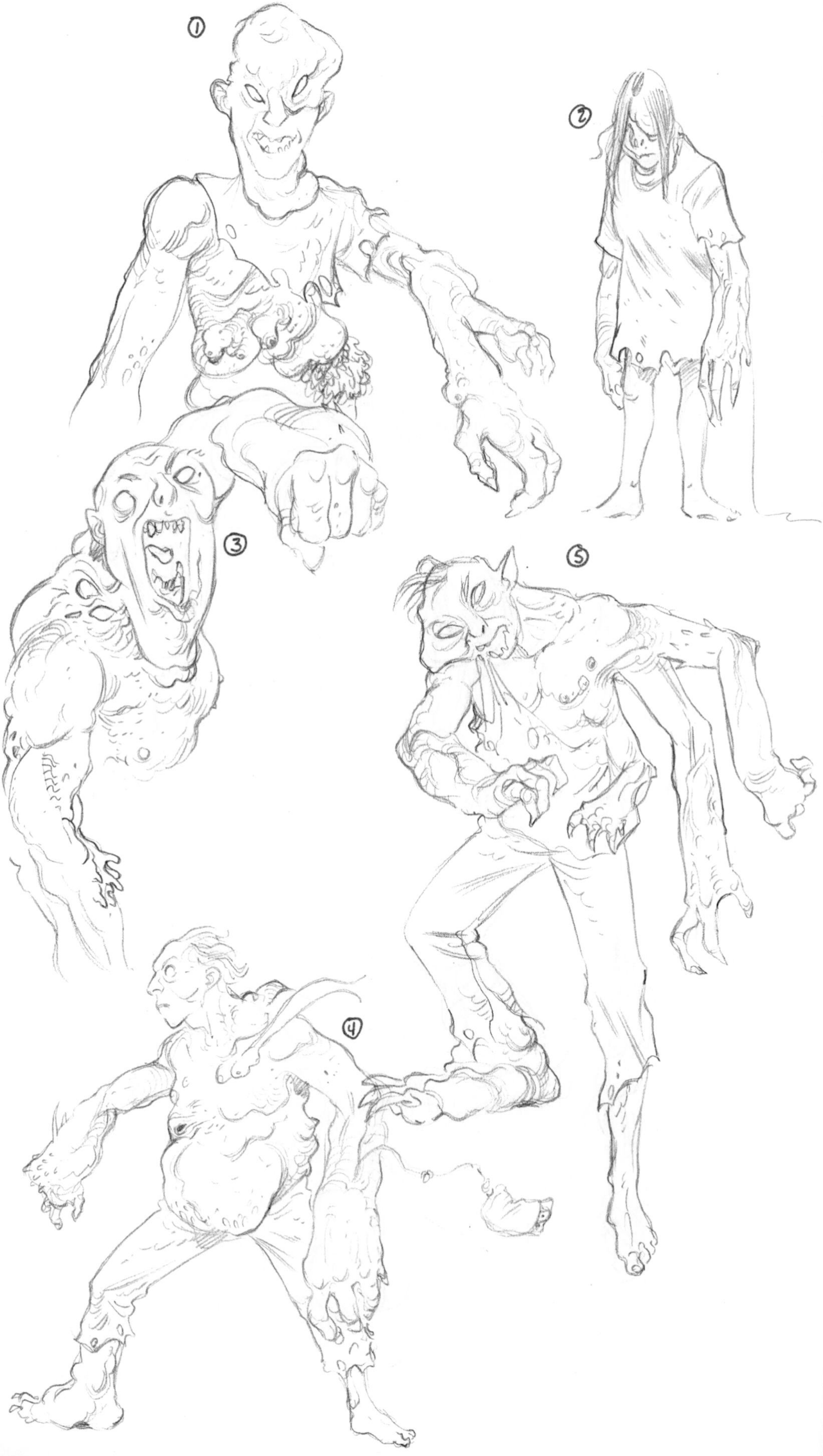

1
2
3
5
4

The unfortunate patients in Salt Lake City.

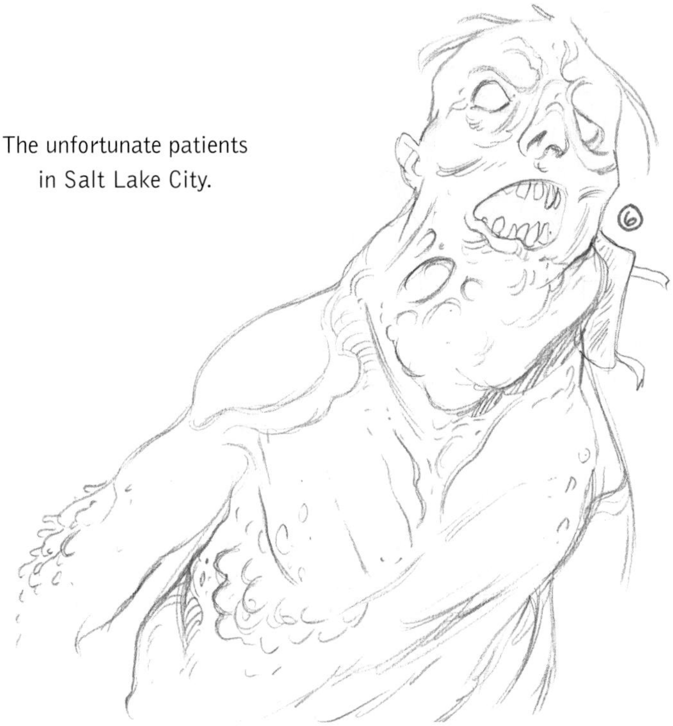
6

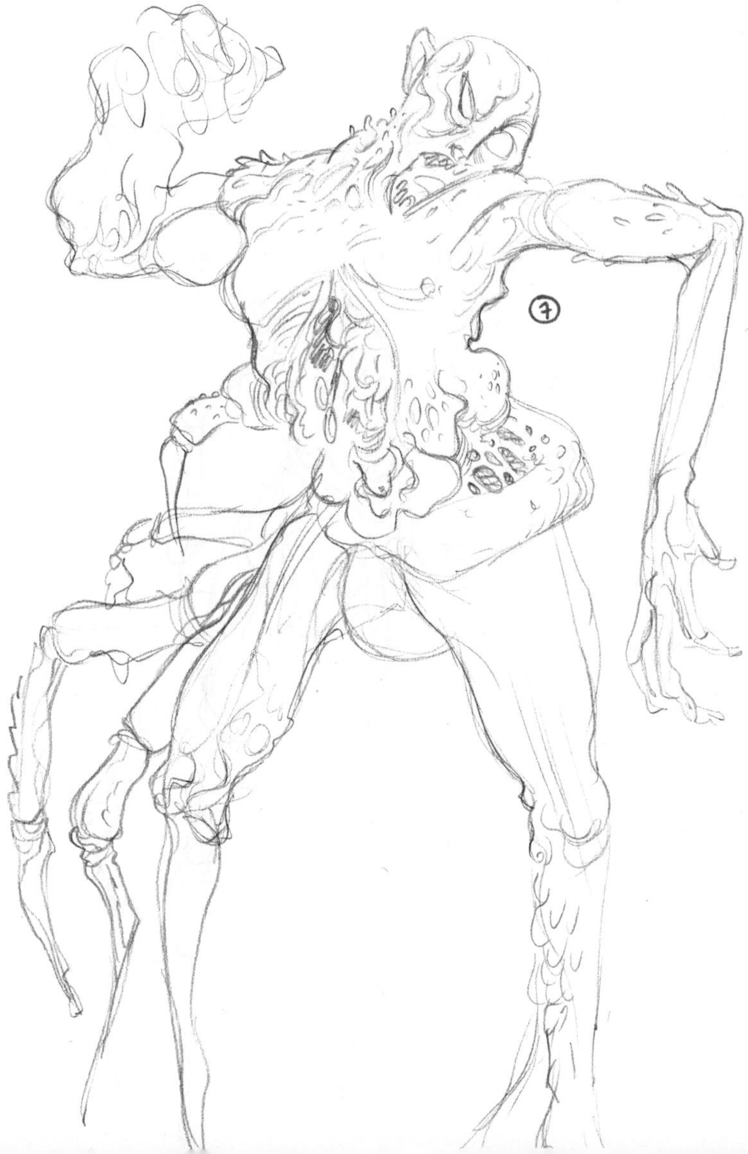
7

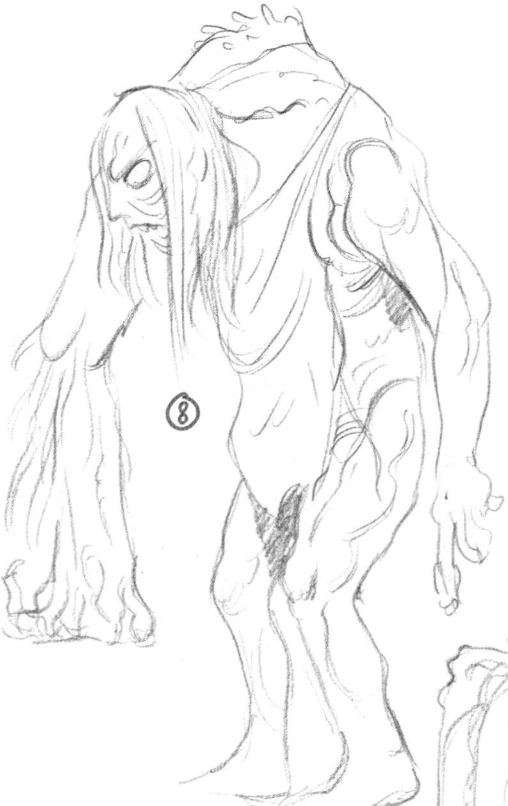
8

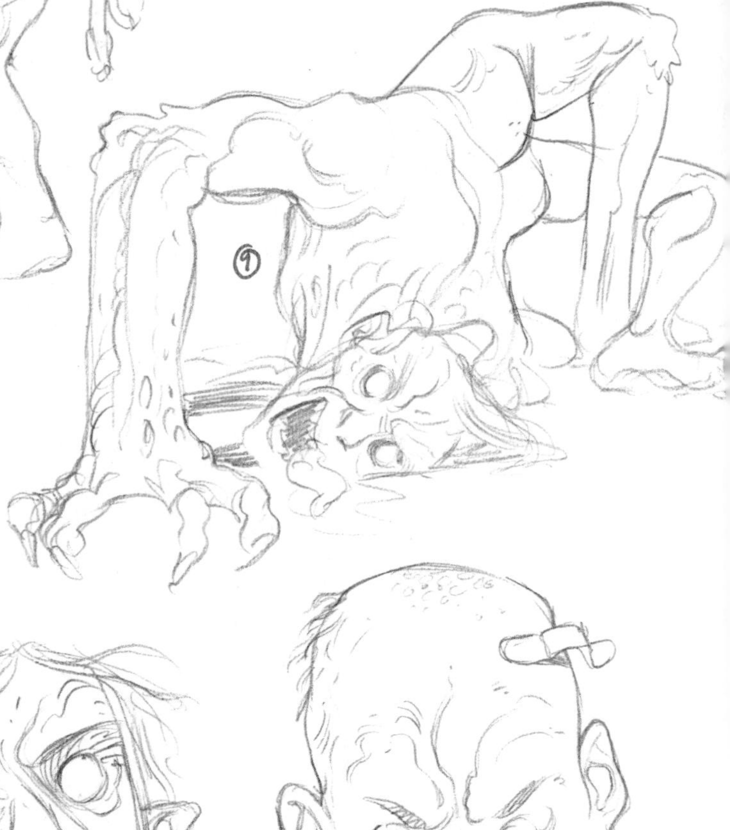
9

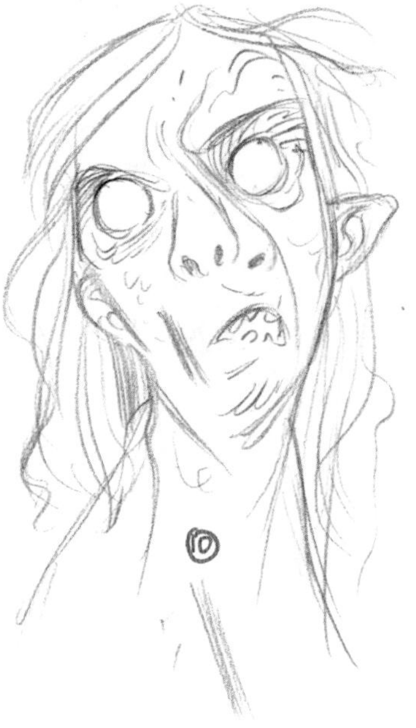
10

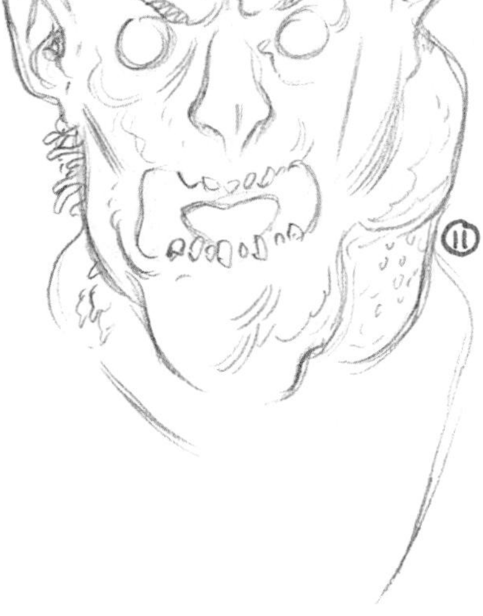
11

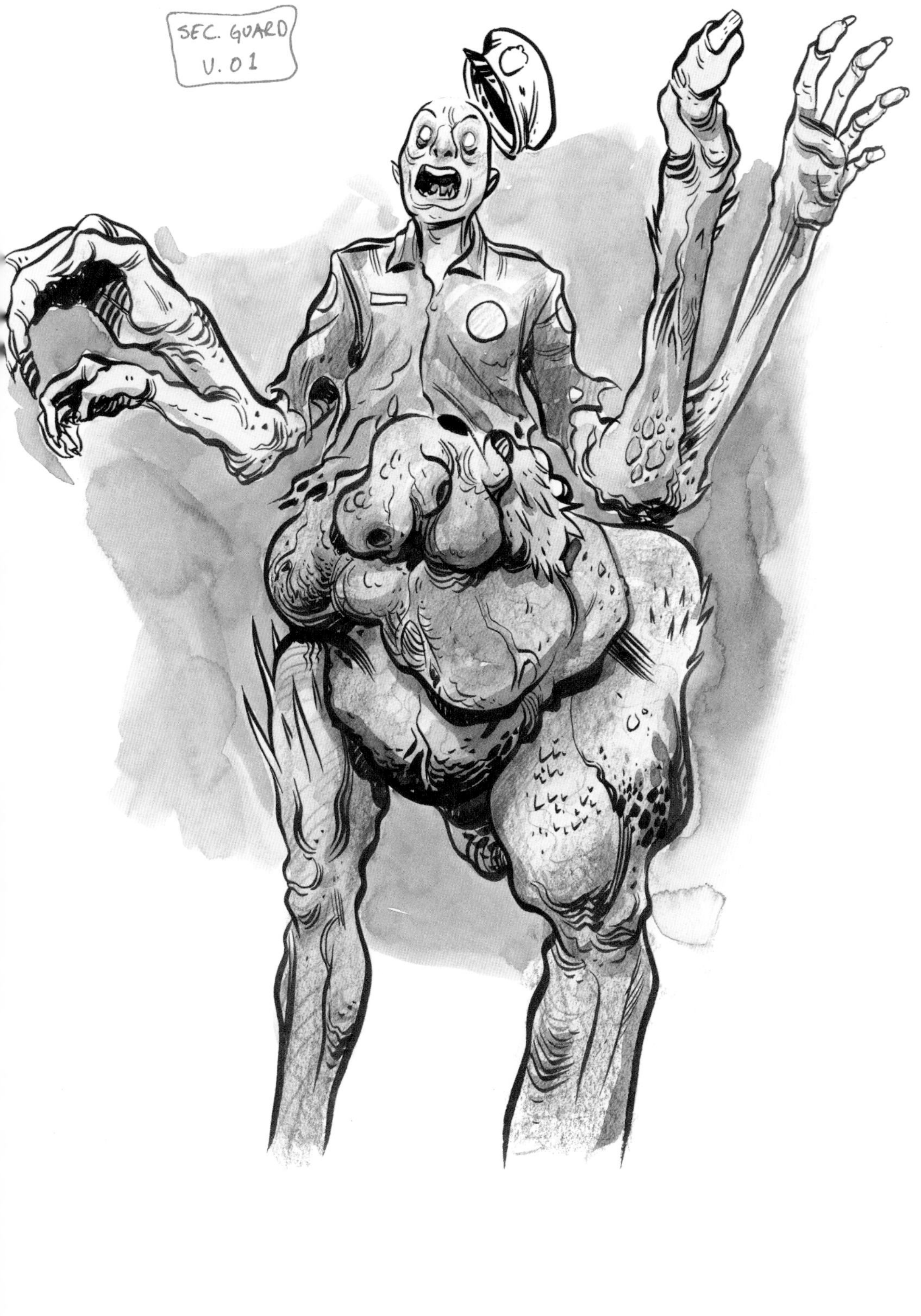
SEC. GUARD
V. 01

MY TAKE ON Rafael's Creature --

①

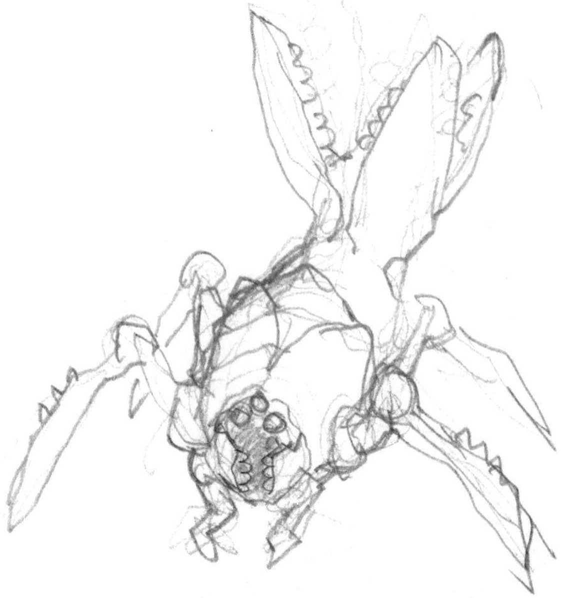

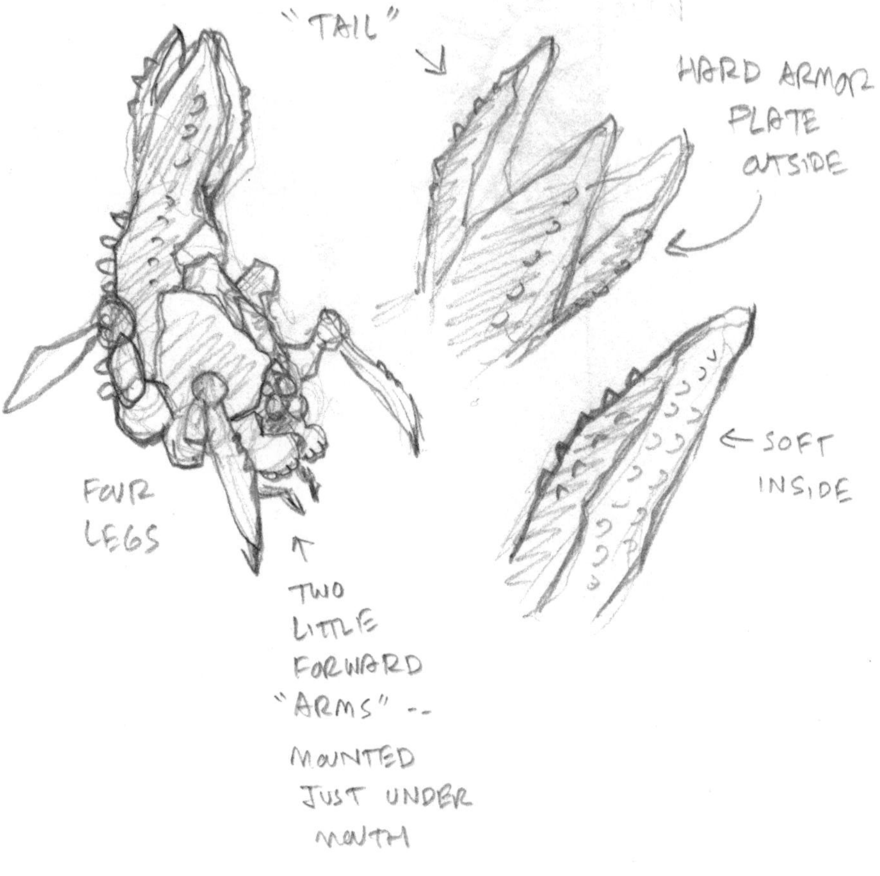
"TAIL"
HARD ARMOR PLATE OUTSIDE
SOFT INSIDE
FOUR LEGS
TWO LITTLE FORWARD "ARMS" -- MOUNTED JUST UNDER MOUTH

Before Rafael began cover sketches for this series, he worked on some Ogdru Hem designs. Our usual process for creating these is to have the interior or cover artist on the book take a pass, and then Mike revises it. Mike jumped in and redrew Rafa's Ogdru Hem, as seen on these two pages, before we decided that it would be better to use the Salton Sea monster, since that one has been appearing in the books since *King of Fear*.

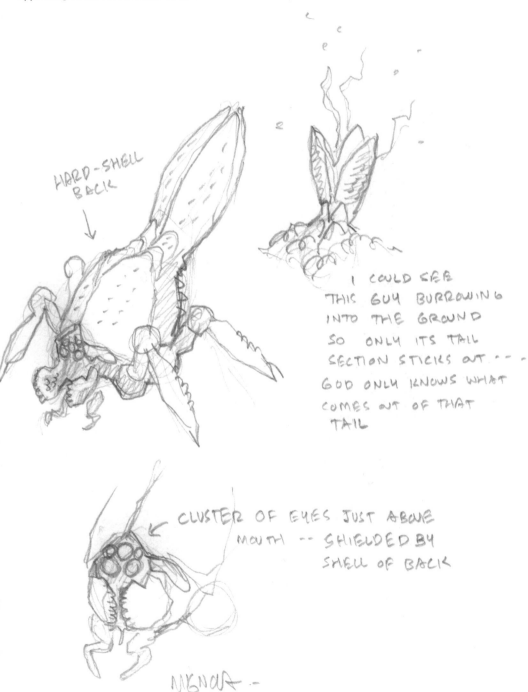

HARD-SHELL BACK

I COULD SEE THIS GUY BURROWING INTO THE GROUND SO ONLY ITS TAIL SECTION STICKS OUT -- GOD ONLY KNOWS WHAT COMES OUT OF THAT TAIL

CLUSTER OF EYES JUST ABOVE MOUTH -- SHIELDED BY SHELL OF BACK

MIGNOLA -

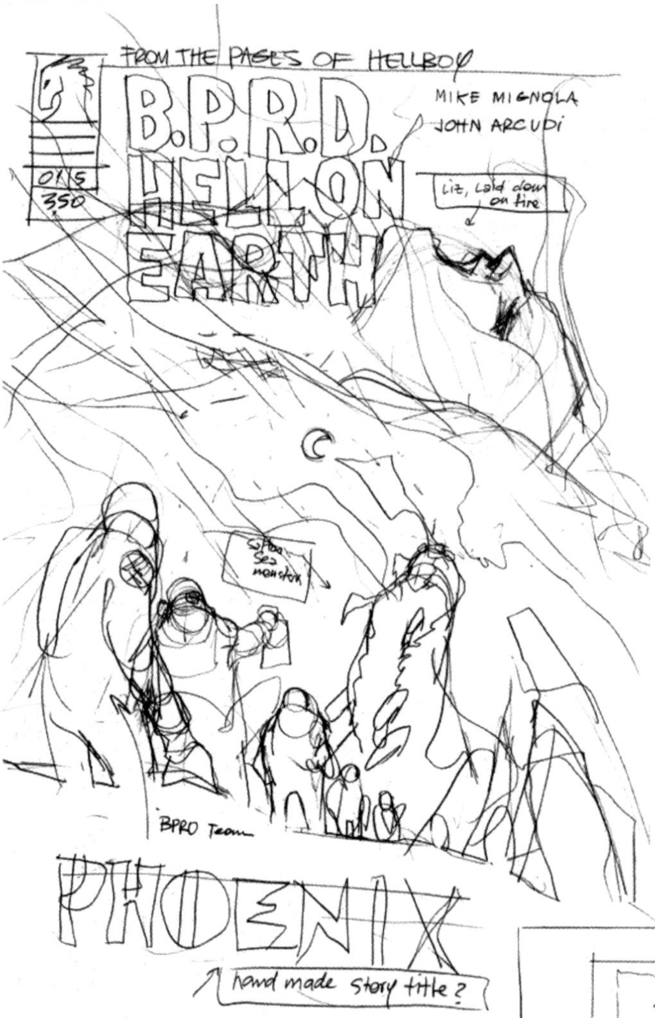
FROM THE PAGES OF HELLBOY
B.P.R.D.
HELL ON EARTH
MIKE MIGNOLA
JOHN ARCUDI
Liz, Laid down on fire
Salton Sea monster
BPRD Team
PHOENIX
hand made story title?

Before Rafa did any sketches, we'd decided to use the Salton Sea monster on the covers, so it's pictured here. Rafa turned in the completed cover on the right, and we gave him some notes that were not meant to be extreme but led him to completely redraw the cover, resulting in the image you see in front of chapter 1 of this volume.

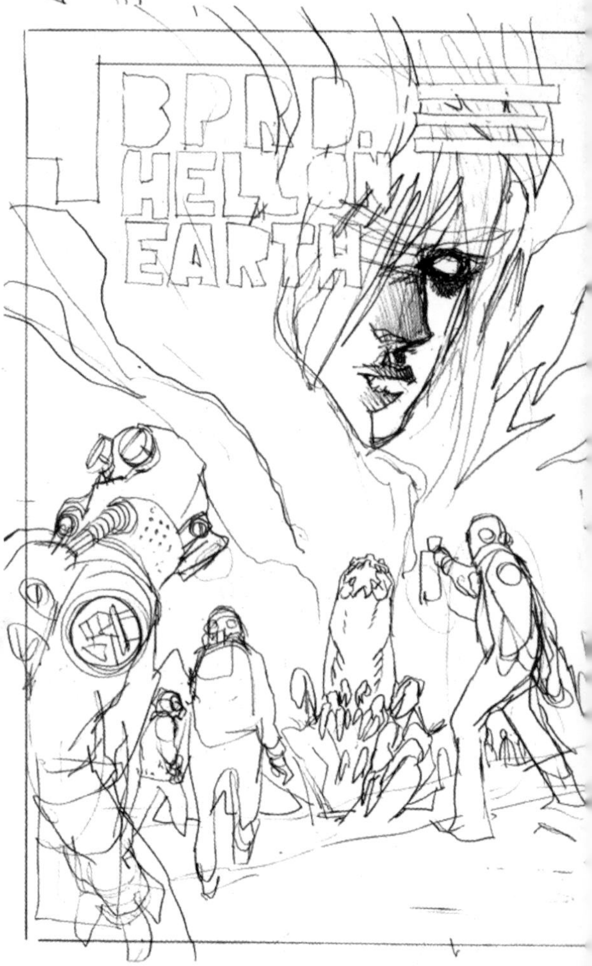
B.P.R.D.
HELL ON EARTH

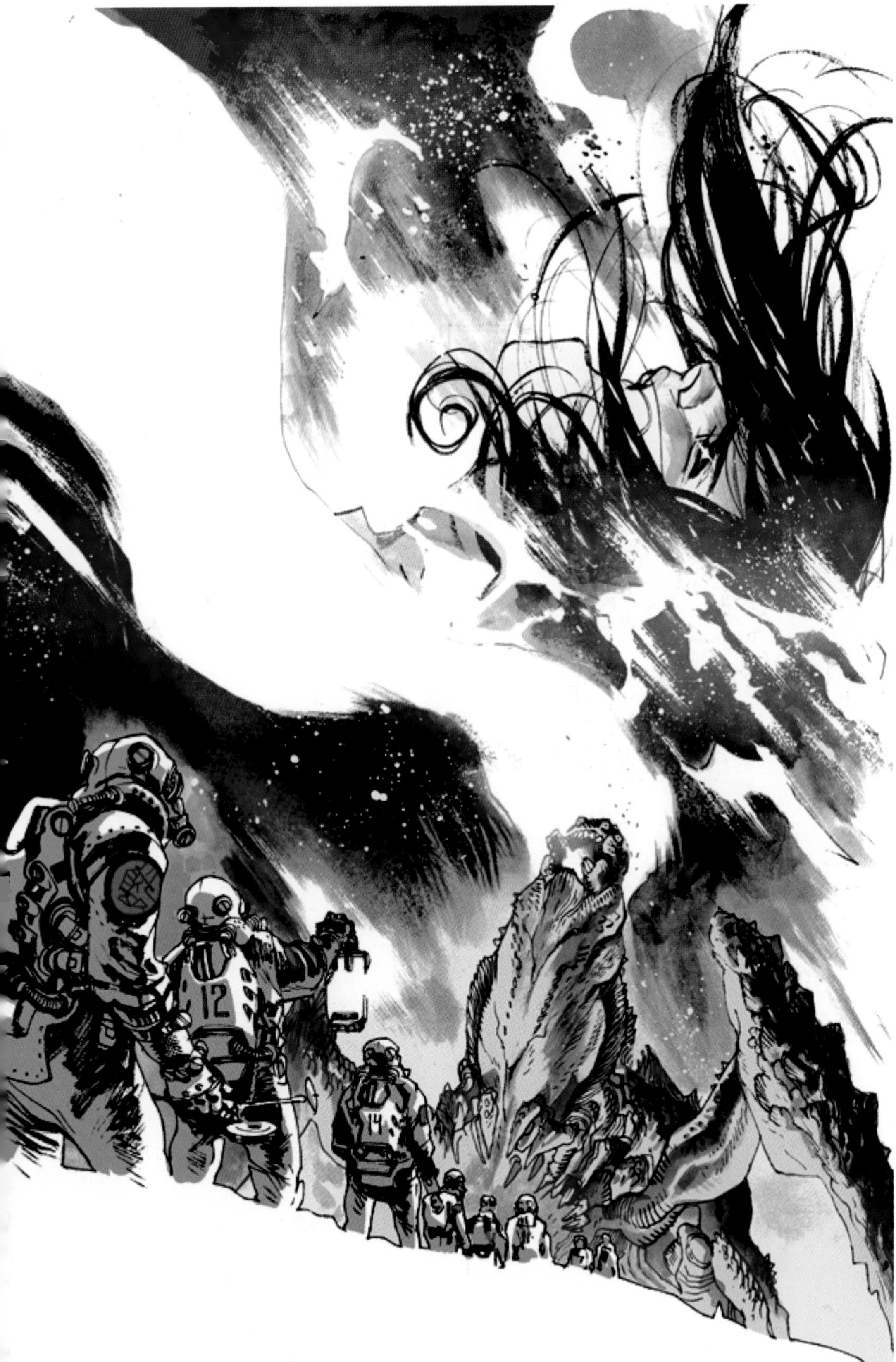

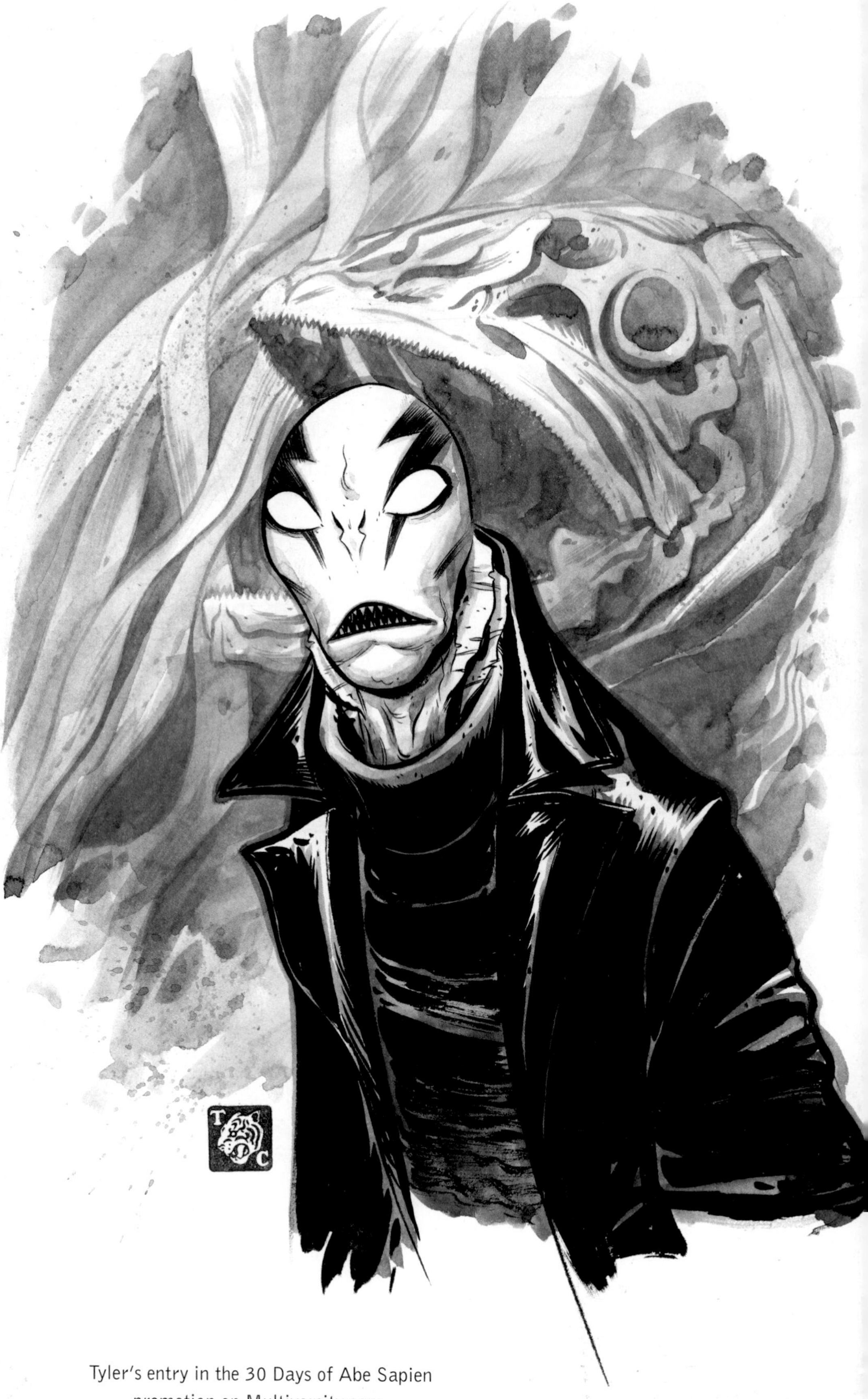

Tyler's entry in the 30 Days of Abe Sapien
promotion on Multiversity.com.

Also by
MIKE MIGNOLA

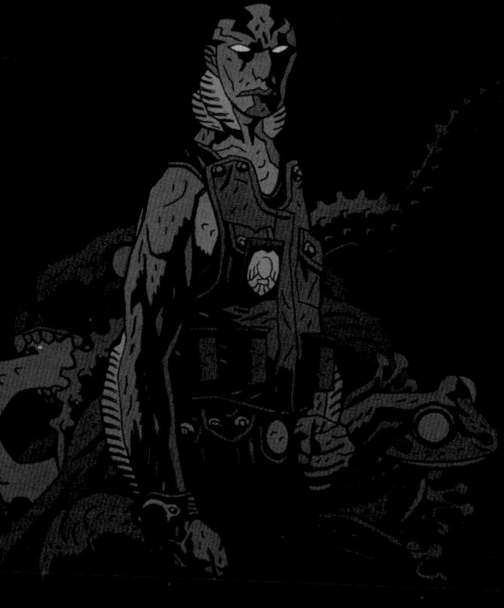

.P.R.D.

LAGUE OF FROGS
olume 1
ith Chris Golden, Guy Davis,
nd others
BN 978-1-59582-609-1 | $34.99
olume 2
ith John Arcudi, Davis,
nd others
BN 978-1-59582-672-5 | $34.99
olume 3
ith Arcudi, and Davis
BN 978-1-59582-860-6 | $34.99
olume 4
ith Arcudi and Davis
BN 978-1-59582-974-0 | $34.99

946
ith Joshua Dysart and Paul
zaceta
BN 978-1-59582-191-1 | $17.99

947
ith Dysart, Fábio Moon, and
abriel Bá
BN 978-1-59582-478-3 | $17.99

948
ith Arcudi and Max Fiumara
BN 978-1-61655-183-4 | $17.99

EING HUMAN
ith Arcudi, Davis, and others
BN 978-1-59582-756-2 | $17.99

AMPIRE
ith Moon and Bá
BN 978-1-61655-196-4 | $19.99

.P.R.D. HELL ON ARTH

EW WORLD
ith Arcudi and Davis
BN 978-1-59582-707-4 | $19.99

ODS AND MONSTERS
ith Arcudi, Davis, and Crook
BN 978-1-59582-822-4 | $19.99

USSIA
ith Arcudi, Crook, and
uncan Fegredo
BN 978-1-59582-946-7 | $19.9

THE DEVIL'S ENGINE AND THE LONG DEATH
with Arcudi, Crook, and
James Harren
ISBN 978-1-59582-981-8 | $19.99

THE PICKENS COUNTY HORROR AND OTHERS
with Scott Allie, Jason Latour,
Harren, Max Fiumara, and
Becky Cloonan
ISBN 978-1-61655-140-7 | $19.99

THE RETURN OF THE MASTER
with Arcudi and Crook
ISBN 978-1-61655-193-3 | $19.99

A COLD DAY IN HELL
with Arcudi, Peter Snejbjerg, and
Laurence Campbell
ISBN 978-1-61655-199-5 | $19.99

ABE SAPIEN

THE DROWNING
with Jason Shawn Alexander
ISBN 978-1-59582-185-0 | $17.99

THE DEVIL DOES NOT JEST AND OTHER STORIES
with Arcudi, Harren, and others
ISBN 978-1-59582-925-2 | $17.99

DARK AND TERRIBLE AND THE NEW RACE OF MAN
with Allie, Arcudi, Sebastián
Fiumara, and Max Fiumara
ISBN 978-1-61655-284-8 | $19.99

LOBSTER JOHNSON

THE IRON PROMETHEUS
with Jason Armstrong
ISBN 978-1-59307-975-8 | $17.99

THE BURNING HAND
with Arcudi and Tonci Zonjic
ISBN 978-1-61655-031-8 | $17.99

SATAN SMELLS A RAT
with Arcudi, Fiumara, Joe
Querio, Wilfredo Torres, and
Kevin Nowlan
ISBN 978-1-61655-203-9 | $18.99

WITCHFINDER

IN THE SERVICE OF ANGELS
with Ben Stenbeck
ISBN 978-1-59582-483-7 | $17.99

LOST AND GONE FOREVER
with Arcudi and John Severin
ISBN 978-1-59582-794-4 | $17.99

THE AMAZING SCREW-ON HEAD AND OTHER CURIOUS OBJECTS

ISBN 978-1-59582-501-8 | $17.99

BALTIMORE

THE PLAGUE SHIPS
with Golden and Stenbeck
ISBN 978-1-59582-677-0 | $24.99

THE CURSE BELLS
with Golden and Stenbeck
ISBN 978-1-59582-674-9 | $24.99

A PASSING STRANGER AND OTHER STORIES
with Golden and Stenbeck
ISBN 978-1-61655-182-7 | $24.99

NOVELS

LOBSTER JOHNSON: THE SATAN FACTORY
with Thomas E. Sniegoski
ISBN 978-1-59582-203-1 | $12.95

JOE GOLEM AND THE DROWNING CITY
with Golden
ISBN 978-1-59582-971-9 | $99.99

HELLBOY

by MIKE MIGNOLA

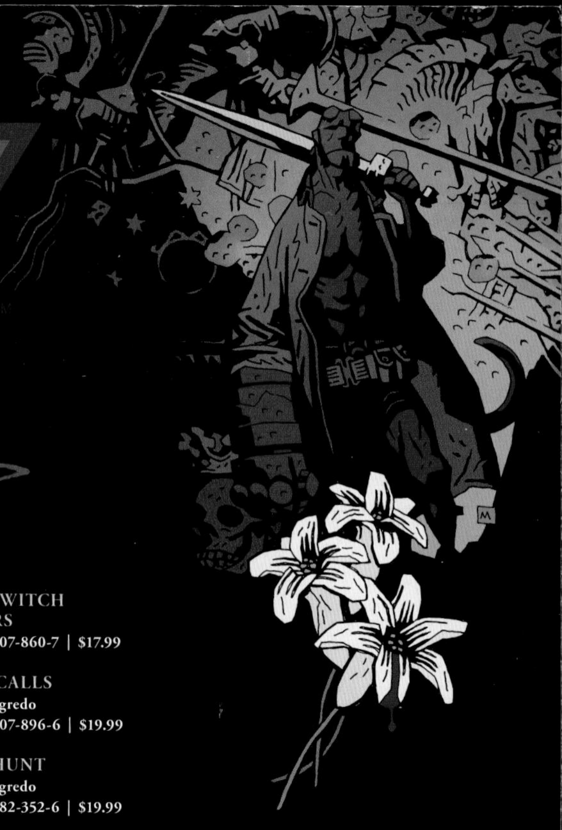

HELLBOY LIBRARY EDITION VOLUME 1:
Seed of Destruction and Wake the Devil
ISBN 978-1-59307-910-9 | $49.99

HELLBOY LIBRARY EDITION VOLUME 2:
The Chained Coffin and The Right Hand of Doom
ISBN 978-1-59307-989-5 | $49.99

HELLBOY LIBRARY EDITION VOLUME 3:
Conqueror Worm and Strange Places
ISBN 978-1-59582-352-6 | $49.99

HELLBOY LIBRARY EDITION VOLUME 4:
The Crooked Man and The Troll Witch
with Richard Corben and others
ISBN 978-1-59582-658-9 | $49.99

HELLBOY LIBRARY EDITION VOLUME 5:
Darkness Calls and the Wild Hunt
with Duncan Fegredo
ISBN 978-1-59582-886-6 | $49.99

HELLBOY LIBRARY EDITION VOLUME 6:
The Storm and the Fury and The Bride of Hell
with Duncan Fegredo, Richard Corben, Kevin Nowlan, and Scott Hampton
ISBN 978-1-61655-133-9 | $49.99

SEED OF DESTRUCTION
with John Byrne
ISBN 978-1-59307-094-6 | $17.99

WAKE THE DEVIL
ISBN 978-1-59307-095-3 | $17.99

THE CHAINED COFFIN AND OTHERS
ISBN 978-1-59307-091-5 | $17.99

THE RIGHT HAND OF DOOM
ISBN 978-1-59307-093-9 | $17.99

CONQUEROR WORM
ISBN 978-1-59307-092-2 | $17.99

STRANGE PLACES
ISBN 978-1-59307-475-3 | $17.99

THE TROLL WITCH AND OTHERS
ISBN 978-1-59307-860-7 | $17.99

DARKNESS CALLS
with Duncan Fegredo
ISBN 978-1-59307-896-6 | $19.99

THE WILD HUNT
with Duncan Fegredo
ISBN 978-1-59582-352-6 | $19.99

THE CROOKED MAN AND OTHERS
with Richard Corben
ISBN 978-1-59582-477-6 | $17.99

THE BRIDE OF HELL AND OTHERS
with Richard Corben, Kevin Nowlan, and Scott Hampton
ISBN 978-1-59582-740-1 | $19.99

THE STORM AND THE FURY
with Duncan Fegredo
ISBN 978-1-59582-827-9 | $19.99

HOUSE OF THE LIVING DEAD
with Richard Corben
ISBN 978-1-59582-757-9 | $14.99

THE MIDNIGHT CIRCUS
with Duncan Fegredo
ISBN 978-1-61655-238-1 | $14.99

HELLBOY: THE FIRST 20 YEARS
ISBN 978-1-61655-353-1 | $19.99

THE ART OF HELLBOY
ISBN 978-1-59307-089-2 | $29.99

HELLBOY II: THE ART OF THE MOVIE
ISBN 978-1-59307-964-2 | $24.99

HELLBOY: THE COMPANION
ISBN 978-1-59307-655-9 | $14.99

HELLBOY: WEIRD TALES
VOLUME 1
ISBN 978-1-56971-622-9 | $17.99
VOLUME 2
ISBN 978-1-56971-953-4 | $17.99

HELLBOY: MASKS AND MONSTERS
with James Robinson and Scott Benefiel
ISBN 978-1-59582-567-4 | $17.99

NOVELS

HELLBOY: EMERALD HELL
By Tom Piccirilli
ISBN 978-1-59582-141-6 | $12.99

HELLBOY: THE ALL-SEEING EYE
By Mark Morris
ISBN 978-1-59582-141-6 | $12.99

HELLBOY: THE FIRE WOLVES
By Tim Lebbon
ISBN 978-1-59582-204-8 | $12.99

HELLBOY: THE ICE WOLVES
By Mark Chadbourn
ISBN 978-1-59582-205-5 | $12.99

SHORT STORIES

Illustrated by Mike Mignola

HELLBOY: ODD JOBS
By Poppy Z. Brite, Greg Rucka, and others
ISBN 978-1-56971-440-9 | $14.99

HELLBOY: ODDER JOBS
By Frank Darabont, Guillermo del Toro, and others
ISBN 978-1-59307-226-1 | $14.99

HELLBOY: ODDEST JOBS
By Joe R. Lansdale, China Miéville, and others
ISBN 978-1-59307-944-4 | $14.99

AVAILABLE AT YOUR LOCAL COMICS SHOP OR BOOKSTORE! • To find a comics shop in your area, call 1-888-266-4226
For more information or to order direct visit DarkHorse.com or call 1-800-862-0052 Mon.–Fri. 9 AM to 5 PM Pacific Time.
Prices and availability subject to change without notice.

DARK HORSE BOOKS
DarkHorse.com